$\mathscr{G}$ LOBAL $\mathscr{S}$ EX

~~KEY TEXT~~
REFERENCE

GLOBAL SEX

DENNIS ALTMAN

THE UNIVERSITY OF CHICAGO PRESS
CHICAGO AND LONDON

DENNIS ALTMAN is professor in the School of Sociology, Politics, and Anthropology at La Trobe University, Melbourne, Australia. He is the author of numerous books, including *Defying Gravity: A Political Life* (1997) and *Power and Community: Organizational and Cultural Responses to AIDS* (1994), and journal articles.

The University of Chicago Press, Chicago 60637
The University of Chicago Press, Ltd., London
© 2001 by The University of Chicago
All rights reserved. Published 2001
Printed in the United States of America

10 09 08 07 06 05 04 03 02   2 3 4 5

ISBN: 0-226-01606-4 (cloth)

Library of Congress Cataloging-in-Publication Data

Altman, Dennis.
  Global sex / Dennis Altman.
    p. cm.
  Includes bibliographical references and index.
  ISBN 0-226-01606-4 (cloth : alk. paper)
  1. Sex customs. 2. Globalization. I. Title.

HQ16.A38 2001
306.7—dc21

                                                    00-036884

⊚ The paper used in this publication meets the minimum requirements of the American National Standard for Information Sciences—Permanence of Paper for Printed Library Materials, ANSI Z39.48-1992.

For Anthony Smith again—and our nephews and nieces:
Daniella, Eleanor, Francesca, Kate, Meredith, Peter, Raul, and Thomas

Contents

Preface: Sex and Politics

While I was writing this book sexual scandals shook two very different governments, those of the United States and Malaysia. Of course the nature and gravity of the scandals were very different; while President Clinton's sex life was exposed to ridicule and humiliation, former deputy prime minister Anwar Ibrahim was arrested and beaten after allegations of various "sex crimes," including sodomy. In April 1999 he was convicted of attempts to corrupt justice by seeking to cover up the allegations, and sentenced to six years in prison.

In the case of attacks on Clinton, hypocrisy was, as Russell Baker put it, "at its most hilarious when it comes from employees of vast media empires which thrive on exploitation of sex and violence."[1] Nonetheless the attacks were serious enough to lead to his impeachment by the House of Representatives and a protracted trial in the Senate. While his opponents claimed that the issue was Clinton's lying, it was only in an atmosphere where the media felt able to expose any aspect of sexual behavior that lying was required. The attacks on Clinton might well be seen as the logical extension of a growing media interest in celebrity sleaze; after Prince Charles's widely reported comment that he wished he were Camilla Parker-Bowles's tampon, a semen-stained dress seemed almost anticlimactic.

The attacks on Anwar were more serious, a stark reminder that in many parts of the world sexual "misconduct" (as interpreted by those in power) remains a powerful weapon for social and political control. Ironically by publicly accusing Anwar of sodomy Prime Minister Mahathir broke the de facto ban on public discussion of homosexuality in Malaysia, despite his claimed reluctance to do so.[2] Nor was Anwar the only high-level politician to be accused of sodomy in 1998. For most of the year former president Banana of Zimbabwe was also on trial, accused of sodomy and indecent assault. He was found guilty in the beginning of 1999 and sentenced to ten years' imprisonment. Ironically Banana, the country's first postcolonial president, fell foul of laws which were a legacy of colonialism; the irony was all the greater since he was himself a Methodist minister. As in the case of Anwar the trial and the resulting public discussion of homosexuality broke a number of taboos.[3] Both cases, too, illustrated a reverse "orientalism," whereby "the west" was cast as the source of sexual decadence, which colonial Europeans had long associated with "the east" or "the south."

The attacks on Anwar's alleged behavior are more easily understood as opportunism by a power-hungry prime minister determined to dispose of a protégé turned rival, just as the original investigations into Clinton's behavior were pushed by right-wing ideologues determined to destroy him. At the same time the attacks on Anwar for his alleged sexual misbehavior reflected a peculiarly Malaysian version of the same punitive moralism applied against Clinton, a set of views that Jeremy Seabrook referred to as "an alliance of frozen Victorian colonial morality and Islamic rhetoric, allied to an orgiastic consumerism."[4] Since the presidency of Richard Nixon Republicans have used the language of "family values" to defend economic policies which are helping undermine the very structures which made the "traditional" family possible. In a somewhat similar way Mahathir quite systematically used the language of Islamic morality to cut down his rival, while maintaining a determination to further economic growth and industrialization. The Malaysian situation was somewhat complicated by the fact that Anwar's supporters included both fundamentalist Muslims and Malaysians committed to genuine democratization, and by Mahathir's opposition to the demands of the International Monetary Fund for further restrictions in government spending and deregulation of the currency.

What links these examples is the invocation of certain standards of sexual propriety which are in practice disregarded by large sections of the population, and the presence of a global media. Images of a tearful Monica Lewinsky or a bloodied Anwar Ibrahim were circulated instantaneously to far larger audiences than ever existed before, and became part of everyday conversation among people who neither know nor care where Malaysia is nor what constitutes the impeachment process. The trial of political leaders on charges related to their sexual behavior might also be seen as the logical end of the liberationist slogan "The personal is the political," which John MacInnes claims has become the "essential political aphorism" of the past fifty years, replacing the "public conflicts and struggle . . . over the right to vote, strike or work [with] increasing conflicts over the right to a particular identity, or conversely, the social obligation to develop a particular form of identity."[5]

These two examples are related to the particular personal itinerary which led me to writing this book. Both the United States and Malaysia are countries where I have spent time, in the case of the former some seven years of my life. One of the striking aspects of the burgeoning literature on globalization, some of which will be cited, is the extent to which authors draw on serendipity as much as scholarship for their examples. The very nature of writing about "the global" means we must appear at home everywhere, yet at the same time none of us can know more than a small fragment of the world. Thus Thomas Friedman takes the metaphor which gave him the title for his book *The Lexus and the Olive Tree* from the contrast between a newspaper story from Palestine and the Japanese bullet train in which he was traveling when he read that story.[6] Salman Rushdie, unsurprisingly, sets *The Ground beneath Her Feet*, his novel of the global, in Bombay, London, and New York. Another version of that story could just as easily move from Tehran to Berlin and Tokyo.

Two further obstacles arise in writing about "globalization." The term itself is, after all, an attempt to describe a world which is constantly changing as one writes, making any statement about it at best provisional. Moreover almost all those who write about "globalization" are at the same time its beneficiaries. Those who use the mainstream media to articulate their criticism of contemporary trends tend to belong clearly to the world Mary Kaldor describes when she evokes the division between "those members of a global class who can speak English, have access to faxes, e-mail and satellite television, who use dollars or deutschmarks or credit cards, and who can travel freely" and those "who live off what they can sell or barter or what they receive in humanitarian aid, whose movement is restricted by roadblocks, visas and the cost of travel, and who are prey to sieges, forced famines, landmines, etc."[7]

Like Friedman and Rushdie I have drawn heavily on my lived experience in a number of parts of the world to develop my argument. A perceptive reader may guess that while writing this book I have spent time in Manila and Johannesburg, not in Lagos and Caracas, even while I try to pay attention to the latter. Some of the most telling examples I cite have been found by hazard, by reading a particular newspaper on an airplane or by coming across a little-known novel in a secondhand shop. While I have tried to read widely, I have made particular use of the *Economist* (which I see as the house organ of a certain sort of enlightened liberal globalization), of the *International Herald Tribune,* favorite reading whenever I travel, and of the lesser-known *New Internationalist,* which provides a welcome antidote to the neoliberal boosterism of the other two. But the fact that I read overwhelmingly English-language sources (and am capable of reading only one other language, French), suggests how necessarily limited my view of the global will be. I am particularly conscious of the rich Latin American literature on sexuality and feminism, to most of which I lack access.

This book, too, owes a great deal to my involvement over the past decade in the interconnected world of international HIV/AIDS politics and the global gay/lesbian movement. Those worlds have introduced me to extraordinary people, and given me particular insights into a number of countries very different from my native Australia, and for this I am very grateful. (For more details see the acknowledgments.) But while these are my own activist roots, and have inevitably influenced my knowledge and perceptions, I have tried to move beyond them in writing *Global Sex.* Above all, my reading about the politics of gender inequality, reproductive health, and violence against women has made me a more committed supporter of feminism.

In its obeisance to certain conventions of research and citations, this is a work of scholarship, whose aim is in part to establish a connection between scholars of sexualities and those of political economy and international relations, who in general have had little to say to each other. But to the extent that all writing must be autobiographical, even where it takes shelter behind the appurtenances of footnotes and learned quotations, this is also my own account of a very complex and problematic set of relationships which could be told in many ways. Nor do I make any claim to "objectivity," if by that we mean a refusal to take sides or to make political and moral choices. I rather like E. L. Doctorow's comment that "[w]e . . . did not make such a sanctimonious thing of objectivity, which is finally a way of constructing an opinion for the reader without letting him know that you are."[8] I hope that anyone who reads *Global Sex* will know exactly where I stand.

Introduction:
Thinking about Sex and Politics

How—and why—do we connect two of the dominant preoccupations of current social science and popular debate, namely globalization and the preoccupation with sexuality? Or, more concretely, is the increasing globalization of the world—understood as both "the compression of the world and the intensification of consciousness of the world as a whole"[1]—affecting the ways in which sexuality is understood, experienced, and regulated?

It is the argument of this book that changes in our understandings of and attitudes to sexuality are both affected by and reflect the larger changes of globalization. Moreover, as with globalization itself, the changes are simultaneously leading to greater homogeneity and greater inequality. As all but insignificant pockets of the world's peoples are brought within the scope of global capitalism, a consumer culture is developing which cuts across borders and cultures, and is universalized through advertising, mass media, and the enormous flows of capital and people in the contemporary world. Increasingly sexuality becomes a terrain on which are fought out bitter disputes around the impact of global capital and ideas.

Gilbert Herdt has written of the long neglect of sexuality in the social sciences at large: "Until quite recently, the social sciences remained preoccupied with gender but had scarcely begun to conceptualize desire, notwithstanding the prodding of Foucault."[2] His point remains valid, even if we need to recognize that often sex has relatively little to do with desire. It is of course true that in recent years certain sorts of studies of sexuality, often coded in the arcane language of literary and cultural theory, have become academically fashionable. It is also true that these studies are largely ignored in the burgeoning literature on globalization written by political scientists and economists. Equally those who do concern themselves with questions of sexuality and gender often ignore questions of material and institutional power. Alison

Murray came closer to the truth when she warned that "[t]he academy has progressed from women's studies to gender to sexuality, getting closer to the cunt of the matter while continuing to marginalise class, race and alternative subject-voices,"[3] a view echoed in Nancy Fraser's concerns that contemporary "difference" feminism ignores political economy.[4] A good example, as we shall see, is the paucity of material analyzing pornography and prostitution as industries rather than as problems of morality.

Sex is framed by social, cultural, political, and economic factors—and remains a powerful imperative resistant to all of these. Perhaps this explains the resistance to theories of social constructionism, which its critics see as attempts to tame something which survives all human attempts at control.[5] The tension is summed up in a passage from a piece Michael Ignatieff wrote about the bathhouses of Budapest, a legacy of Turkish occupation:[6] "The Kiraly isn't a gay bathhouse: the pleasure of the place consists precisely in its blurring of sexual boundaries, in its acceptance that gay and straight belong here together . . . I ask my masseur as he works his way up my calves, Is there more sex now than under Communism? He shrugs. The question seems ridiculous in this place. In the time zone of the bathhouses, regimes come and go, along with their styles in moral censure. Only the pleasures of the body endure."[7]

But however seductive the phrase, "the pleasures of the body" cannot be separated from the world outside. People who are undernourished, sick, pregnant, old, or threatened by potential violence will experience their bodies very differently, and only when political and economic conditions allow can we engage in certain "pleasures." Indeed bodily pleasure is often shaped by political and economic conditions; a sex worker in a Calcutta brothel is unlikely to experience her body in ways similar to that of her customers (or indeed to that of a high-class "escort" in Manhattan). Beryl Langer has observed that "[w]hile the tortured body is as emblematic of global postmodernity as the playful lycra/leather-clad body, it receives much less attention from theoretical explorers of the 'postmodern condition.'"[8] Yet torture often comes with sexual overtones, which is reified and trivialized in some pornography.

Sexuality is an area of human behavior, emotion, and understanding which is often thought of as "natural" and "private," even though it is simultaneously an arena of constant surveillance and control. What is understood as "natural" varies considerably across cultures and is policed by a large range of religious, medical, legal, and social institutions. Equally there are many ways of understanding the links between sex and politics, ranging from the regulation of contraception and abortion through to espionage, where sex has been central, or so at least novelists like to believe. (Though it was the head of the CIA, Allen Dulles, who once said: "So long as there is sex it is going to be used in espionage.")[9] Societies regulate sex through religious and cultural prohibitions, ceremonies and rules; through legal, scientific, hygiene, and health policies; through government restrictions and encouragement; and through a whole range of practices which form part of everyday life, and constitute what Gayle Rubin termed the "sex/gender system."[10]

Almost all "traditional" (by which I mean preindustrial) societies appear to be organized with strong homosocial components, so that men and women often exist in largely separate worlds, and marriage and heterosexual sex is highly regulated through ceremony and ritual, usually involving extended families. The best example of this sort of social organization is found in those tribal societies where men and women live separately, as in the famous "longhouses" of Borneo, and married couples spend only relatively short periods of time together. As societies "modernize," the sharp distinctions based on gender decline, and along with these changes comes the development of the nuclear family as the central unit of social organization and the development of ideologies of companionate marriage based on reciprocal love and respect. Until the 1970s more than half the marriages in South Korea were arranged through go-betweens; now "marriages for love, not family-arranged partnerships, have become the norm."[11] As the expectations of marriage grow, so too do the probabilities that those who are disappointed will seek to end them, leading to rising divorce rates.[12] These are of course ideal typologies, but they help make sense of the ways in which larger socioeconomic structures frame assumptions about sexuality and gender. They also explain the extraordinary rapidity of changes in the sex/gender system over the past century, as more and more people are forced to negotiate the transition between very different orders. It is not uncommon for middle-class urban dwellers to find themselves looking after relatives from the hinterland with whom they share very few common values.

Even so, the most "modern" society retains particular assumptions around sexuality and gender derived from earlier periods, and often enforced through religious and cultural ideologies. Think, for example, of the ways in which certain sports are constructed as essential tests of masculinity, and of the long battle of women to have their sporting prowess recognized as equally valid to that of men, as in the struggle to establish a professional women's tennis circuit. Team sports have played a central role in the creation of both individual and national styles of masculinity, whether it be English cricket or football in Uruguay, for whom victory in the 1924 and 1928 Olympics was a decisive moment in nation building.[13]

Sports, too, are an arena where one sees a range of sexual restrictions and inhibitions; is it too fanciful to see an element of homoerotic sublimation in contact sports, especially football, matched by the strong taboos against footballers "coming out"?[14] (Footballers who *do* come out gain considerable notoriety, as in the case of David Kopay in the United States; Ian Roberts in Australia; and, most tragically, Justin Fanashu in Britain, who committed suicide after being accused of sex with a minor.) In the case of women, team sports are often an arena for lesbian contacts to be established, and not only in western countries, as Kim Berman has noted of the Soweto Women's Soccer Club in South Africa.[15]

As these examples suggest, sexuality and gender are inextricably interconnected, and often regulated through similar ideological and institutional means. I agree with Spike Petersen and Jacqui True when they write: "Whereas gender is not always the most salient or oppressive dimension at work in a particular context, we believe gender always shapes the expression of other dimensions (e.g., racist policies are also gendered); and insofar as gender identities are integral to our sense of self and personal security, it often profoundly shapes our commitments to particular lenses."[16] This is one reason why transgender behavior or display outside permissible spaces—whether such spaces be the *bedarche* role in Native American societies or the Mardi Gras festivals in contemporary New Orleans or Sydney—are so unsettling.

Almost all societies establish very clearly gendered rules and expectations around sexuality, so that while most societies, for example, place a particular value on female virginity this is rarely the case for men. Indeed in some societies a girl who has been raped is treated as "dishonored" and hence unfit for marriage, even though she was powerless to preserve her virginity. Equally, in many societies a raped wife is regarded as fit only to be divorced or, in the worst of cases, to be killed. In a study drawing on seven countries in Africa, Latin America, and Asia/Pacific, Gary Dowsett and

Peter Aggleton comment that "[a]s the best marker of the double bind for young women, virginity is still held as important in two ways: as a guarantee of the value of a potential marriage partner, and as proof of the character and worthiness of each young woman in the eyes of her partner, family and community." Yet they point to the decline of virginity before marriage as a consequence of modernization, the demand to earn money, and the impact of youth culture, which "increasingly validates a 'surrender to love.'"[17]

It is an oversimplification to suggest that all cultures organize sexuality around the enhancement of male pleasure above female, but it is rare to find cultures where the reverse is true. Indeed many cultures and religions teach women that to enjoy sex is a sign of immodesty: one study quotes a Nigerian woman as saying "Hausa women usually do not show any sign of enjoyment during sex because their husbands will think they are wayward."[18] Anthony Giddens has noted that the sexual "double standard" is central to almost all nonmodern societies,[19] but it appears to persist well into modernity. Thus Gail Pheterson's framework of "the interplay between psychology and sociology, between notions of female honor and male nobility,"[20] used to analyze sex work, applies to most human societies, though it takes very different forms. The provision of male sexual pleasure is part of sexual regimes in societies marked by the imperative to produce—namely those in the early stages of industrialization—as much as in those dominated by the imperative to consume. Prostitution and pornography flourish in both, and are largely created as means of satisfying male "desire" through the services, in both the corporeal and fantasy realms, of women. The reverse of this is the very common practice of defining sexual desire as something "nice women" do not experience, and the construction of women as either madonnas or whores, no matter that the reality is almost always more complex. No equivalent divide appears to exist for men.

Certainly the growth of "consumer society" has tended to create at least the possibilities of recreational sex for women as well as for men, with the growth of male strippers catering to women-only audiences, the basis for the enormously popular film *The Full Monty*. But overall the imbalance remains, and is symbolized by the numbers of "swingers" clubs and bars which allow free admission to women in order to balance the numbers of men.

Both the political/economic order and dominant patterns of sexuality and gender reflect what R. W. Connell has termed "hegemonic masculinity," namely "the configuration of gender practice which embodies the currently accepted answer to the problem of the legitimacy of patriarchy, which guarantees (or is taken to guarantee) the dominant position of men and the subordination of women."[21] Every society treats men and women differently, and in very few does this difference favor women. In practice, as Connell demonstrates, the nature of this masculinity may shift, and indeed certain women may well find ways of successfully benefiting from its structures while many men will be severely punished or disadvantaged for their failures to uphold the premises of hegemonic masculinity. The advantage of this conceptualization is that it allows for the structural inequalities suggested by terms like "patriarchy," while also recognizing that these inequalities are created through human action, and impinge very differently on different individuals.

Religion is central to sexual regulation in almost all societies, although its impact has steadily declined in most western democracies over the past half century, with the major exception of the United States. Indeed it may well be that the primary social function of religion is to control sexuality and gender in the interests of hegemonic masculinity. Ironically those countries which rejected religion in the name of Communism tended to adopt their own version of sexual puritanism, which often matched those of the religions they assailed. Whether it be Catholicism, Hinduism, Islam, or Communism, religions tend to claim a particular right to regulate and restrict sexuality, a right which is often recognized by state authorities. As Marta Lamas wrote of Mexico: "All local and federal battles over sexuality have focussed on the same issue—whether to affirm or question traditional Catholic morality."[22] Even though the Mexican revolution of 1917 established a secular state, the influence of the church remains very large, and is often exerted through religious organizations such as Opus Dei and the Legionnaires of Christ. Similar comments could be made about the tension between religious and secular forces in countries as different as Israel, Ireland, Turkey, and post-Communist Poland.

All too often sex is regulated through violence. "Violence is the quintessential, testosteronic expression of male entitlement,"[23] David Landes wrote in speaking about Islamic cultures, but his words are clearly applicable beyond them. There is evidence that domestic violence is widespread in most societies, and it is rare for police and legal systems to provide adequate resources to prevent it. As Silvana Paternostro wrote of Mexico: "An average of eighty two rapes are committed every day in Mexico City. Women's fears

are even more justified, given the police officers themselves have been participants in sex crimes. In 1990, five policemen rampaged the city raping at
least nineteen young women."[24] It is tempting to ascribe such figures to the
Latin cult of machismo,[25] but these and other accounts from South America—
in Argentina it is reported that 65% of women have been beaten by a man
at least once, more than three-quarters of the time by their husband[26]—are
repeated in very different societies. Moves to outlaw wife beating in Papua
New Guinea were rejected by the (overwhelmingly male) Parliament on the
grounds they were contrary to "traditional family life."[27] In the same way it
is only recently, and in a limited number of countries, that rape within marriage has been recognized as an offense.

 When men act out their sexual fears they are likely to be distorted into
violence, and there is some evidence that sexual violence is a growing part
of the current global disorder.[28] Thus rape is used by men both in the name
of preserving tradition and in making revolution. As Lillian Ng described the
experience of a woman in China: "The red book of Mao held in front of
my eyes was my anaesthetic, my moral support, my encouragement, while I
burned with pain, scorched by cramps, the fire in the pit of my stomach that
rose from the furnace that was my passage of yin."[29] Meanwhile adulterers,
prostitutes, homosexuals—or those suspected of being any of these—are
routinely raped, stoned, tortured, and killed in countries with governments
as different as Guatemala and Iran. Those who publicly flout the gender/
sexual order seem particularly vulnerable to violence, so that for sex workers
and transsexuals the anticipation of violence is often, as Richard Parker
wrote of Brazil, "an explosive potential that permeates daily life."[30]

 The triumph of liberal capitalism at the end of the Cold War has also
meant new outbreaks of local conflicts and unrest, as conflicts increasingly
become power and ethnic struggles within countries, with correspondingly
huge civilian casualties. Under conditions of civil war sex becomes as much
a realm of torture as of pleasure, as shown in widespread rape in Rwanda,
former Yugoslavia, or Sierra Leone.[31] Manuel Carballo of the International
Centre for Migration and Health has estimated that 40,000 women were
raped in the war in Bosnia "and we don't believe these figures are particularly unique or unusual."[32] There were further reports of mass rape by Serb
soldiers as part of the "ethnic cleansing" of Kosovo, with suggestions that
one of the aims was to impregnate Albanian Muslim women. Rape, of

course, can also be used against men, and indeed seems particularly prominent in the ethnic battles in former Yugoslavia.[33] Linda Grant has suggested
that the rapes in Bosnia were connected to the availability of pornography
in post-Tito Yugoslavia, but without any firm evidence, which is unfortunately true of many of the claims made about pornography.[34]

   More convincing is Nikos Papastergiadis's claim that the use of rape in
Bosnia was different from the accounts of rape in previous warfare, because
it was a conscious part of the policy of "ethnic cleansing" and involved "a
new extreme of brutality."[35] Unfortunately his argument would probably
hold in a number of other contemporary situations of ethnic and civil conflict. Even without war, rape may be increasing. Evidence from countries as
dissimilar as Papua New Guinea and South Africa suggests that rape (often
"pack rape") is becoming increasingly common as a response to the massive
dislocations of contemporary life.[36] Indeed it is widely believed that a woman
is raped every five minutes in South Africa. As Graeme Simpson and Gerald
Kraak argue, many young men who feel powerless and marginalized in a
world of rapid change will turn to violence, and rape "becomes a way of
symbolically reasserting their masculine identity."[37]

   Such phenomena are often described as being the "unintended consequences" of modernization, often with the implicit assumption that they will
pass with growing affluence. This is probably the point to note my unease
with terms such as "development" which imply some sort of linear progression toward a future possessed already in the rich world. I have tried to avoid
speaking of "developed" and "underdeveloped" countries for this reason,
and more often speak of "rich" and "poor." This does, however, group together countries with very different cultural backgrounds and political systems—Denmark and Saudi Arabia are both "rich" countries for example—
and at times I have had to use the rather clumsy terms "western" and "nonwestern" where the emphasis is on culture rather than economics. I do so
uncomfortably aware that the sort of oppositional definition here is both
loaded and inaccurate: both contemporary Japan and traditional villages in
Papua could be described as "nonwestern" but to lump them together is to
deprive the term of any real meaning. In the same way concepts of "modernization" tend to imply a linear progression toward a single end point which
is usually coterminous with American capitalism,[38] so that terms such as
"modern" and "traditional" need to be understood as ideologically loaded
ideal types.

Increasingly the institutions and ideologies which link sex and politics are themselves being globalized, as concerns around gender, sexuality, and the body play a central role in the construction of international political, social, and economic regimes. It is the complexity of these interconnections that is the central theme of this book.

The Many Faces of Globalization

BANGKOK 2000 / VIENNA 1900

By the end of the twentieth century Bangkok had become a significant world city, not only because of its size (perhaps 12 million people in the metropolitan area) and its centrality to the Thai economic boom—whose dramatic collapse in 1997 triggered mass recession in Asia—but also as a center of nightlife and sexual excess which attracted tourists in large numbers. In the words of Bruce Rich: "In the brave new era of the global . . . Bangkok has become the global brothel."[1] This perception is echoed in a number of feminist analyses of prostitution.[2] A couple of years earlier a similar reference in, of all places, the Longman's English dictionary caused heated debate within Thailand, a ban on the book by the police relying on a section in the Publications Act about matters offensive to moral standards, and the reissue of the dictionary with a revised entry on Bangkok.[3] Bangkok was equally known for its traffic jams and the resulting pollution, so that high levels of lead have been found in the umbilical cords of newborn babies,[4] and its cityscape of huge postmodern skyscrapers rising cheek by jowl with old slums. As William Greider put it: "Bangkok was thriving and Bangkok was declining."[5]

How different was this from the great cities of the previous century—and how far could one see the same forces (economic growth, large-scale migration, great inequalities, sexual excess, cultural upheavals) in Paris, London, or New York in 1900? From ancient Rome to contemporary Bangkok cities play a special role in the ways we imagine the history of sex. Think of the imagery evoked by Berlin, Tangiers, and Paris in the interwar years; "swinging London" or "hippie San Francisco" in the 1960s; Rio de Janeiro or New Orleans and their Mardi Gras festivals; prostitution in Amsterdam and Hamburg. These images grow both out of popular culture and from socioeconomic reality: the sexual attraction of these cities cannot be sepa-

rated from the industries (prostitution, bars, dance halls, discos) which were
the basis of their reputation. In some cases tourism was a major factor, as in
Havana in the 1950s[6] (a legacy not forgotten by the Castro government).
There may have been as much prostitution in Turin or Toronto as in Berlin
or Shanghai in the 1930s, but if so it does not form part of how we imagine
these cities.

Only a few cities can base their economies on sex (true for some towns
near naval bases or mining camps). Yet sex is a central part of the political
economy of all large cities, especially those which are growing fast and therefore home to many who are uprooted, transient, desperate—or newly rich
in times of political or social upheaval. Under such conditions what is often
hidden becomes revealed: this would seem true of Chinese and Russian cities
since the 1990s with their rapidly flourishing prostitution and their flashy
new rich.

The view of Bangkok as "the global brothel" grew out of its status as
the major center for American GIs on "rest and recreation" during the Vietnam War when 700,000 U.S. military took leave in Bangkok[7] (the most lasting memory of the musical *Chess* is the song "A Night in Bangkok"). Writing
of John Lennon's visit to Bangkok in 1976, Albert Goldman, in a generally
reviled biography, says: "When John walked out of the world-famous Orien-
tal Hotel . . . he would have been accosted by steerers, who would have presented him with their comically garbled cards, reading, 'You haven't had
your job blown until one of our girls does it' . . . Having sex with these girls
is the closest thing in the world to legally sanctioned child abuse, which is
why Thai whores are the favorites of jaded men."[8] By the mid-1980s an
underground travel guide proclaimed Bangkok "the world's most open city"
and there was the beginning of a large-scale HIV epidemic which led to
some organization among sex workers, most particularly through the group
EMPOWER, based in the entertainment district of Patpong. Had the South
won the Vietnam War it is possible that Saigon (now Ho Chi Minh City)
would occupy the role now taken by Bangkok. Twenty years later Ho Chi
Minh City, like Phnom Penh in neighboring Cambodia, is fast developing its
own even seedier version of the Bangkok sex trade.

But neither widespread prostitution nor the importation of foreign sex
workers is new. In his autobiography Stefan Zweig wrote of growing up in
Vienna: "The present generation has hardly any idea of the gigantic spread
of prostitution in Europe before the [First] World War . . . At that time fe-

male wares were offered for sale at every hour and at every price, and it cost a man as little time and trouble to purchase a woman for a quarter of an hour, an hour or a night, as it did to buy a package of cigarettes or a newspaper."[9] By late nineteenth century Buenos Aires was infamous in Europe for its "white slave trade,"[10] and in Rio de Janeiro at the same time not only was prostitution widespread, but many of the workers were recent immigrants. From the late nineteenth century on there was an international trade specializing in eastern European Jewish women, so that the term *polaca* came to be used for prostitute.[11] There was indeed a "global network" of Jewish prostitution by the turn of the century, built on "the consequences of European religious bigotry, rigid Jewish laws, and their combined impact on family structures and poor Jewish women."[12] The indignation at the widespread sex industry in modern cities such as Bangkok or Rio is often uninformed by any historical sense.

It is tempting to use Zweig's comments to compare Bangkok with Vienna a century earlier because of the central role of Freud in creating our perceptions of sexuality as central to social life—Freud published the *Interpretation of Dreams* in 1900—and the images of Vienna as a decadent fin de siècle city. (Peter Hall, who includes Vienna among the six cities he surveys as "cultural crucibles," refers to it as "the city as pleasure principle.")[13] Not for nothing is Vienna sometimes seen as the first postmodern city[14]—or, perhaps, the city where, as Callinicos wrote, "one is tempted to say, the twentieth century was invented."[15] It was also, noted Callinicos, a major industrial city, and a center of social democracy. Vienna of course was a center of theorizing about sex and avant-garde art, theater, and music, while Bangkok can be seen rather as a center of sexual consumption: the cerebral made flesh. Much of the art of pre–World War I Vienna involved an exploration of sexuality which was radical for its time, as in the paintings of Oskar Kokoschka, Egon Schiele (of whom John Updike wrote "he shares with his fellow Viennese Freud a dispassionate and rather melancholy sexual realism with an eye to psychopathology"),[16] and Gustav Klimt.[17] The Viennese were very taken by the works of Oscar Wilde, reflected in Richard Strauss's adaptation of his play for the opera *Salome*, and in Arthur Schnitzler's play *La Ronde* (1903) the characters are linked by a cycle of infidelity.[18]

Both Austria-Hungary at the start of the last century and Thailand at the start of this are cases of old-established monarchies moving uneasily toward democracy, and both were the undisputed cultural, political, and eco-

nomic centers of their realms, though Vienna was a cosmopolitan city, seat
of an empire which embraced a dozen languages and cultures, while Bangkok
is the seat of a kingdom which remains remarkably homogeneous. The most
significant exception are the Chinese, whom many have compared to the
Jews in Europe; as with Jews in Vienna the Chinese in Bangkok are both
assimilated and separate. The obvious difference is that Vienna was central
to world intellectual/artistic developments in ways which are not true for
any contemporary Asian city except perhaps Tokyo. Yet at same time there *is*
a political and even an intellectual ferment in Bangkok reflected in its student
movements and perhaps its architecture.

Both cities grew rapidly due to industrialization, but in Vienna far
more attention was paid to planning, to housing, to public transport, to welfare. Vienna's population doubled between 1840 and 1870, and in the late
nineteenth century Vienna took its modern shape, just as the modernization
of Bangkok was beginning. Bangkok's recent growth between 1960 and 1990
was more rapid, and less well planned, reflected in the squatters' shacks
which straddle canals and railway lines in the shadow of vast postmodern
skyscrapers—hotels and shopping malls display architectural achievement
rather as public buildings and cultural centers did a century ago.[19] While
in nineteenth-century Vienna a great boulevard circling the inner city was
built for military reasons,[20] in late-twentieth-century Bangkok expressways
were built to deal with the unmoving traffic jams, and there was considerable confusion and corruption surrounding attempts to build an elevated
rail system through the city center, which finally opened at the end of the
century.[21]

Bangkok's growth was that of the "tiger boom" in which foreign capital played a far larger role than the state, and has produced the sort of lop-
sided "development" seen in so much of the world. The new inequalities of
the global economy are symbolized for me in the unhappy elephant whose
owner I once saw begging for tips outside Robinson's department store on
the prosperous shopping strip of Sukhumvit. The gap between the bourgeoi-
sie and the workers of late-nineteenth-century Vienna was probably less than
the gap between the newly rich in the upmarket condominiums and the
squatters of Klong Toey.

I don't want to make too much of the comparison, but it is worth reflecting that much of what we see as new, both in terms of globalization and
sexual commodification, accompanied earlier social change and industrial-

ization. The real point of thinking about contemporary Bangkok and fin de
siècle Vienna is to remind us that neither globalization nor widespread concerns about sexuality are new.

WHAT'S NEW ABOUT GLOBALIZATION?

This discussion of Bangkok foregrounds the link between economic and social change and different expressions of sexuality—but it also questions the
too easy claim that "globalization" is totally unprecedented in world history.
There is an argument that globalization was already well under way in the
nineteenth century, through the rapid expansion of world trade, the major
migrations from the Old World to the New, and the impact of new technologies such as the railway and the telegraph. Others trace it back to the expansion of Europe from the fifteenth century on, or even to conceptions of the
world in Greece and Rome.[22] For the last several millennia, trade and religion have assured the dispersion and mixing of cultures. Wars, whether the
wars of European conquest or the huge conflagrations of the twentieth century, have long been major sources for the export of new social and cultural
patterns.

　　The experience of crowding into the newly industrializing cities of Europe in the nineteenth century had its parallels with what is now happening
in Bangkok, Mumbai, and Lagos. Peter Beinart and others have pointed out
that world trade in 1913 was at similar levels to those of 1992,[23] though this
was certainly not the case for capital flows. (Nor does it allow for the new
forms of trade now possible through the Internet, and the rapid means of
transport which allow for hothouse flowers—and human organs—to be
shipped across the world in less than a day.) The devastation caused to African societies by the slave trade and later by the expansion of mining in colonies such as the Congo, Rhodesia, and South Africa foreshadowed the equal
devastation brought by much economic "development" in our time. More
than 150 years ago Marx wrote: "Constant revolutionizing of production,
uninterrupted disturbance of all social conditions, everlasting uncertainty
and agitation distinguish the bourgeois epoch from all earlier ones. All fixed,
fast-frozen relations, with their train of ancient and venerable prejudices and
opinions, are swept away, all new-formed ones become antiquated before
they can ossify."[24] And in 1927, in a French science fiction novel, Theo Varlet
wrote: "The rhythm of life has accelerated on our planet and humanity

forms more and more one block, a single organism which moves together in
the same way."[25]

Globalization became a key buzzword in the 1990s—and found trans-
lations into a number of languages. (It has been claimed that the term is
more used in Thailand, where it is known as *lokaphiwat*, than anywhere else
in the world.)[26] Arguments about the meaning of globalization echo the now
overrehearsed argument about what is new in postmodernism: of course
what we call globalization has its precursors in previous periods just as "postmodern" is an irritatingly imprecise term which can be used to cover a vast
range of human activities. Even so I would agree with David Held when he
argues: "What is new about the modern global system is the chronic intensification of patterns of interconnectedness mediated by such phenomena as
the modern communications industry and new information technology and
the spread of globalization in and through new dimensions of interconnectedness: technological, organizational, administrative and legal, among others, each with their own logic and dynamic of change."[27] We should also
bear in mind that part of globalization means that modernity in its broadest
sense, meaning the sort of social assumptions and institutions connected with
industrial capitalism, is changing the life experiences of millions of people
just as parts of the world which have long experienced modernity are moving
into a condition which some term postmodernity. Without entering into the
enormous and complex arguments around these terms, postmodernity is
best understood, at least for my purpose, as a further stage of capitalism, or
what Ulrich Beck terms a "second modernity."[28]

In a globalizing world, with technologies quite different from those of
pre–World War I expansion, time and space themselves take on different
meanings,[29] and no aspect of life remains untouched by global forces. Yet
most people still operate within particular local spaces, and there is constant
tension between the local and the global.[30] I still experience a difference
between reading the Melbourne *Age* over breakfast at home, and reading
its headlines on the web in a smoky Internet café at Geneva Station. The
difference is not merely one of forms of media, it is based upon my different
physical proximity to the world it describes. Despite the rhetoric about the
global village, a term first coined by Marshall McLuhan in the early 1960s,
and the "end of geography," almost all of us remain linked to particular
places, even if we may also feel part of communities which are not primarily
defined by a shared space.[31]

While much of this book concentrates on what is sometimes called the "developing world," the phenomenon of rapid change is apparent everywhere. Tony Judt wrote of France, arguably of all major countries the one with the greatest historical continuity: "Whereas the France of, say, 1956 had been in most important respects fundamentally similar to the France of 1856—even down to a remarkable continuity of geographical patterns of political and religious allegiance—the France of 1980 did not even resemble the country just ten years earlier."[32] Exaggerated? Perhaps: there are certainly small towns in France where one can still imagine oneself in the days of the Second Empire and the French have a peculiar genius in preserving their past in ways unmatched elsewhere. Halfway across the world, in the island territory of New Caledonia (now on its way to independence) you can find traditional French meals served by Kanaks speaking Parisian French. Yet even France cannot resist the remaking of the world which has reduced it from an imperial center to a major second-rate power, increasingly integrated into a social, economic, and political union with its former rivals. Nor, according to Judt, is France likely to escape one of the sadder consequences of rapid and ubiquitous change, namely the widespread decline of the study of narrative history, which is in turn linked to increasing confusion about what is and is not important in historical memory. Similarly Julian Barnes talks of the death of *la France profonde,* killed off by "war, peace, communications technology, mass tourism, the unfettered free market, Americanization, Eurification, greed, short-termism, smug ahistoricism."[33]

The impact of multinational firms, able to move capital and factories across the world in search of both markets and cheap workers, of electronic media and the Internet, of the vast apparatus of consumerism, means that increasingly national boundaries are unable to contain ideas, money, or even people. The British Empire may have brought new ideas and products to the Indian subcontinent, but there is a qualitative difference in a world where it could be estimated (in 1998) that in five years the number of households in Pakistan with access to satellite television had escalated from 70,000 to some millions.[34] The decentralization of control over Chinese television and the growth of satellite transmission has meant a rapid increase in the amount of foreign programming available to the average Chinese, 80% of whom have some access to television.[35] In similar fashion the greatest growth in Internet domain names is occurring in middle-income countries, though North America remains dominant. Indeed American technological superiority is symbolized by the fact that its Internet addresses are the only ones which do not bear a country code, rather as British stamps are the only ones not to bear the name of the country. In both cases being first sets norms to which others must conform.

Migration has become more complex than in previous periods, as the end of European empires meant that millions have moved from ex-colonies to the metropolis, with large numbers of people maintaining either voluntary or involuntary ties to several countries during their lifetimes.[36] The large-scale movement of people from the "third world"—West Indians and South Asians to Britain, North and West Africans to France, Central Americans and Caribbeans to the United States—means what Iain Chambers has termed "the return of the repressed, the subordinate and the forgotten in 'Third World' musics, literatures, poverties and populations as they come to occupy the economies, cities, institutions, media and leisure time of the First World."[37] Only too typical of the contemporary world are accounts of virtual concentration camps in Lithuania where "[t]hirteen Somalis had spent three months in the dark, three metres underground in horrifying conditions. They never saw the light of day except during the daily exercise hour. They suffered from eye problems. It was terribly hot. The air was heavy, unbreathable."[38] What twenty years ago would have seemed bizarre—namely east African refugees in a small Baltic state—has become part of the contemporary condition.

Meanwhile the colonial class who ran the European empires from their redoubts in Delhi and Algiers have to some extent been replaced by a new class of expatriates, who serve multinational companies or international agencies rather than national states, and often act as new vectors for ideas and fashions. These "new cosmopolitans" are very visible, but it remains true that the great majority of those who migrate are fleeing desperation in search of possibility.[39] Both the privileged and the desperate cross frontiers, so that the banking executive and his cleaner in Singapore or Los Angeles may each have come from elsewhere, but their experiences are separated by a class divide which is no less than that between the rich and poor of nineteenth-century colonialism.

Again it is difficult to argue that this is unprecedented: the experiences of Eritrean refugees in Italy, of Bangladeshi migrant workers in the Gulf, of Salvadoran "illegals" in Texas and California, all have their precursors in the huge migrations of the nineteenth century. In a study of Filipino workers in the Middle East Jane Margold argues that "the international political economy that interpenetrated with individual lives had splintering effects, selecting muscles and energy and denying human totalities."[40] No argument there, but was this not also the experience of millions of Africans shipped across the Atlantic during the slave trade, or indeed of young Irish women or Chinese laborers who came to the United States in the nineteenth century? Nor is the huge migration from countryside to city which is producing shantytowns and squatters in almost every large city of the poor world new, though in sheer scale it is even greater than the urban growth of nineteenth-century industrialization. Remember that in the 1920s over half the adult males in New York City were of foreign birth, and many of those born in the States were poor black immigrants from the rural South.[41]

What does seem true is that fewer and fewer parts of the world can cling to any sense of racial or ethnic homogeneity, as large-scale migration has remade the cities of the rich world in the past thirty years. There are now more foreign-born residents in Switzerland than in Argentina, and even Japan, perhaps the most closed rich country in the world, has well over 100,000 immigrants a year, mainly from other parts of Asia. Questions of citizenship and multiculturalism, long central to the politics of settler and colonial societies, have become key issues in the metropolis, with political groups like the National Front in France and the Freedom Party in Austria appealing to illusory memories of racial homogeneity. While countries such as the United States, Canada, and Australia had long defined citizenship as something which could be attained by immigrants, it was not until the end of the twentieth century and the election of a Social Democrat government that Germany changed its immigration laws to allow millions of people born in Germany the right to full citizenship.

It is estimated that up to a 100 million migrants and 20 million refugees change countries each year; more than 35 million people work overseas and 10 million have been displaced from their land by environmental degradation.[42] Temporary movement across frontiers is also huge. The economies of many small countries, particularly in the Caribbean, depend increasingly upon tourism for survival, just as countries such as Bangladesh and the Philippines rely more and more heavily on remittances from overseas workers.[43] In addition the huge internal migration within countries can change the ethnic and environmental balance of entire areas, as in the dispossession of Indian tribes through the "settlement" of the Amazon or the Indonesian *trans-migrasai* project which has moved three-quarters of a million people into West Papua (West Irian).[44] Local resentment at these shifts lay behind the considerable ethnic violence which followed the collapse of Suharto in 1998, such as that against Madurese immigrants in Kalimantan (Borneo).[45]

Appadurai claims that what is new is that "diaspora is the order of things": "The United States, always in its self-perception a land of immigrants, finds itself awash in these global diasporas, no longer a closed space for the melting pot to work its magic, but yet another diasporic switching point, to which people come to seek their fortunes but are no longer content to leave their homelands behind."[46] Millions of people manage to move back and forth between several countries, maintaining loyalties to both (one of Australia's richest men is both the owner of the Melbourne Football Club and a major donor to right-wing causes in Israel). Ethnic politics and tensions are now part of the experience of most countries, though this should not necessarily be seen as negative. The replacement of the unquestioned assumptions of superiority which accompanied European invasions in the past three centuries with the often troubled debates around multiculturalism and pluralism is surely an important gain.

Appadurai is one of a significant group of expatriate Indians, both academics and writers, whose invention of a whole set of ways of understanding the contemporary expatriate experience has given birth to both postcolonial theory and one of the richest bodies of imaginative writing in contemporary English. Of course it would be absurd to reduce postcolonialism to a collective autobiographical undertaking of south Asian academics, but it is equally impossible to avoid the extent to which its project is directly related to their experience of balancing their sense of being outsiders at the same time in both Mumbai and New York, Karachi and Manchester. If the dominant imagery of the migrant, torn between a homeland which rejected him and a diaspora where she was uncertain of her place, used to be found in Jewish writings, today our dominant imagery comes from south Asian writers. At the same time "postcolonialism" is a term used to cover three very different historical movements: the expropriation of indigenous peoples, the colonization of existing societies, and the development of settler societies. Of course all three occurred often at once: thus Europeans in South Africa dispossessed the original inhabitants while encouraging migration of other Africans and then Indians whose labor they could use in the growing settler economy. When one goes to countries such as Malaysia or Fiji or much of the Caribbean, it is not at all clear who has the best claim to "real" postcoloniality.

Nonetheless there is a sense in which the postcolonial condition, which Leila Gandhi has characterized as "a relationship of reciprocal antagonism and desire,"[47] remains central to much of my project. When I write of globalization I am drawing on imagery which is also that of postcolonial writers, whether it be the strange juxtaposition of postmodern architecture and squatters' shacks in the booming metropolises of the "developing" world or the rapid change in racial and ethnic composition of my own home cities of Sydney and Melbourne. Globalization, after all, is used to describe what is happening within the rich and poor worlds as well as between them, and my emphasis is on the latter.

Most writers agree that globalization involves the simultaneous strengthening and weakening of national and local boundaries. The borders of the international state system remain, and indeed they have become emblematic of a world which technology unites but human endeavor further segments. Sometimes one crosses from one continent to another with barely a whiff of interrogation; other borders—the tunnel through the Alps from Switzerland to Italy, the barbed wire and concrete blocks of San Diego/Tijuana, the slow ferry from Singapore to Indonesia's Bataam Island—seem designed to demarcate the boundaries of separate cultures, as if computer screens and passport controls could preserve national differences against the steady flow of information and ideas and images through the ether.

As the powers of the nation-state are eroded, either due to international economic forces or to new supranational institutions, parochial and separatist forces threaten it from within, as the events following the end of the Cold War in the Balkans and the Caucasus tragically illustrated. Globalization shifts the sense of what is local, as technology seems to obliterate any sense of distance and once-local concerns become universalized. In 1998 there was huge controversy over the entry of a number of foreign competitors in Australia's preeminent horse race which is so widely followed that Melbourne Cup Day is a public holiday in the state of Victoria. Yet this concern was matched with a certain pride in the growing international reputation of the cup; one newspaper reported that a farrier "flew halfway around the world just to check the horse's feet . . . and flew out the same day in just another example of global shrinking."[48]

Ironically globalization is often taken to mean a certain homogenization of cultures just when the influence of postmodern thought is to focus on
difference, hybridity, pastiche. Yet globalization does not abolish difference
as much as redistribute it, so that certain styles and consumer fashions are
internationalized while class divides are strengthened, often across national
boundaries. The yuppie businesswoman with her portable phone in Kuala
Lumpur or São Paulo has more in common with her counterpart in Stutt-
gart or Minneapolis than do either with the rural or urban poor of their
own societies. Yet even the poor know what is happening elsewhere, and
increasingly demand access to global products.

It could be argued that globalization is merely another term for the
further stage of capitalism, and the incorporation, through neoliberalism and
international institutions such as the World Bank and World Trade Organization, of larger parts of the world than ever before into the capitalist system.[49] By neoliberalism I mean policies which, in the name of the free market
and greater competition, have urged an end to restrictions on foreign investment; privatization of government-owned enterprises; reduction in the
powers of unions; corporate deregulation; deficit reductions; the downsizing
of the public sector, often through a process of "out-sourcing"; and steady
cuts in public expenditure on health, education, and welfare. To a greater or
lesser extent these policies have been adopted by almost all western governments since the 1980s, though at the time of writing there seems to be growing resistance in at least some countries as the alleged benefits of the freer
market are less and less apparent and as unemployment remains stubbornly
resistant to the claims of freeing up the labor market. In particular, a number
of former Communist countries in eastern Europe experienced a resurgence
of leftist politics once it became clear that the loss of certain guaranteed state
services and welfare accompanied the move to a market economy.[50] The
danger, as Zygmunt Bauman has pointed out, is that the role of the state
will steadily shrink so that it comes to concentrate above all on the provision
of "law and order," "an issue which inevitably translates in practice as or-
derly—safe—existence for some, all the awesome and threatening force of
the law for the others." While we might associate this development particularly with recent trends in the United States, Bauman illustrates it with examples from France and Germany.[51]

These policies have also been urged on "developing countries," and in
the name of "structural adjustment" became conditional for support from

the World Bank and the International Monetary Fund for poor economies over the past several decades. Just as there is now some resistance to their impact in rich countries, so the failure of developing economies over the past few years, and the dramatic "crashes" in countries as distinct as Indonesia, Brazil, and Russia, has led to increasing hostility to the idea that the unregulated market will necessarily achieve unproblematic growth. Indeed "structural adjustment," which was a result of interventions by international agencies in response to the "debt crisis" of the 1970s and 1980s, was a crucial mechanism in economic globalization. As a condition of financial assistance the World Bank and IMF pushed governments toward an emphasis on export production, privatization of government-owned enterprises, import liberalization, and a reduction of domestic spending in order to control inflation and repay foreign debt.[52] Little wonder that demonstrators in various countries waved placards proclaiming "IMF = I'm fired." Richard Cornwell of the South African Institute for Security Studies has argued: "The contradictions between the imperatives of democratisation and structural adjustment have become apparent: at the very moment when democratisation stimulates popular demand for better social and welfare services, structural adjustment requires that this be denied. In broad terms this has played a significant part in further undermining the state's claim to legitimacy in the eyes of its own citizens."[53]

In 1998 the United Nations Development Programme (UNDP) estimated that "[t]he burden of debt repayment and servicing is so great for many countries that it cripples their ability to make advances in human development or inroads in addressing poverty."[54] As one example Mozambique, despite some relief through the World Bank's Heavily Indebted Poor Countries Initiative, was paying $275,000 a day in debt service in 1999—almost three times its expenditure on health services.[55] Little wonder there is growing international pressure to wipe out the debt of the world's poorest countries, in thirty-one of which (predominantly in Africa and Central America) the per capita foreign debt *exceeds* the per capita GNP.[56]

The neoliberal project is capable of achieving impressive economic figures, but it brings with it conspicuous consumption and growing inequalities as the global market seems to generate wealth ever more divorced from real human needs, reminding us of Marx's warnings about the fetishization of commodities. No longer does capitalism generate jobs for all; in the rich world economic growth is generated by booming consumption while increasing numbers of jobs are lost to the new industrial zones of the poor world. Such transfers of jobs do not necessarily bring the benefits claimed by the exponents of neoliberal development. Jeremy Seabrook quotes one academic as saying: "All Bangladesh has become an export processing zone . . . People do not participate because they are not citizens of their own country, they are subjects of a global power structure . . . our lives are governed by decisions taken elsewhere, by the World Bank, by GATT, by IMF structural adjustment programs."[57] This shift of manufacturing jobs to poor countries brings with it a rapid increase in the female workforce, especially in industries such as garments and electronics assembly.

Criticism of this aspect of globalization underlies the approach of William Greider in *One World, Ready or Not*, where he writes: "The market process is, as its advocates claim, a source of vast creative energies—the sales-and-profit incentive that leads individuals and enterprise to invent and multiply output. Yet this same mechanism also generates the brutal swings and manic excesses—the herds of reckless investors, the false hopes of producers, the relentless drive to maximize return—that create so much destruction and human suffering, subordination and insecurity."[58] That Greider seems to be echoing the language of nineteenth-century Marxism merely indicates that such analysis is more relevant today than many post-Marxists wish to acknowledge. After all, as Paul Smith points out: "Marxism is fundamentally constituted upon the analysis of capital, and in the current conjuncture capitalism's 'triumph' and its fundamentalism should encourage a strengthening of the forms of Marxist analysis."[59]

At the same time the retreat from seeing the state as central in guaranteeing equality and providing a wide range of services has also been global in nature. There are obvious connections between Reagan's and Thatcher's attacks on unionism, the move to privatization which has affected almost every country on earth, and the pressures from the World Bank and IMF on poor countries to cut back spending on education, health, and public services in the apparent belief that this would promote greater economic efficiency and growth. The dominant ideology of globalization has meant a consistently increasing gap between rich and poor, which is remarkably uniform— it is one of the few features that, say, Chile, Hungary, and New Zealand share over the past two decades. Boosters of globalization see the tower blocks and smart new restaurants and shops which have remade cities like London since Thatcher or Toronto in the 1990s; its critics look at the same streets and see the increasing number of people forced to survive in the gutters. There are some genuine examples of economic growth due to market reforms which have carried the great majority of the population with them, but examples of these are harder to cite after the massive economic downturns across much of the world since 1998. (Up to then one would certainly have cited South Korea and Malaysia; a few countries in eastern Europe such as Poland, Estonia, and Slovakia; and some provinces of various Latin American countries, such as Ceará in the generally very poor northeast of Brazil.)[60]

The retreat from a state-run economy and state provision of services is going on even in countries which are nominally socialist. Early in 1999 I visited Vietnam, where the government is trying to achieve capitalism with a Communist face, rather as in China. *Doi moi*, the reformist policies adopted over the past few years, imply the development of a market economy and the encouragement of foreign investment without any loosening of the grip of the party apparatus. In the north this is tenable; in Ho Chi Minh City, where anyone over forty has memories of pre-Communist control, there is more discontent. Ho Chi Minh City is a low-rent version of Bangkok, with motor scooters rather than cars jamming the streets and polluting the air. The rate of building has slowed: several new hotels remain unopened, because of the fall off in regional travel, but at night the streets were packed with people, eating at sidewalk cafés, cruising the streets, packing the new bowling alleys which seem to be the high point of HCMC night life.

But not everyone on the streets is living well. The economic boom of the last few years is producing its own underclass, victims of both the decline in government support and the disintegration of traditional village life. Sex workers roam the streets on motor bikes, looking for customers, and at night will perform quick handjobs in the park for a few thousand dong (perhaps equivalent to a U.S. quarter). Street kids constantly accost foreigners trying to sell them cards, maps, stamps—one boy followed me for blocks and finally spat out "Fuck you mister" when he realized I did not intend to buy yet more cards. The use of hard drugs is increasing; over the last few years opium has largely been replaced by heroin, which comes overland from the Golden Triangle. I visited a drug rehabilitation center outside Ho Chi Minh City, where hundreds of young men and some women are put through intensive withdrawal and retraining programs, sometimes at the demand of their families. It was less oppressive than I'd anticipated—in the late afternoon kids were playing ball games in the yard, to the rather incongruous music of a recorded Beethoven symphony—but the staff are frank that within a year up to 80% are injecting again. Many of them will become infected with HIV, of which more later.

Little wonder that so much futuristic writing paints a twenty-first century which is remarkably like the grimmest memories of the nineteenth, with megacities scarred by violence, crime, pollution, and fear,[61] a far cry from the optimistic futurism of conventional science fiction writers such as Isaac Asimov. The image of the megacity also reflects the rapid urbanization of almost all parts of the world, so that even in countries the size of China and India the village peasant no longer makes up the majority of the population[62] and the number of urban agglomerations is constantly increasing. Michael Dutton reminds us that this process is akin to the steady industrialization and urbanization of England over several centuries.

> It is in *Capital* that Marx explains the general effects of the tendencies unleashed as a result of the English laws around enclosure and vagrancy. It is with an understanding of these . . . legal changes that one can begin to see the significance of the collapse of the Chinese household registration laws and the tightening of laws against vagrancy in China. In other words, to understand the key dynamics producing human rights abuses in China today, it is necessary to take Queen Victoria's advice and "close your eyes and think of England!"[63]

For some of its defenders globalization is linked inextricably to the triumph of democracy, and American policy, particularly in the post–Cold War world, has adopted a triumphalist view which sees capitalism and democracy as mutual prerequisites, arguing that liberal economics and politics cannot be separated. This is a view which has been strenuously contested by authoritarian regimes in what used to be called the "tiger" economies of Asia; whether their dramatic slowdown of growth at the end of the century proves or disproves either case remains an open question. It is as plausible to argue that the opening of the Chinese economy will lead to greater democracy as it is to suggest that growing affluence will keep most Chinese content with an authoritarian political system. Certainly the end of apartheid in South Africa, and the undoubted gains for democracy, have meant if anything a greater economic gulf, with the flight of white business from downtown Johannesburg to guarded shopping malls and housing estates north of the city. Equally the end of military regimes in most of Latin America in the past decade, while undoubtedly an important step forward for human rights, has not been necessarily accompanied by greater equality. Some Latin American critics argue that "[d]emocracy and capitalism have proved time and again to sing a poor duet because they elide questions of social justice."[64] There are signs at the beginning of this century that the assumptions of neoliberalism are being questioned in the highest echelons of the World Bank, if not yet in the IMF.

In his article (later book) "Jihad versus McWorld" Benjamin Barber warned that there are two possible futures facing much of the world. One of these stresses retribalization, the other the triumph of "one commercially homogenous global network," and both are "bleak, neither democratic."[65] I was reminded of Barber's pessimism when I came across a newspaper publicity supplement sponsored by the Tunisian government which proclaimed that its "competitive economy is based on an open, tolerant and modern society": "The capital's . . . modern district is clean and bustling, with sidewalk cafes, shops bearing international brand names, jeans-clad strollers and even a home-grown hamburger outlet."[66] No mention, needless to say, of secret police or the extent to which Tunisia is a country generally regarded as one of the less democratic in Africa. Free-market economics can produce increasing political and social strains, of which there are growing numbers of examples.

It is fascinating how strongly McDonald's has become an index of globalization.[67] In a welcome variation Thomas Friedman uses Kentucky Fried Chicken to sum up the appeal of Americanization in Malaysia, though he also claims to have originated the thesis that "no two countries which both have a McDonalds will go to war with each other" (or, as he terms it, "the Golden Arches Theory of Conflict Prevention").[68] That particular piece of neoliberal folk wisdom was ended by the war in Kosovo, when having McDonald's outlets gave Serbia no protection against NATO bombings. Shared consumerism proves not to guarantee anything about political outcomes. It is, of course, a particular formulation which conveniently avoids the American base of McDonald's, which in many countries symbolizes what Canada's leading business paper termed "the devouring of corporate Canada": "Let's talk oneness. One retailer (WalMart), one fashion (Gap), one food (McDonald's), one beverage (Coca Cola), one entertainment (Hollywood), one hang-out (Starbucks). To be at one with the world is to be at one with the United States. And this could not be truer of Canada. Awash in American culture and products, Canada is going one step further and selling the last of its prized possessions—its top stock market companies—to the United States."[69]

A couple of years ago Tuathail, Herod, and Roberts wrote: "The neoliberal-induced traumas of Mexico, with its peso crisis, international bailout, endemic political corruption, assassinations, bankruptcies, income polarization, narco-capitalism and political rebellions may well be paradigmatic for the future of many states in our current world order."[70] Globalization does break down borders, and hence the reach of the state, but the rapid move toward a global liberal order—liberal in both economics and politics—is more complex than its boosters believe. In many societies, ranging from China to Egypt, governments are banking on a mix of increased affluence and persistent repression; in others, particularly in Africa but also in central Asia and parts of Central America, economic failure is accompanied by a collapse of social and political order. In the best of cases—some parts, perhaps, of South America and eastern Europe in the past few years— one gets increasing wealth accompanied by increasing freedom, but the more common path appears to be a combination of authoritarian governments with growing inequalities and increasing lawlessness. Such conditions are almost the perfect recipe for the (re)emergence of fundamentalist religious and nationalist movements—and for what Kevin Bales has termed "the new slavery," characterized by forced labor, often linked to debt bondage and fraudulent contracts.[71]

The neoliberal push means decreasing support for welfare services while international investors are protected, in what Stephen Gill terms the "new constitutionalism" of the global political economy. In the end there is no inevitable path to democracy and prosperity. Anatol Lieven warned that "Russia in the 1990s has repeated the experience of many other weak states under the lash of the free market: they have not reformed but crumbled; and the collapse of the traditional order has led neither to democracy nor to economic progress, but to the rule of corrupt elites whose effect has been precisely to stifle both real democracy and economic efficiency."[72]

Whichever view is accepted, both the critics and the exponents of globalization agree that it has changed almost all aspects of life irreversibly. As

Lester Thurow put it: "In a very real sense the global economy has become physically embodied in our ports, airports and telecommunications systems. But most important, it is embodied in our mind-sets."[73] At the level of what Thurow terms "mindsets" there is also the question whether globalization is just another name for "Americanization," whether this is taken to refer to American military and economic influence or to the alleged cultural hegemony of the United States, which extends to even the most hostile states such as Iraq and Serbia.[74]

A democratic, neoliberal world, protected by a *pax Americana:* this is presumably what George Bush had in mind in those heady days after the collapse of the Berlin Wall when he coined the phrase "the new world order." The phrase has become less fashionable than it was in the early 1990s, when Harold Pinter even wrote a short play about torture using the phrase.[75] Some commentators would soon dismiss it as "chimerical . . . wrong on every count,"[76] as Bush's optimism gave way to a general sense of pessimism about the future might of the United States, reflected in Neal Stephenson's comment in his futuristic novel *Snow Crash* that "[t]here's only four things we do better than anyone else: music, movies, microcode (software), high-speed pizza delivery."[77] Stephenson's book reflected the then current fear of Japan as a major economic threat to the United States, and a few years later William Greider postulated the decline of the United States, in part tied to a declining U.S. dollar.[78] A year or so later this forecast seemed unnecessarily pessimistic, and the financial crises of east Asia underlined the role of the World Bank and IMF, in both of which the United States has a dominant role.

"Not since Rome claimed both imperial and spiritual precedence," Martin Walker has written, "has a single political entity managed to achieve such a double preeminence."[79] Indeed it is arguable that the twenty-first century is even more likely to be "an American century" than the preceding one.[80] No other country possesses the sheer might in economic and military power, and optimistic scenarios for the growth of European unity or the recovery of the "tiger" economies of east Asia are less convincing than the continuing dominance of American technology, agriculture, and media. It is just as easy to postulate a world increasingly shaped by American might as it is to postulate a steady decline of America. In an increasingly decentralized world New York, Washington, and Los Angeles remain dominant centers of wealth, power, and the imaginary unrivaled by any others.

TOWARD A GLOBAL CULTURE?

> *On the street, Palestinian students still burn the occasional American flag when the United States bombs Iraq. But inside Flamingo's, the posters on the wall are a pantheon of American pop culture—James Dean, Elvis Presley, Marilyn Monroe, Clint Eastwood and Charles Bronson.*
>
> —*Lee Hockstader, "West Bank Jazz," 1999*

As more of the world is drawn into the global economy, others find themselves following American cultural fashion; the clothes may be mass-produced in China or Bangladesh, but the styles imitate Los Angeles.[81] One sees the dominance of the American imaginary in the proliferation across the world of bars and restaurants and discos with American names. One current gay guide lists the Disco Hollywood on Ghengis Khan Avenue, Ulan Bator, and while it would obviously be a mistake to assume that it is equivalent to a similarly named disco in Los Angeles, the name reminds us that to be "American" is in many places to be "modern." I recall being driven around the city of Casablanca in 1996 by a guide who was genuinely excited that a McDonald's had opened near the city's most famous mosque. A more sinister example of the symbolism of American cultural dominance was the blowing up of Planet Hollywood in Cape Town by unknown terrorists in August 1998.

The impact of America may of course be at a mythological level, as in the case of the *bantut*, transgendered men studied by Mark Johnson in the Filipino island of Sulu, who relate to an America none of them have experienced firsthand.[82] This is echoed by the Swahili *mashoga* (or "passive homosexual") who told Deborah Amory that if s/he could be anyone, s/he would be Madonna.[83] Again this is not new; the image of America as "the promised land" has a long history, and the idea of it as a model for modernity was already important in nineteenth-century Europe. For the narrator of Salman Rushdie's *Ground beneath Her Feet*, America is "the open-sesame . . . which got rid of the British long before we did."[84] Even where other cultural influences seem important, the influence of the United States may be seen; discussing the Japanese impact on Taiwan, Leo Ching notes that "Japanese mass culture itself is still plugged into every trend of Western, especially American, pop culture."[85] One of the most popular Chinese television programs of the 1990s was the series *Beijingers in New York*, which was filmed in New York and seen by many critics as "a good textbook for a market economy," even as the

Ministry of Culture stressed it revealed the excessive materialism of American culture.[86]

Of course other popular cultures flourish: Indian films, African music, Egyptian radio, Mexican soaps. Known as *telenovelas,* the soaps are successfully exported to more than 100 countries, and have been claimed to be Mexico's largest export.[87] In the same way Brazil has a huge television industry, and TV Globo is the fourth largest commercial network in the world. Indeed television in most countries is dominated by locally produced shows, though often shows which draw on American themes and production values. Japanese cartoons are widely circulated through Asia, and in Korea at least have been attacked as morally corrupting.[88] *Of course* American pop culture draws increasingly on overseas influences, whether it be the story of Eva Perón or games such as Nintendo and Pokemon. Thinking again of fashion, one might note the importance of Paris, Milan, and Tokyo—but it is only when their styles are taken over by Hollywood that they are disseminated effectively across the world. No other large nation is both so insulated from the rest of the world and so able to export its views. The American popular conception of Mexico, a strange mix of exotic fears and fantasies, is far closer to the view of Mexico held by the rest of the world (at least the non-Spanish-speaking world) than anything Mexico itself can create, despite the successful marketing of its *telenovelas.* Like children across the world my own introduction to Mexico came via the crude stereotypes of siestas and sombreros in Warner Brothers cartoons.

Equally world events—the death of Princess Diana, the election of a pope, the World Cup—need not take place in the United States, but increasingly the ways that such events are perceived will reflect the dominance of the United States in world communications. This is reflected in the ways in which the Olympic Games have become vast events in which television rights and sponsorship, above all within the United States, are central. At least two-thirds of the television rights for the summer games, and a higher percentage for the winter event, are sold to American networks, and the United States has correspondingly greater influence within the International Olympic Committee. Holding the Olympics in a city outside the United States can be an enormously significant way of further incorporating that city into the global communications economy, as was most obvious when the 1988 Seoul Games marked the emergence of South Korea as a significant "developed" economy.[89]

For all the talk of "world culture"—and the undoubted evidence of constant American borrowings from diverse sources—it remains true that, unlike flows of capital, the flows of cultural influence tend to increasingly favor the United States, and overseas-owned corporations often contribute to this. Or, as Beryl Langer put it: "Producers of 'Canadian' popular culture confront an audience socialised into *American* music, film and genre fiction. Whatever they produce can only be a 'Canadian version' of 'the real thing.'"[90] By the 1960s half the non-Communist world's movie theaters were dominated by American movies;[91] three decades later Hollywood, the *Economist* has estimated, provides 80% of world film viewing and 70% of television fiction.[92] (In reverse only 1% of movies shown in the United States originate in Europe.)[93] At the end of the last century Arnold Schwarzenegger (originally an Austrian, but now American through both career and marriage) was allegedly the world's most popular film star,[94] and his replacement will almost certainly be Hollywood based. Both in such former world centers of filmmaking as France and Britain, and in the bulk of the "developing" world, American films dominate mass culture, partly because of the massive marketing machines that include ownership of cinemas across the world and complex retail tie-ins, which allow Warner Brothers and Disney shops to proliferate in shopping malls across the globe.[95] Increasingly "pop" culture unabashedly promotes the consumer goods produced by major corporations, whether it be through designer labels on clothes, movie tie-in promotions, television "infomercials," or rap music which extols its links to the commercial world.

Even though the *Economist* recently argued that "flogging American culture around the world has turned out to be trickier than the big companies first thought," its evidence for this is the need for MTV (which reaches 320 million households worldwide) to increase its local content[96]—much of which, one assumes, is a repackaged if hybridized version of MTV Central. The Walt Disney Company, argues Wayne Ellwood, "may just be the single most powerful and influential force in the globalization of Western culture"[97] and Maio claims that it deliberately made the animated film *Mulan*, about a legendary Chinese woman warrior, as a means of breaking into the Chinese market.[98] While regional and local cultures can sometimes flourish, even if they must increasingly coexist with a global culture in which English is becoming the undisputed lingua franca,[99] government attempts to protect local film and television industries, as in France and Korea, have not proved particularly effective. (Nonetheless it is true that what is acceptable on most European television stations remains marginal in the United States. American television may now have a plethora of gay characters in their situation comedies, but they are far less likely to depict actual homosexual behavior than are the Dutch, the Spanish, or the British.)[100] Commenting on a Malaysian government attempt to promote local films through video outlets one film industry spokesman said: "There are not enough local titles to sell. Furthermore, no one wants to rent them."[101]

It is hardly surprising that Mahathir can simultaneously worry about western influences and the decline of English-language proficiency in Malaysia, which gives Malaysians a comparative advantage in accessing the larger world. Foreigners, whether they be movie stars or British royalty, achieve ultimate celebrity status by becoming in some sense American. It is revealing that after the Italian fashion designer Gianni Versace was shot (in Miami) the *Economist* could write about him as "a good American."[102] But why not? Before her death even Princess Diana, mother of the future king of England, was rumored to be considering a move to the United States and her former sister-in-law, the duchess of York, had already become a regular on U.S. television. (One of the oddities of writing this book was the number of times references to the British "royals" seemed to capture so much of what is changing in the global regulation of sexuality.)

Sexuality is a useful domain in which to test the alleged dominance of the American. Christopher Hitchens identifies "sexual freedom" as the first in a list of ingredients of what constitutes the New World in the European imagination.[103] As Robert Kaplan described a bus ride in post-Soviet Uzbekistan: "On the panel behind the driver's seat, facing the passengers, was a poster of a nude American pinup whose large and glossy breasts seemed to fill the bus as it bumped along the road. *The promise of the West,* I thought."[104] Certainly, as will be argued further, the United States remains a model which has heavily influenced certain global trends in sexuality, whether we think of identity politics, sexology research, or the politics of moral backlash. But at the same time we need to beware of assuming that growing homogenization of consumption makes for the eradication of national—or local—cultural differences.

The anthropologist Arjun Appadurai argues for the impact on the nation-state of mediascapes: "In many countries of the Middle East and Asia the lifestyles represented on both national and international TV and cinema completely overwhelm and undermine the rhetoric of national politics."[105] But what is striking about the contemporary world is that more and more of us coexist with contradictions, so that the audience who watches *Baywatch* in Chennai or Asunción will not necessarily see it in the same way, nor draw the same conclusions for their own behaviors and beliefs as do audiences in Los Angeles or Lexington. Cynthia Enloe points to the different ways in which the film *Rambo* was understood, absorbed, and rejected in various countries when it became a world hit in the 1980s and was viewed "by people as different as Filipino guerillas and anti–Cold War Finns," as well as becoming a nickname for a Russian commando.[106] To adopt the style did not necessarily mean adopting the politics associated with the original.

Culture and religion continue to mold sexual values and behaviors in ways which are not apparent if we only look at the common consumption of goods and images. Of course we must be careful in making this argument not to forget that over half the world's population have never made a phone call, and that there are many parts of the world which do not have access to radio let alone television and the Internet. Once again technology, for all the hype about its contribution to democratization, generates its own class divides. A shopping mall in Milan, Taipei, or Caracas will increasingly carry similar brands, but this does not by itself eradicate cultural differences, as Appadurai stresses in his discussion of globalization. On the other hand it can lead to what the Thai political scientist Kasian Tejapira has termed "cultural schizophrenia."

> Thus pseudo-chemically sublimated Thainess is returned to us in a solid but useless, irrelevant and fossilized or mummified form right from a temple, theater or museum . . . Thus apart from Coke—the promoter of the value of Thainess, we have, in this official Year to Campaign for Thai Culture [1994], such Thai-Thai advertising campaigns as "Singha Beer—the pride of the nation," "Thai Life Insurance—the life insurance company of, by and for the Thais" . . . No matter how spurious their claims to Thainess may be under scrutiny, the fact that these commodities have indeed been turned into signs of Thainess has changed Thainess willy-nilly into one identity option among many others in the free market of a limitless plurality of commodities and/or brand names.[107]

HREE

Sex and Political Economy

I use the term "political economy" to signal that I am discussing sexuality in the context of larger socioeconomic factors which create the conditions within which sexual acts and identities occur. These factors include the *economic,* as growing affluence allows—and forces—new ways of organizing "private" life, and as sexuality is increasingly commodified; the *cultural,* as images of different sexualities are rapidly diffused across the world, often to be confronted by religious and nationalist movements; and the *political,* in that state regulation plays a crucial role in determining the possible forms of sexual expression. For example there is a far more overt "gay" world in Manila than in Singapore, despite the considerable gap in wealth, in part because of different political regimes. A more dramatic example comes from Spain, which after the death of Franco and the resulting democratization saw a rapid growth of apparent sexual permissiveness, reflected in the films of Pedro Almodóvar. It might at times be appropriate to add a fourth category, the *epistemological,* as particular ways of understanding human beings and the worlds they make are diffused globally.

A political-economy perspective means we have to recognize class, gender, race *but also* the role of the state; that is, we need to think in terms of structures rather than specific issues or identities. As long as political and economic structures maintain most women as subordinate in most areas of life, as they do in most parts of the world, we cannot escape the fact that any discussion of sexuality must recognize differences of gender which are an unknowable mix of the biological and the social. I say unknowable because despite the current vogue to attribute a great deal to genetic influences we cannot stand outside human society and say this is the essence of being "man" or "woman": there are clear biological differences, most obviously the ability to give birth, but the meanings attributed to these differences are inescapably social. Biology imposes certain limits within which humans construct their worlds, but these too are changing, and indeed becoming less and less meaningful with developments such as in vitro–fertilization births and cloning.

Others have sought to link political economy to sexuality, and as Nancy Folbre has shown, sexuality was an issue for the founders of modern economic thought.[1] The rebirth of second-wave feminism saw some interest in applying economic analyses to sexuality,[2] often around issues such as child care and housework. In general, however, current theorizing around sexuality tends to place great stress on questions of discourse, representation, and identity, often at the expense of material reality. The approach of this book is in some ways an attempt to return to earlier attempts in this century to link a Marxist and a Freudian reading of social life, though in a very different context from that of the Frankfurt School and theorists such as Herbert Marcuse (whose later work was a significant influence on my early writings). I am less utopian, now, than was Marcuse during the upheavals of the late 1960s;[3] the experience of both the gay movement and the AIDS epidemic has produced its own pragmatic reckonings, of which more later. At the start of this century Freud's pessimism about "human nature" seems unfortunately all too justified. Nor is it easy to reconcile the Freudian and Marxist traditions; Joel Kovel expresses the difficulty when he writes: "Each had a terrible truth to it—and each negated the other."[4]

Nonetheless there is in Freud an attempt to link an exploration of the personal with larger historical forces, to find ways of explaining the mix of self-interest and irrationality which underlies social life. If we are prepared to understand concepts such as libido or the superego, or grand historical myths such as that of *Civilization and Its Discontents* as metaphors rather than as literal truth, they offer ways of illuminating the ways in which political economy intersects with the psychological to create particular regimes of sexuality and gender. What makes it possible to link Freud's theories to those of Marx is that both understood the way in which a great deal of what is taken for granted is constructed by human beings, for Marx through the relationship of social and economic forces in history, for Freud through their impact on the unconscious. Both thinkers were hostile to religion, but a Freudian reading makes more sense of just how it is able to operate so frequently as "the opiate of the masses," to borrow Marx's term.

My approach has something in common with the work of two American anthropologists, Michaela di Leonardo and Roger Lancaster,[5] of feminists working to gender international relations (particularly Jan Pettman[6] and Cynthia Enloe) as well as with such writers as R. W. Connell, Nancy Fraser, Richard Parker, and Jeffrey Weeks, whose works will be cited frequently. It is an approach that could be called neo-Marxist, and shares much of the criticism of postmodern theory as too inclined to concentrate on the textual and the discursive, and insufficiently interested in institutions and political and economic structures.[7] At the same time it recognizes that not all power relations are based on economic conflict, and that sexuality and gender are arenas in which we need a more nuanced understanding of human understandings and action than is true in either orthodox Marxist or postmodern discursive analyses. This is not to deny the attempts of some scholars to find ways of incorporating older Marxist and Freudian critical theory into postmodernity. In her remarkable study of body politics in Guatemala, the anthropologist Diane Nelson develops the idea of "fluidarity," which she sees as "'pink' in the sense of Marxist, with close attention to class relations, but also as 'Freudian,' attune to the work of desire and the unconscious."[8]

The use of Marxism does not mean, however, that I believe all forms of oppression and exploitation can be reduced to economic relations, and here I draw on Nancy Fraser's very useful distinction between "injustices of distribution and injustices of recognition," both of which she claims have material consequences and both of which need to be countered to achieve social justice.[9] She argues that the former injustices require political-economic restructuring, while the latter require cultural or symbolic change: "It could also involve recognizing and possibly valorizing cultural diversity. More radically still, it could involve the wholesale transformation of societal patterns of representation, interpretation, and communication in ways that would change *everybody's* sense of self."[10] Fraser's analysis is particularly useful in that it goes beyond the crude idea that we need to choose between distributive and identity politics, and suggests that each has a place in developing better and more just societies.

The present period is one which has to be understood as marking an enormous expansion of the reach of capitalism, both in terms of geography and in terms of everyday life, but without thereby assuming that everything is reducible to questions of economic power. However, the postmodern vogue for reducing questions of inequality and power to matters of discourse is even more misleading. Discussing this in relation to the work of Judith Butler,

Teresa Ebert argues: "[She] provides an analytic of power in which we do *not* have to confront the global relations and systematicity of power; in which we do *not* have to deal with the most serious consequences of power operating in dialectical relation to the mode of production and the division of labor— the consequences . . . of exploitation."[11]

Sex has always been present in exchanges between peoples; one can see harbingers of today's globalization in the trade in youthful slaves in the Roman Empire or in the sexual exchanges which accompanied early Chinese, Arab, and European explorers. The introduction of syphilis into Europe following Columbus's "discovery" of the New World reminds us of the ways in which sexual contact almost inevitably goes hand in hand with other forms of cross-cultural contact, and is an integral part of colonization and exploitation. Outbreaks of syphilis in Uganda in the early part of the twentieth century were associated by some British colonial authorities with the impact of colonialism and Christianity on traditional Bagandan society.[12] The end of the Cold War meant a rapid change in attitudes about sexuality in eastern Europe.[13]

In Leonard Bernstein's version of Voltaire's *Candide* there is a wonderful song, sung by Dr. Pangloss in eighteenth-century Lisbon, about the transmission of "a dear souvenir" which passed from "a seafaring Scott" via "a sweet little cheat in Paree . . . a man from Japan . . . and a Moor from Iran" back to Westphalia and his sweetheart Paquette.[14] With the great imperial expansion of Europe which began in the sixteenth century came a vast array of different sexual arrangements, all ultimately based on maintaining the dual superiority (through gender and race) of the imperialist male. That male was usually but not always white; Japan established brothels through east Asia to accommodate the expansion of Japanese business after its defeat of China in 1895 led to the conquest of both Korea and Taiwan.

Sexuality is a domain enormously influenced by global forces, both economic and cultural, but also one that has been underresearched and theorized. Here I am speaking of both behavior and emotions; while it is impossible to say much about global change in behavior there will sometimes be evidence for change through a careful study of survey research, police reports, STI figures, and so forth. R. W. Connell claims that at least in the United States there is persuasive evidence for a rising rate of heterosexual intercourse outside marriage and a move for women's patterns of behavior to become more like men's.[15] In similar ways research suggests that sexual behavior appears to be changing in similar ways in Japan, which has the world's highest use of condoms (in part because the contraceptive pill was not available until 1999, making Japan the last significant country to approve its use).[16] The decision led to an extraordinary article by conservative commentator Francis Fukuyama, who claimed that it would undermine Japanese social stability, based on "the social bargain on which Japanese society has traditionally rested, in which male resources were exchanged for female fertility."[17] Given that condoms are widely available in Japan, and that countries which have not only allowed but promoted the pill have long had far higher birthrates than Japan, the argument seems bizarre.

Evidence collected as a consequence of HIV-prevention programs has shown a rise in the use of condoms in a number of countries,[18] and some reports of a decline in adolescent sex in a couple of countries, most notably Uganda. However, reports from Thailand suggest an increase in premarital sex among teenage girls, and correspondingly less reliance on prostitutes by adolescent males.[19] While one might expect various fluctuations in sexual behavior following particular campaigns, the impetus of globalization is almost certainly to both break down existing taboos (e.g., the very high premium on premarital virginity for women) and lead to a gradual convergence of sexual behavior across different societies.

Sexual mores and values have constantly changed as societies have come in contact with outside influences and new technologies. While the emphasis in this book is on more recent and sometimes dramatic change, these are often best understood as a continuation of a very long historical process which involves centuries of trade, slavery, colonization, and large-scale shifts in the nature of economic and technological structures. To speak of "traditional values" is often to adopt a totally ahistorical attitude toward human behavior, which assumes a static continuity which is likely to be true only in small and very isolated societies. It is not at all clear that the changes in sexuality in, say, post-Communist Russia or rapidly industrializing China are any greater than those wrought by the Atlantic slave trade of the eighteenth century or the massive urbanization of nineteenth-century Europe. What is different, however, is a far denser and faster system of diffusing ideas, values, and perceptions, so that a certain self-consciousness about and understanding of sexuality is arguably being universalized in a completely new way.

There are various transnational surveys which attempt to measure changes in attitudes to a whole range of social issues across both time and space, and in one overview of these Ronald Ingelhart has claimed to find evidence of a shift from what he terms "materialist" to "postmaterialist" values in a number of countries. A full discussion of his argument goes beyond the scope of this book, but it is interesting that he shows significant shifts toward a more permissive view on abortion, divorce, homosexuality, and extramarital sex in all but two of twenty countries surveyed between 1981 and 1990.[20] The two exceptions are South Africa and Argentina, but it is my hunch that particular political circumstances in the two years surveyed might explain this, and that a rather different result would be likely had the latter year been somewhat later. The twenty countries were largely North Atlantic democracies, though they included Mexico, Hungary, Japan, and South Korea as well as Argentina and South Africa; what is interesting is the rapid shift away from "traditional" values about sex in Catholic countries such as Mexico and Spain. (I leave aside for the moment the extreme skepticism with which we must read such survey data, especially given that even apparently equivalent questions change their meaning through translation, and there are very difficult issues in ensuring appropriate sampling, etc.) Overall the evidence suggests that in rich countries at least there is a converging move toward a more permissive set of attitudes on matters sexual, even if national differences remain significant.

Equally it is difficult to fully grasp the ways in which the emotional and "inner life" are altered by the larger changes wrought by political economy. If Giddens is right "globalization" is "a shorthand [term] for a whole series of influences that are altering not just events on the large scale but the very tissue of our everyday lives."[21] This is echoed in the less sociological description of Don DeLillo: "But even as desire tends to specialize, going silky and intimate, the force of converging markets produces an instantaneous capital that shoots across horizons at the speed of light, making for a certain furtive sameness, a planing away of particulars that affects everything from architecture to leisure time to the way people eat and sleep and dream."[22]

These changes are part of everyday life for greater and greater numbers of people. I was once asked in a seminar where I had spoken of the apparent universalizing of gay identities whether the apparent increase in gay romance in some countries was a product of "soap opera or Chinese opera." The emphasis on foregrounding "the personal," most obvious in American television and magazines, is disseminated through a global media, which carries *The Oprah Winfrey Show* or *Who Magazine* to anywhere that has television and newsstands. With this comes a particular way of understanding identity and relationships which is as culturally specific to early-twenty-first-century consumerist capitalism as Freud's analyses were to early-twentieth-century bourgeois Vienna, and is reflected in phenomena such as the rejection of arranged marriages and women claiming the right to sexual pleasure.

One can see these shifts in accounts of Japanese life, where the last several decades have seen revolutionary shifts in the willingness of women to accept their traditional subordinate role. This shift is evoked by the narrator in the novel *Memoirs of a Geisha,* who claims of the man she loved that "[n]othing in life mattered more to me than pleasing him."[23] Contemporary Japanese women reject arranged marriages, are more likely than men to initiate divorce, and have become increasingly willing to pursue cases of sexual harassment and rape.[24] (Indeed new terms have been invented to cover cases such as a married couple who live apart or a weekend-only marriage.) Yet this does not mean that sexual life in Japan is simply becoming westernized. The hypocrisies of Japanese sex remain rather different, meaning that the gap between what can be said and what is in practice accepted would seem shocking to most westerners. Nicholas Bornoff gives the example of "moppet cheesecake": "In the West the concept of pornography for adolescents would be almost as outrageous as child pornography. In Japan, however, where basic attitudes towards sex are down-to-earth despite the paradoxical formalities and official injunctions curtailing them, such magazines raise only the eyebrows of the more puritanical."[25] In the same way there is a large homosexual world, but very little open acknowledgment of its existence of the sort that has now occurred in most western countries.

It is not true, of course, that the globalization of emotions runs in one direction, or indeed that the north is always the source of change. In her formulation of "the world economy of passion" Marta Savigliano argues: "Parallelling the extraction of material goods and labor from the Third World, the passion-poor core countries of the capitalist world system have been appropriating emotional and affective practices from their colonies for several centuries . . . The Third World's emotional and expressive actions and arts have been categorized, homogenized, and transformed into commodities suitable for the First World's consumption."[26] While I am uncomfortable with the simplistic assumption of the poverty of northern passion, her comments are a reminder of the ways in which globalization always involves reciprocal and often contradictory influences. Certainly the rich world has long looked to the hot zones of the world for images of sexuality, whether they be the Polynesian paintings of Gauguin, the sexual adventures of several generations of French artists and writers in North Africa, or the flamboyance of Latin American samba and tango. Echoing Savigliano, Jose Quiroga has written that "Cuba has always been linked to the outside world by the threads of desire."[27]

In the 1920s the African American singer Josephine Baker became famous for a show which played on the association in white audiences between negritude and sex: "[She] entered a stage jungle by dusk (of course), and crawled along the trunk of a fallen tree on all fours; there, to the beat of native drums, she came across the sleeping body of a young white man, for whom she launched into her dance."[28] The appeal of the apparently savage darkskin was repeated by the Cuban Alicia Parla, who became famous in the 1930s for her erotically charged rumba dancing, and the Brazilian Carmen Miranda in the 1940s and 1950s. Since the 1960s Jamaican reggae music has been a potent influence on the outside world,[29] joining a range of other cultures in the shopping malls of the world under the sobriquet "world" (i.e., nonwestern) music. Even today western theatrical entrepreneurs promote African dancers as embodying a particular sensual savagery.

More recently the patterns have to some extent become multiple, so that in the imagination of many in the poor world it is the north which represents sexual exoticism. Such exoticism can be conjured up as either an evil against which traditional protections need be invoked, or a fantasy to be sought after, as in the appearance of eastern European women in the brothels of Bangkok and Dubai. (There were already elements of this view of the north during the time of European empire, when some of the colonized constructed white women as both desirable and unattainable.)

While it is tempting to write about globalization as if the script ran in one direction, the reality is that human contact and conquest has always changed perceptions of what is natural behavior, and much current postcolonial theory can be profitably used to read back into the long histories of imagining ourselves through contact with those who can be defined as different. The colonial enterprise changed both the colonizers and the colonized, as Neville Hoad has argued persuasively in discussing the invention of homosexuality as a category in nineteenth-century scientific thought. "The perception of male homosexuality amongst the subject people of empire," he writes, "is mobilized both by groups seeking to stigmatize homosexuality fur-

ther and by those wishing to depathologize and decriminalize it." As Hoad
points out, the connection between the invention of the homosexual category
and the expansion of empires is linked in narratives such as the anxiety about
moral decline found in writers like Josephine Butler and in Sir Richard Bur-
ton's rather fanciful invention of the "Sotadic zone," namely almost anywhere with a non-British climate which he claimed facilitated the existence
of "pathological love."[30]

Sexual ideologies cannot exist independent of larger political, social,
and cultural contexts, and any meaningful liberationist position must simultaneously recognize the links to certain privileges in this position which are
often unavailable to most women and children. To the phrase "pleasure and
danger," which Carole Vance took as the title of an anthology on sexuality,[31]
Jill Matthews has added the concept of "obligation," arguing that for women
sex is almost always "embedded in a network of power relations, and their
position in this network is usually incoherent."[32] For most women in the
world sex and reproduction carry considerable dangers—disease, unwanted
pregnancy, infertility, and severe obstetric complications—which may well
outweigh the possible pleasures, and again underline the extent to which the
experience of sex is gendered.[33] It is not surprising that women's movements
have often been associated with campaigns for greater sexual morality, which
often have been equated with forcing men to accept more responsibility for
their actions. At the same time many feminists themselves have warned of
the danger of divorcing reproduction from sex: "Sexual desire is entangled
with broader questions of pleasure, with the aesthetics of the body, with the
pleasures of a more diffuse sensuality and collective sociability, and sometimes with the pleasures of fecundity."[34]

Certain regimes of gender are themselves being globalized, as Cynthia
Enloe has demonstrated in her account of the "banana republics" of Central
America, where sexist ideologies and a division of labor along gender lines
help maintain low wages and the dominance of foreign corporations. Yet the
standard literature of political economy and international relations largely
avoids this dimension. It ignores, as Enloe writes about her introduction to
the study of international relations, "what the connections might be between
international debt, foreign investment, and militarism on the one hand and
rape, prostitution, housework and wife-battering on the other. The message
one came away with from those books was: the former are inherently 'serious' and 'political'; the latter are 'private' and probably trivial."[35]

Consider, too, the role of globalization in the creation of new gender and family structures. R. W. Connell, whose work has influenced mine for more than twenty years, has argued that we should see "global markets and multinational corporations as key sites of the making and transformation of a global gender order."[36] Of course in assessing these changes we have to remember that in many parts of the world dominant sexual ideologies are themselves the products of earlier imperialist expansion, and of the missionaries who accompanied traders and soldiers. "Traditional" views of sexuality and gender in much of Africa, the Caribbean, and the Pacific owe as much to colonialism as to precolonial culture. Indeed the idea of a precolonial tradition is often a problematic concept for the millions of people who are descended from the mass migrations of nineteenth-century empires—African slaves to the Americas, Indian laborers to Fiji and South Africa, Chinese workers to Malaysia and California. Whose tradition are we talking about in countries which have undergone radical reshaping of their demography due to foreign domination? Is it African culture or imperialist Christianity which continues to criminalize homosexuality in Zimbabwe, and put President Banana on trial?

Gender and sexuality come together through the family, and family structures themselves, far from being fixed or "natural" as moral conservatives insist, are ultimately dependent on social and economic structures. Perhaps the most significant change for millions of people caused by greater affluence, urbanization, and foreign influences is the decline of marriage based on social and economic arrangements between families, versus the far more individualist assumptions about marriage as ways of achieving love and personal fulfillment. With these changes in marriage comes, in turn, a decline in the extended family, which is causing huge problems in the majority of countries which do not have state welfare systems and depend on families to care for the young, the old, and the sick. Even as wealthy a state as Singapore legally requires children to take responsibility for their aging parents as part of propping up "traditional" (or "Asian") values.

John MacInnes argues that "modernity systematically undermines patriarchy,"[37] and certainly one of the themes of fundamentalist movements opposed to modernity (the Taliban, the Amish, the Lubavitchers) is their rigid patriarchal attitudes to women and children. At the same time the male "flight from commitment," which Barbara Ehrenreich noted for the United States some time ago,[38] is taking place across the globe, as neoliberal economics lead to the collapse of more and more families under the pressures of economic hardship and movement from country to city. One report from Chile claims: "Nationally, 25 per cent of households are headed by a woman, but they are concentrated in poor areas like Reneca where the figure rises as high as 50 per cent. Most of these women's partners either disappeared during the Pinochet years or abandoned them in the Latin American machismo culture of multiple mistresses."[39] While I think this explanation places too little emphasis on the implications of the larger socioeconomic changes of the Pinochet regime, the figures underline the double jeopardy of globalization: once the economic boom slows down not only does it leave millions without jobs, but also without the informal security nets provided in the past by extended family and village communities. Under such conditions of social disintegration, corruption and crime flourish.

Just as was true in nineteenth-century Europe and North America, "traditional" family forms break down with urbanization, industrialization, and affluence, but the pace of change means that in some cases people may move in one generation from the extended family of precapitalism to the post–nuclear family of consumer capitalism. (The highest percentage of households headed by women is not in the affluent west, but rather in Botswana and Barbados.)[40] A few years ago I was on Bataam Island, an Indonesian outpost a short ferry ride away from Singapore. Going into town in the evening, I was struck by the large number of teenagers flocking to discos, teenagers who had moved away from their villages and families because of the opportunity for work in new factories. The club scene, complete with its designer drugs, is by no means confined to western countries; there has been considerable controversy over the use of ecstasy in Asian countries over the past few years. Runganaga and Aggleton have noted that in Zimbabwean discotheques and nightclubs "[y]oung men also learn from one another how to arouse women sexually by kissing and smooching, behaviors which were rarely seen in former times, and actions that cause offense to some rural peoples today."[41]

The more affluent travel abroad to find sexual freedom, or at least its illusion; perhaps the contemporary version of nineteenth-century British and French homosexual tourists in North Africa and Southeast Asia are the Chinese gay men portrayed in films such as *Wedding Banquet* or *Happy Together*[42] or the single Japanese women tourists in Bali or Hawaii, sometimes referred to as "yellow cabs."[43] Some western countries have begun to accept persecu-

tion of homosexuality as a reason to grant refugee status. There is another
sort of travel in search of sexual freedom, that of women crossing borders in
search of abortions, as is the case for thousands of Irish women who have
been forced to go to Britain because of the strictness of the Irish laws or large
numbers of European women who seek abortions in the Netherlands.[44] In
recent years some women have fled China, fearing compulsory abortions
because of the "one child" policy: in a widely reported case in Australia in
1997 an eight-and-a-half-month-pregnant woman was deported to China
and apparently underwent an abortion ten days later.

Such examples only emphasize that movement between and within
countries has very different meanings for the rich and the poor. Economic
"development" means that hundreds of thousands are forced to turn to sex
work. This is evident in Chinese cities where in 1991 official figures suggested
200,000 people were *arrested* for prostitution, with the actual number working
clearly far higher.[45] Such figures in turn reflect a general collapse of the puritanism of Mao's China, with growing affluence creating new opportunities
and interest in sex, mild perhaps by western standards but revolutionary be-
side the mores of even fifteen years ago.[46] Similarly Vietnam by the late 1990s
was estimated to have 60,000 prostitutes, although "since prostitution is illegal and often occurs in veiled settings, such as karaoke bars and hotels, others
believe the number is much higher."[47] The women who offer quick handjobs
in the parks late at night in Ho Chi Minh City are there as a direct consequence
of the economic—but not political—liberalization of the past few years.

That there is a close link between liberalization and major changes in
sexual behavior is suggested in a story in *Asiaweek* in early 1999 about the
Chinese city of Nanjie in central China. Here local authorities have preserved an earlier version of Communist austerity: "There is no pollution
from such Western decadence as karaoke bars and discos, and township
leaders insist that Nanjie has no crime, no prostitution, no premarital sex
and no unplanned babies. 'There was only one divorce last year. We strictly
live according to the thoughts of Chairman Mao' says Wang Jinzhong, vice
party secretary. It is almost as if Nanjie were a Communist theme park."[48]
Allowing for the particular views of the reporters—it is odd to see karaoke
described as "western decadence"—the report suggests that it is probably
impossible to maintain the sexual rigidities of revolutionary China once economic liberalization is encouraged. In a country with a transient population
of between 80 and 120 million, mostly young men, social dislocation seems

inevitable.[49] By the end of the century sexually transmitted infections were escalating rapidly, and Chinese authorities themselves were attributing this to the impact of market reforms.[50]

It could be argued that the changes in family structures and values have been slower in much of Asia, both Communist and non-Communist, than one might expect, but they are occurring, and are reflected in certain Asian unease about globalization: "When Asian spokesmen (at least the male ones) say they do not like Western values, what they often mean is that they do not like Western sexual roles; the individualism that is problematic for them includes not only freewheeling political protest but freewheeling protest within the family."[51] Under President Suharto the Indonesian state tried systematically to maintain "traditional values" through explicit rules for sexual conduct among civil servants[52] and carried on the opposition of Indonesia's first president, Sukarno, to "decadent" western music: "In the late New Order, punk, death metal and other 1990s headbanging genres, adopted from the Euro-American scene, have come to signify a gesture of generational opposition to the ageing regime, led by an old man."[53] Not surprisingly the emergence of new political movements and politics in post-Suharto Indonesia involved considerable numbers of women unwilling to continue the subservient role laid down for them in the New Order. Similarly the modernizing rulers of Malaysia adopted policies of considerable intervention in family and gender structures to promote both economic growth and political quiescence.[54]

There is ongoing debate about how markedly and how rapidly economic change is leading to social change, particularly in terms of family and gender structures. There are considerable insights into this from the literature of HIV/AIDS—but these suggest considerable variations between countries. Thus a UNAIDS report in Thailand suggests that the extended family is breaking down and stresses the centrality of mothers in care.[55] On the other hand (and writing of Africa) Carael, Buve, and Awusabo-Asare claim that "[f]requently the changes perceived to follow from modernization are found to be less dramatic than initially supposed. Cross-cultural survey results showed that disparities in sexual behavior between urban and rural areas, after controlling for age and marital status, were considerably less than expected."[56] It is probable that new sorts of social pressures are required to maintain "traditional" forms of behavior as the environments in which they developed change—thus the concern of fundamentalists of all stripes to maintain such traditions, often through quite draconian social controls. It is probably also true that the greater wealth and "modernity" of Thailand is the crucial difference, rather than any particular cultural tradition.

Such social controls create new victims, usually women and children who are punished because they have already been violated. Consider, for example, reports that in Jordan a quarter of all homicides are "honor killings," punishments of women for allegedly defiling their family's honor through sexual misbehavior.[57] Currently there is a campaign to repeal that section of the country's penal code which provides that "[h]e who discovers his wife or a female relative committing adultery and kills, wounds or injures one or both of them is exempted from any penalty."[58] Increasing numbers of children, often born to women who have been raped or coerced into sex, are abandoned, so that numbers swell in orphanages in Moscow and Casablanca.[59] In many countries governments provide no services for single mothers or illegitimate children, and in a few, particularly in Latin America, it is not unknown for police to regard such children as fit only for extermination. Although it is hard to get reliable figures, women with dependent children constitute a major part of the world's poorest populations. As was true of industrialization in nineteenth-century North Atlantic countries, the rapid changes of the contemporary economy are producing demands which many governments are neither ready nor willing to accept.

In western countries not marrying is becoming the norm, as is increasing recognition of a wide range of family structures including single-parenting, communal households, and homosexual couples. The changes are rapid: until the 1970s "cohabitation" was illegal in most American states. This range is reflected both in the popularity of television programs which reflect new forms of relationships (e.g., the largely unattached singles of *Seinfeld* or *Friends*) and in the anxiety around the family which is reflected in the politics of "family values." In the same way reports that more women are contemplating the possibility of life without marriage or children are coming from at least the more affluent parts of Asia,[60] although the acceptance of single mothers and couples living together without marrying remains far less than in most western countries.

Except in a few rich enclaves outside the "first world" the availability of housing is a significant restriction on the development of growing numbers of single-parent and indeed single-person households now common in most of the western world. However, middle-class and educated women in "developing countries," while clearly a minority, can count on the availability of cheap servants, which makes careers easier to manage than for most comparable western women. It is worth remembering that it took approximately a hundred years of industrialization before western countries recognized the possibility of the single woman as anything but a figure of either fun or pity.[61] (On some readings the gap between Jane Austen's Bennet family waiting at home for proposals of marriage and the single women searching for love and relationships in *Sex and the City* is not all that great.) Such a development requires changes both in the economic order, to allow women to hold well-paying jobs, and in the ideology which defines women in relation to the family.

While debates around the post–nuclear family are most obvious in the United States, they are by no means confined to that country. The first national recognition of same-sex partnerships came in Denmark in 1989 and arguments about state recognition of homosexual relationships have now extended to almost all of Europe.[62] In 1998 a new magazine was launched in France, called *Le Mensuel des Nouvelles Familles* (The monthly of the new families), whose advertising poster showed two middle-aged men gazing adoringly at what appears to be an empty pram. By the 1990s France had a higher rate of births outside marriage than Britain or the United States, and in 1998 there was bitter debate over a proposal known as the Pacte civil de solidarité (Civil solidarity pact). The proposed law recognized cohabiting couples (both hetero- and homosexual) "who cannot or do not wish to marry," and was bitterly opposed by the Right,[63] who brought 100,000 people onto the streets of Paris in a protest march at the beginning of 1999. Shortly afterward the Senate amended the proposal to cover only heterosexual couples, but its opposition was finally overruled by a vote in the Assembly in October 1999. In Canada the supreme court ruled in 1999 that the definition in Ontario's family law of "spouse" as a person of the opposite sex is unconstitutional—and in an echo of American responses, the House of Commons promptly declared that "marriage is and should remain the union of one man and one woman."[64]

The idea of "gay marriage" became a major issue in the United States in 1996, following a case in the Hawaii Supreme Court which seemed likely to recognize same-sex marriage as constitutional. In response Congress passed—and President Clinton signed—the Defense of Marriage Act, which would have refused recognition of such a ruling in Hawaii in other states. (The Hawaiian decision was preempted by a constitutional amendment, supported by a 70% vote in a referendum, which grants the legislature the power "to reserve marriage to opposite-sex couples."[65] The fight has now shifted to other states, with Vermont the most likely battleground at the time of writing.) But while the idea of "gay marriage" has been a major issue for both sections of the gay/lesbian and the Christian right movements in the United States, it has had an impact elsewhere. There have been reports of homosexual marriages in countries as different as Japan, Argentina, and Vietnam, and in bizarre agreement with American fundamentalists, the Vietnamese National Assembly outlawed gay marriage in 1996 after reports of a couple of ceremonies which were held in Ho Chi Minh City, without any legal standing. In the Philippines there has been considerable debate around the legal status of same-sex partnerships, while the 1998 gay- and lesbian-pride parade in Johannesburg took as its theme "Recognise Our Relationships."

One might of course ask whether this threatens to put the movement too far out of touch with the gut feelings of the great majority of South Africans. Sue Willmer makes this argument vis-à-vis Mexico: "The prominence given to the marriage issue has provided the religious right with fertile ground on which to organise opposition to the lesbian and gay movement. To what extent has the same-sex marriage movement benefited lesbians in the context of a country where religion, tradition and family values have so clearly been a source of their marginalization and where economic dependence remains a reality for the majority of women?"[66] Similar comments have been made by the Fiji NGO Coalition on the Right to Sexual Orientation, which has pointed to fears of homosexual marriage as a major scare tactic being used by moral conservatives to push for the elimination of discrimination on grounds of sexuality from the Fiji Constitution.[67] Yet when I discussed the issue with people in South Africa it became clear that the demand was an important one for large numbers of black and colored homosexuals, who saw it as necessary to win acceptance within their often deeply religious families and communities. The campaign for recognition of our relationships and "the right to a family life" was not, as I had originally assumed, a copy of American rhetoric but rather the logical extension of gains already won through the inclusion of equality based on sexuality within the new South African Constitution. Material produced by the National Coalition

for Gay and Lesbian Equality for the 1999 South African elections stressed
that full equality encompasses equality in adoption, custody, and parenting
of children and full and equal recognition of gay and lesbian relations.[68]

More surprisingly the Namibian high court, in a 1999 immigration
case, ruled that homosexual relationship should enjoy legal equality. This
was particularly controversial as the government had already declared its
intention of criminalizing homosexuality as "inimical to true Namibian culture, African culture and religion."[69] The clash between universal concepts
of human rights and essentialist views of African tradition captures some of
the basic contradictions of globalization.

Nonetheless, Willmer's comment reminds us that even where the same
phenomenon seems to exist, in this case same-sex marriages, social and cultural differences will mean the phenomena bear very different meanings and
significance in different settings. Underlying this discussion is the constant
tension between the anthropological emphasis on cultural continuity and the
emphasis of political economy on change. Think, for example, of different
explanations of the prevalence of sex work in Thailand—in the argument
that this is an integral part of Thai culture there is a danger of essentializing
a "Thai sexuality" and ignoring socioeconomic contingencies which will
shape the ways in which cultural norms are constantly remade and reimag-
ined. It is equally silly to ignore the ways in which cultural, religious, and
historical factors will change the ways in which global forces impinge on
particular societies: prostitution has a different history in Thailand than in,
say, Ireland or Paraguay.

Globalization makes it harder and harder to see societies as self-
sufficient, or to ignore the ways in which we are all products of exogenous
influences, like the Coke bottle which falls from heaven in the South African
film *The Gods Must Be Crazy* and affects everyone in the film. Peter Drucker
writes of the idea of "combined and uneven social construction," arguing
that "[d]ifferent indigenous starting points, different relations to the world
economy, and different cultural and political contexts can combine to produce very different results . . . It can help us understand how some indigenous forms of sexuality can be preserved within a global economy and culture, changing to a certain extent their forms or functions; how new forms
can emerge; and how indigenous and new forms can be combined."[70]

Specifically there are a number of contemporary developments which
bear on sexuality, all of which are the subject of later chapters: the rapid

commodification of sex, the impact of new technologies, the partial globalization of the "sex industry," the academic discovery of sex as both discourse
and field of study, the impact of the HIV/AIDS epidemic, the universalizing
of certain identities, and the emergence of questions of gender and sexuality
as central to contemporary political debates around human rights and international relations. Globalization must be understood as occurring at both
discursive and institutional levels, as will be examined in some detail in the
discussion of the AIDS epidemic.

*F*our

The (Re)Discovery of Sex

Within rich societies over the past few decades there has been a marked politicization of sex. This is a product of both consumer capitalism and political
movements, even if it is difficult to disentangle which is more important.
Within the scale of roughly a generation the "double standard" has moved
from being "taken for granted" to a central concern in relations between
women and men, as women have demanded the right to social and economic
equality, and along with this equal access to pleasure and protection from
harassment. The rapidity of the changes is marked yet again by the marital
histories of the British royals: while Princess Margaret had to renounce her
desire to marry a divorcé in 1955, four decades later she and three of Queen
Elizabeth's children had undergone widely publicized divorces. At the same
time the open expression of homosexuality has gone from being a radical
political gesture to a phenomenon associated with niche marketing to the
extent that some theorists speak of a "postgay" world, meaning one in which
sexual identities no longer have political significance.[1]

Of course "body politics" are older than we sometimes recognize, as in
late-nineteenth-century campaigns against Chinese foot binding and early-
twentieth-century ones against female circumcision in Kenya.[2] Attempts to
regulate sexual and gender behavior was an integral part of the colonial
practice, as in the British outlawing of *sati,* or wife burning, in India in 1829.
Since the late nineteenth century there has been an important strain in western scientific thought which has attempted to develop a "science" of sexuality, ranging from the development of psychoanalysis to the contemporary
vogue for genetics and sociobiology. Kenneth Dutton attributes the beginning of the social exploration of the body to the nineteenth-century French
sociologist Émile Durkheim,[3] and since the late nineteenth century sex has

been a major preoccupation of law, medicine, and science, often, as Foucault argued, creating new categories and assumptions through official surveillance. As part of these developments the regulation of the body moved from the religious sphere and became increasingly controlled by science, as in the first legislation (in 1919) covering "cosmetic therapy" in the United States.[4]

Writing in 1961 Dennis Wrong complained that "[a]s soon as the body is mentioned the specter of biological determinism raises its head and sociologists draw back in fright. And certainly their view of man is sufficiently disembodied and non-materialistic to satisfy Bishop Berkeley, as well as being de-sexualized enough to please Mrs. Grundy."[5] But Wrong was writing shortly before the counterculture led to a new interest in sex and the body—and a youth movement determined to contest social taboos. This interest was played out in somewhat different ways for men and women; whereas men saw the counterculture as a way of escaping conventional restraints on both appearance and behavior, leading to a great deal of experimentation with sex and drugs, for women the changes helped politicize their personal lives.

The "second wave" of western feminism was in part a reaction against male assumptions that while everything should change nothing should alter their rights over women, symbolized by the alleged comment of black-power leader Stokeley Carmichael that the only place for women in the revolution was prone. The publication of the enormously popular *Our Bodies, Ourselves* by the Boston Women's Health Collective in 1973 marked a new step in women's awareness of the body as a central terrain of politics. The existence of a large and vibrant feminist movement allowed space for lesbians—even if they sometimes had to argue for inclusion—which was not available to gay men in the aftermath of the countercultural movements. Even today's "men's movements" are strangely uncomfortable with exploring homosexuality.

From the late 1960s on, the literature about sex has become huge, ranging from self-help soft erotica to highly academic theoretical studies of "the body," building on new styles of history, anthropology, and cultural studies which grew simultaneously from developments in most of the humanities and social sciences and were influenced both by the new style of post-1960s politics and theorists (to name the most obviously fashionable) such as Barthes, Foucault, and Deleuze and Guattari. Foucault in particular introduced two key concepts into our understandings of the body: the idea of "biopower" and that of the "inscribed body": "The body is the inscribed surface of events (traced by language and dissolved by ideas), the locus of a disassociated self (adopting the illusion of a substantial unity) and a volume in perpetual disintegration."[6]

Often theorists such as Foucault are cited without any reference to either the changed material circumstances or the political movements which both influenced their work and made it so popular with a new intellectual generation. It seems likely that the new emphasis on "reading" sex and the body in western countries represents a response to mass consumption and affluence, and to the politicization around sexual matters in the late 1960s and the 1970s. It is somewhat odd that an interest in the body—by definition something which is material—so often accompanies a stress on "representation" which seems to conflate the depictions of popular culture with the material experience of the lived world.[7] It is also likely that the fashion for analysis of representation and discourse is in part the reaction of a generation who felt disenfranchised from political engagement by the apparent triumph of conservatism, at least in most of the English-speaking world, in the 1980s.

The contemporary interest in the body, suggests Bryan Turner (who has been in part responsible for this interest in academic circles), stems from "the emphases on pleasure, desire, difference and playfulness which are features of contemporary capitalism."[8] Others have expressed similar views, more harshly. The Swiss critic Jean Starobinski claims it is "only superficially banal [to conclude] that the present infatuation with the different modes of body consciousness is a symptom of the considerable narcissistic component characteristic of contemporary Western culture."[9] Rosalyn Baxandall suggests that the body may be perceived "as the only remaining locus of possible control and autonomy, in an increasingly invasive and precarious society."[10] And Emily Martin has suggested that "[o]ne reason so many of us are energetically studying the body [is] precisely that we are undergoing fundamental changes in how our bodies are organized and experienced." She goes on to suggest "a dramatic transition in body perception and practice, from bodies suited for and conceived in the terms of the era of Fordist mass production to bodies suited for and conceived in the terms of the era of flexible accumulation."[11] There is a parallel here to arguments both John D'Emilio and I have made about this change from an economy marked by an emphasis on production to one dominated by consumption in the rise of gay/lesbian identities and communities from the 1960s on.[12]

Turner ignores gay analyses, a tendency reflected in a great deal of contemporary feminist theorizing about the body which either ignores or is contemptuous of male homosexual experience and theory, so that writers such as Gayle Rubin and Judith Butler are too often read by feminists without any sense of the ways in which they were influenced by the gay/lesbian movement of the 1970s and 1980s.[13] Feminist theorists *do* read Foucault, but usually without recognizing that his homosexuality was not just an incidental biographical fact. Foucault was more influenced by the radical French gay movement which emerged from the events of May 1968 than is apparent from his more scholarly writings. That he at one point denied that his work was related to gay liberation[14] only emphasizes the extent to which he wrote in response to the particular neo-Freudian intellectual writings of the 1970s French movement. More recently of course both postmodernists and feminists have taken an interest in "queer theory," often without acknowledging its origins in the gay/lesbian movements of the 1970s.[15]

Given the availability of new technologies of reproduction, surgery, and communication, it is hardly surprising that we are fascinated by bodies in new ways: a world which has experienced artificial insemination, gender reassignments, routine plastic surgery, and cybersex is one where bodies seem far less immutable than in any previous time. At least one strand of second-wave feminist thought, represented by Shulamith Firestone's now largely forgotten book *The Dialectic of Sex,* saw the possibility of using technology to "free" women from their biological role in reproduction.[16] While she couldn't have foreseen it, new genetic techniques may indeed make it possible for a child to be produced from the chromosomes of two women—or, indeed, to be cloned from one. The enormous sales of Viagra when it was put on the market in 1998 suggested that men were equally keen to use technology to counter what previous generations would have accepted as an inevitable part of aging.

At the same time the contemporary cult of the body is in some ways a reaction against the excesses of consumer capitalism, so that we drive to gyms which have taken on all the appurtenances of luxury hotels, and sedentary businessmen jog around city blocks, inhaling polluted air. The sort of physical fitness which came through daily activity has now become another commodity to be marketed via exercise classes, television programs, and the creation of a new industry of personal trainers, dietitians, and aerobics instructors—and if all else fails, plastic surgeons. The marks of aging and overeating—which in other societies at other times have been venerated—are now to be denied, so that, as Agatha Christie put it in one of her later books: "Great-aunts aren't much like that nowadays ... nor grandmothers nor great-grandmothers, if it comes to that. The Marchioness of Barlowe ... a great-grandmother ... her face a mask of pink and white and her hair platinum blonde and I suppose an entirely false figure, but it looked wonderful."[17] Today the marchioness could take advantage of silicone implants, liposuction, chemical peel, cheek and chin augmentation, and an increasing array of other surgical interventions.

Just as biochemistry and genetic engineering is breaking down the traditional limits of the "natural" body, so too the relationship between humans and machines has begun to alter our understanding of the break between the "natural" and the mechanical. Donna Haraway's celebrated discussion of the cyborg which she defined as "a cybernetic organism, a hybrid of machine and organism, a creature of social reality as well as a creature of fiction," brought the term out of science fiction into social theory. (It also recognized implicitly that we were dealing with something more complex and less mechanical than the robot, the central metaphor of much earlier science fiction.)[18] One of the problems with Haraway's piece is that she nowhere defines "cyborg" so as to make clear the boundaries: would *Peter Pan's* Captain Hook, with his primitive prosthesis, qualify? In her 1985 article "A Manifesto for Cyborgs" she wrote that "Foucault's biopolitics is a flaccid premonition of cyborg politics, a very open field."[19] Just what such a politics might be is less clear. In this article Haraway positions herself against certain strands of essentialist feminism—"I would rather be a cyborg than a goddess," she says in her conclusion—and calls for an embracing of the possibilities of science and technology, even as she recognizes the ways in which these are largely controlled by dominant economic forces. (One of her critics has pointed out that "Haraway's myth addresses a First World audience able to realize, in some individualizing form, the body's pleasure in technology.")[20] Nonetheless the article was enormously influential in the development of new ways of thinking about the relationship between technology, gender, and political economy.

It is interesting that it was Arnold Schwarzenegger's depiction of a cyborg in the 1984 movie *Terminator*—who better than the best-known bodybuilder in the world to play a half-human machine?—which introduced the term into the popular consciousness. Three years later Michael Jackson appealed to the cyborg theme, as well as prefiguring the future scandal around his sexuality, in a video for the song "Smooth Criminal," where "Jackson transfigures into a giant robocop-like metallic transformer in a celestial warfare against a child-abducting villain, wins the war, and then returns as 'Michael' in a fairy-tale dance with children."[21] By the end of the twentieth century it could be claimed that "[f]rom fetuses scanned ultrasonically to computer hackers in daycare, contemporary children are increasingly rendered cyborg by their immersion in technoculture."[22]

There is a growing debate on the way in which "virtual reality" allows for new forms of sex, with books like Carole Parker's *Joy of Cybersex* proclaiming a brave new world of virtual sex: "Already the freedom and anonymity of the Internet has taken sex out of our bedrooms and put it on screen where it can be played with, experimented with, bent completely out of shape and then, if we like, brought back home and incorporated into our real lives. We've found a safer than safe-sex alternative and picked up where the free-love generation left off. We've exchanged potentially hazardous physical encounters with less messy and probably more experimental virtual encounters."[23] I think this argument confuses fantasy with actual contact; the world of virtual reality of which Parker writes offers no more than heightened masturbation, and while it is true that many people achieve their most intense orgasms through masturbation this does not replace the need for human interaction which accompanies even mediocre sex. Behind the hype of cybersex is, as Ziauddin Sardar has pointed out, the illusion that the body is "little more than a machine" and thus "even sex and mysticism are reduced to binary communication."[24] Clearly not everyone feels this way: there are a number of sex clubs where the busiest room appears to be that housing machines with free access to the Internet. And the theme is a growing one in science fiction, where virtual reality becomes increasingly merged with corporeal experience.[25]

Perhaps the best way to understand the impact of cyberspace on sex is to recognize its ability to expand the realm of fantasy in ways which break down almost every known barrier, so that a sixty-year-old white woman in Des Moines can appear in cyberspace as a twenty-year-old black stud. In so doing it is likely to expand and at the same time universalize actual sexual experience—at least for the privileged minority who have access to the net. The most striking scene in Patrick Marber's play *Closer,* which was a great success in London in the late 1990s, depicts two men engaged in virtual sex, one of them pretending to be a woman. When they later meet, the man who entered the fantasy in his own persona feels a strong sense of anger and betrayal. Here the role of the market seems dominant; as one critic reflected: "As loneliness is a contemporary epidemic it makes sense that there are plagues of businesses selling computer-assisted romance."[26] The release of the very popular film *You've Got Mail* in 1998 suggested that the email would become as central a device in cinematic romance as the telephone was for Doris Day and Rock Hudson.

The mainstreaming of pornography (of which more later) reflects the more general sexualization of marketing. The use of "sexy bodies"—male and female—in advertising and mainstream newspapers (Murdoch's "page 3 models" in his down-market British tabloids) has become ubiquitous, and with it the creation of a homogeneity of desire through global advertising campaigns and interchangeable glossy magazines, which returns us to the question of the specific American content of "globalization." Of course the control of advertising by transnational corporations does not mean there is an end to specific local content, even if the dominant script remains that of individual consumption and beautiful bodies. Most Asian and African countries—and certainly all Middle Eastern ones—are more restrictive in what is allowed in the media than is Europe, where soft pornography is not uncommonly unrestricted television viewing.

Advertising plays a particular role in the globalization of certain body types, through fashion and film, though there is a certain countering of this by an emphasis on, say, Hispanic or Indian ideas of beauty in some self-consciously national films.[27] The imagery of global capitalism is incorporated into a sense of what is desirable, as in Michael Tan's description of "macho dancers" in Manila gay bars, who "have taken to strutting out with Ray-ban sunglasses and Levi jeans with beepers or cellphones conspicuously clipped on the belt. The dancers eventually strip off their Levis to show—and this is strangely uniform in all the bars—Calvin Klein underwear."[28] The same phenomenon appears to be at work in the extraordinary popularity of the "blond beauty" Xuxa, "the national megastar" of Brazil's very successful television soaps, a popularity which extends across Latin America and to Spanish-language television in the United States. In her study of Xuxa, Amelia Simpson claimed that her much publicized affair with soccer star Pele "enters her biography as a kind of proof of immunity to racism, which then functions as a license to exploit the appetite for the blond and blue-eyed in a country with the largest black population outside Africa."[29] Equally there is a growing eroticization of Caucasian women in Chinese television and advertising.[30]

It could be argued that consumer capitalism creates its own body types, as suggested by this description of late 1990s Moscow: "In Soviet times, the stock image of Russian women abroad was of potato-faced dumplings in polyester dresses and turquoise eyeshade. These days, svelte, Slavic models are the rage on Parisian cakewalks and their many imitators stroll ostentatiously along Moscow's boulevards."[31]

There is a globalization (and a simultaneous limitation) of desirable body images; the very idea of Miss World or Miss Universe implies a single agreed-upon definition of female attractiveness. The concept of the beauty contest has roots in many cultures, but in its contemporary form developed out of the Miss America contests, linked in turn to the promotion of Atlantic City as a major resort. In 1951 the Miss America corporation invented the Miss World contest; Miss Universe followed a year later under rival sponsorship.[32] By 1996 almost every country in Europe and the Americas, plus a significant number of countries in Asia and Anglophone Africa, had entrants in one of these quests, and winners had come from all continents.[33] While contestants are supposed to embody a particular sense of national identity, the standards are those of the dominant commercial interests which fund the competitions, so that the 1992 Miss Universe title went to Miss Namibia, a six-foot white woman.[34] Beauty contests are increasingly ways of combining the commodification of certain body images with the development of a global culture of entertainment, television, and celebrity.

It is probably not accidental that the first places in the old Soviet Union to organize American-style beauty contests were Latvia and Lithuania,[35] whose defections would lead to the rapid disintegration of the Union itself. Similar developments have occurred in China and Vietnam, even if Miss Vietnam contestants are asked questions about their contribution to the nation's poverty-alleviation campaign,[36] and while the Seychelles once banned such contests as unsound, the 1998 Miss World contest was held there—in large part as a ploy to assist the tourist industry. The following year the Tanzanian government reversed its ban on beauty pageants, to allow Kings International Promotions to run beauty contests.[37]

While eating disorders might seem the exclusive privilege of the over-fed, Vanessa Baird quotes evidence of the emergence of anorexia in southern Africa as traditional concepts of beauty are replaced by the superthin images currently fashionable in the rich world,[38] and similar changes have been noted in Fiji since the introduction of satellite television in 1995.[39] Germaine Greer writes of her search for "the whole woman" in terms which combine the nostalgia of colonial anthropology with a critique of the global:

> No sooner had I caught sight of the whole woman than Western marketing came blaring down upon her with its vast panoply of spectacular effects, strutting and trumpeting the highly seductive gospel of salvation according to hipless, wombless, hard-titted Barbie. My strong women thrust their muscular feet into high heels and learnt to totter; they stuffed their useful breasts into brassieres and instead of moth-er's milk fed commercial formulae made with dirty water to their children; they spent their tiny store of cash on lipstick and nail varnish and were made modern.[40]

There are of course nonwestern critics of the obsession with thinness as beauty,[41] and it may be that the defense by many liberal Muslim women of the wearing of the chador is in part a mark of resistance to the globalizing pressures to conform to particular body styles. The Islamic revolution which overthrew the Pahlavi regime in Iran in 1977 placed great stress on the need to cover women's bodies, as opposed to the "immodesty" of western style.[42] As one observer wrote of the wearing of the long gown and the head scarf in Dubai this "is a highly charged political gesture . . . Critiques of the 'West-ern style' of modernization have increasingly centred around the question of women's chastity, modesty and sexuality."[43] It is symbolic that the French fashion magazine *Elle,* which sells 5 million copies a month, launched its thirtieth edition in Turkey at the start of 1999, when that country was in-creasingly polarized between defenders of its secular policies and Islamic val-ues, and an elected member of parliament was forbidden to take her seat when she turned up wearing a head scarf. The previous year up to 4 million Turks are claimed to have demonstrated in support of the right for women to wear head scarves to university. Not all Turks believe that Islam and women's equality are necessarily incompatible. As one commentator wrote: "Why not be like Iran? Turkey has fewer women in universities, the medical profession or the media. The Ayatollah has outstripped Ataturk."[44]

Modern chemicals such as steroids and silicone are used across the globe to reshape bodies to fit the prevailing assumptions of beauty, and to allow the creation of bodies which would have been unimaginable twenty years ago. Gyms, diet, and judicious use of drugs are now producing new body types—both male and female—which make the bodies of previous generations seem wimpish.[45] (The constant emphasis on hugeness in his description of male bodies in Tom Wolfe's novel *A Man in Full* tells us something not only about Wolfe but also about the current American preoccupation with pumping up beyond all previous limits.) It is not surprising that muscular heroes like Schwarzenegger and Stallone are the most ubiquitous symbols of masculinity in the contemporary world, nor that the particularly cretinous American television series *Baywatch* is by some accounts the world's most watched show. In 1995 when I was in Manila I noticed street posters advertising a new gym, with illustrations of muscular (white) men taken, presumably, from overseas gay magazines. The posters seemed to promise a luxurious gym/sauna of the sort found in Paris or Los Angeles, but the gym itself turned out to be an old garage, as small and dark as the other gyms that dot the Taft Avenue area. In the distinction between the image and the reality lies much of the paradox of the apparent "globalization" of postmodern gay identities.

THE GLOBALIZATION OF WOMEN'S BODIES

Women belong to cultures. But they do not choose to be born into any particular culture, and they do not really choose to endorse its norms as good for themselves, unless they do so in possession of further options and opportunities—including the opportunity to form communities of affiliation and empowerment with other women.

—*Martha Nussbaum*, Sex and Social Justice, *1999*

Much of the control and ideology around sexuality is bound up with the politics of reproduction, and the need felt by men to enforce the legitimacy of their progeny and the "honor" of their family. Historically most societies and religions have sought to limit women's sexuality by defining it in terms of their reproductive role, placing very severe sanctions on sexual expression that might threaten male control of reproduction. Speaking of witchcraft the anthropologist Ralph Austen argues: "At a more abstract level, it also seems possible to identify, in both European and African representations of the sexuality of witches, a common concern with the escape of female reproductive power from the enclosed domestic space in which it serves male-dominated communal norms to the open nocturnal realms of self-contained female power."[46] Similar fears help explain male ambivalence toward lesbianism, which has often been ignored because it does not involve the possibility of reproduction, but which can also become the most threatening expression of female sexuality in that it totally excludes men. While there are many historical examples of societies seeking to influence population size, the idea that governments should seek to regulate population through a mixture of persuasion and coercion seems a particular characteristic of the modern state.

Part of "globalization" involves the dispersion of certain discourses and practices. New institutions develop so that reproductive health and HIV become sites for international programming, cooperation, and control which also help create new sorts of identity politics (e.g., the presence of an active lesbian caucus at the 1995 International Women's Conference in Beijing). In the arena of reproductive health, as in that of HIV/AIDS, we see the intersection of various meanings of globalization: *economic*, as major pharmaceutical companies compete for shares of the profitable market in birth control; deep *cultural* clashes, as arguments around contraception and abortion involve major ideological clashes; and *political*, as governments, international agencies, and transnational social movements, including religious ones, fight for control of population policies.

Much of the organizing around women's issues internationally has focused on questions of reproductive rights and health, not surprising given the extent to which women's mortality is linked to issues about childbirth and abortion. (In poor countries up to 30% of deaths among women of child-bearing age are linked to the complications of pregnancy.)[47] Population control has become a highly contested area of global politics, in which the terrain is the actual bodies of women themselves.

Between the world wars a number of countries adopted "population policies," usually aimed at increasing their populations—this was echoed in postwar migration programs in countries like Australia, and in the bans on contraception and abortion in Communist Romania.[48] Indeed the extreme pronatalist policies of the Ceausescu regime influenced Margaret Atwood's dystopian novel *The Handmaid's Tale*. At the same time some governments, influenced by ideas of eugenics and "improving" their population, adopted compulsory sterilization of women regarded as undesirable mothers, whether due to race, abilities, or presumed immorality. Sweden sterilized women with "unmistakable gypsy features," and Norway used radiation on mentally retarded women until 1994.[49] Some governments continue to encourage reproduction. The Singapore government has expressed considerable concern at the failure of well-educated women to marry and have children. Recently

Croatia has adopted a set of laws aimed at increasing the birthrate, in part through "fighting non-womanhood" which appears to be code for severe restrictions on the rights of women as understood by contemporary feminism,[50] while a rapid decline in the birthrate in Serbia following recent wars led at least one politician to suggest taxing couples who did not produce children.[51] And some of the opposition to widespread abortion in Russia— where this is the most common form of birth control—revolve not around the appalling effect this has on women's health but rather on a nationalist appeal to maintain the country's population.[52] Indeed most of the countries of the former Soviet Union and its satellites in Europe still have pronatalist population policies.

Nonetheless, most restrictions on abortion seem the result of religious and patriarchal fears of women's sexuality, and mean that worldwide deaths from botched, usually illegal, abortions amount to *at least* 70,000 a year.[53] It is particularly ironic that these figures include deaths in countries where governments are also committed to family planning, but this merely underlines the irrationality of many of the prescriptions which surround sexual regulation. Indeed some of the programs aimed at reducing population growth involve forced sterilization, often in countries which outlaw abortion because it denies "the sanctity of life." Thus doctors in Peru were estimated to have conducted over 100,000 sterilizations and 10,000 vasectomies in 1997.[54] Yet Peru, along with most of Latin America, has a particularly high rate of mortality from illegal abortions. (In the poor world only China, Vietnam, Cuba, the countries of the former Soviet Union, Turkey, and South Africa allow abortion on request, though several other countries, including Tunisia, Zambia, and Belize, have liberal laws.)[55]

More commonly family-planning programs stress the provision of appropriate contraceptive advice and techniques, often without fully recognizing the extent to which these might disrupt traditional patterns of behavior and understandings of the world. As international development programs have come to stress issues of reproductive health this has meant the increasing globalization of concerns which in previous historical periods have been regarded as private, and certainly outside the scope of international scrutiny. While we might (and I do) applaud international intervention against domestic violence, infanticide, and forced marriages, we should also recognize that such campaigns are also part of the ever growing move to create universal norms which will inevitably mirror the dominant ideological strength of rich countries. Internationally funded family-planning programs, acknowledges the U.S.-based Family Health International, "are in an excellent position to intervene because they represent one of the few institutions to come in contact with most women during their reproductive lives—the time of highest risk for domestic violence."[56] More problematic is the ways in which family-planning programs can become means of changing particular patterns of cultural life, such as the long periods of sexual abstinence which is central to the mores of some African women.[57]

Key players in the global population debate include groups as disparate as the Catholic Church and the International Planned Parenthood Federation. In many countries pressure from the church has retained the illegality of abortion, despite growing demands from women and human rights groups. (After the reunification of Germany the imbalance between the eastern state's liberal abortion laws and the very restrictive ones of the west led to an ongoing political crisis. After prolonged parliamentary debate, an apparent compromise was adopted, only to be overturned by the German Constitutional Court, which further limited the conditions under which abortion was ruled constitutional.)[58] Since the end of World War II population control has been a significant element in international politics, with considerable pressure from the U.S. political establishment to make it a centerpiece of economic "development" in poor countries.[59] Fear of population explosion, usually linked to environmental degradation, has been a major theme of science fiction writing since the 1950s, echoing the concerns of the American foreign-policy establishment.[60] It is interesting that recently the opposite fear of global sterility has emerged as a theme in some science fiction.[61]

Support for population-control programs through international aid is both a reminder of the ways in which such assistance is itself a form of globalization, but has also become a major area of contestation as right-wing pressures have made U.S. support for population control more and more restrictive. (The United States, however, remains by far the major donor for population-control programs.) At the same time various programs of the United Nations are strong advocates of population control, and in 1969 the United Nations Fund for Population Activities (UNFPA) was established to provide assistance in "reproductive health and population issues."[62] It remains a central player in what Betsy Hartmann terms "the population establishment."[63]

It is worth remembering that the first oral contraceptive was tested on

women in Haiti and Puerto Rico before being placed on the American market,[64] and that global contraceptive sales amount to well over $2.5 billion a
year.[65] Pharmaceutical companies based in the rich world have a strong interest in the markets of the developing world, and exert considerable pressure
on governments to adopt "social marketing" of contraceptive pills, a concept
extended to condoms as a means of preventing both pregnancy and transmission of HIV and other STIs. That use of contraceptives without any medical screening or monitoring might be harmful to women's health is often
ignored in a tacit agreement by pharmaceuticals and population-control
bodies to promote maximum use of birth control.[66]

The international women's movement has increasingly asserted that
many existing population programs are coercive of women, and the 1994
International Conference on Population and Development in Cairo saw a
shift of emphasis, at least on a rhetorical level, to one which stressed the
empowerment of women and their rights to control reproduction.[67] The final
recommendations explicitly opposed "the promotion of abortion," however,
a compromise which sufficed to limit opposition to some of the recommendations from the Vatican and a handful of Catholic and Islamic countries.[68]
(Some governments—Iraq, Lebanon, Saudi Arabia, and the Sudan—boycotted the conference.) Implicit in this shift was a recognition of a feminist
position on sexuality and reproductive rights, and even though the final declaration has only exhortative impact this is an important gain for women's
equality. A follow-up conference five years later nudged (or fudged?) toward
greater realism in calling for abortion to be "safe" in countries where it is
legal,[69] and raised the possibility of reexamining criminal sanctions where
they apply.

Nor is coercion by the state, as in China's "one child" policy or forced
sterilization in countries such as Peru and Bangladesh, the only obstacle
faced by women in controlling their sexuality. Arguing that women should
control reproduction means recognizing that this is possible only if women
have genuine choices, which are impossible in situations where girls can be
forced into marriage, men can take extra wives (but not vice versa), and
women can be divorced if they fail to produce male sons, all of which are
forms of coercion on women enforced through social and religious institutions. Indeed while many human rights and feminist groups have denounced
the Chinese government's punitive attitudes toward limiting reproduction,
one of whose consequences is a rise in infanticide and the abandonment of

baby girls,[70] China's policies are arguably not as dependent on a view of women as subordinate as are many religious practices. China has a far lower rate of death from abortion—which is freely available—than most countries of comparable economic standing, and has recently softened its "one child" policy.

It is impossible to divorce the "sexual revolution" from the very major shifts in gender order over the past century which continue to change fundamentally the ways in which women and men understand themselves and each other. Part of the process of globalization is the rapid dispersion of these shifts, often leading to uncomfortable tensions as when claims for equal rights for women conflict with claims for preserving cultural tradition. The example often given is female "circumcision,"[71] but this avoids the uncomfortable fact that most "traditions"—including those based on western Christian teachings—subordinate the needs and desires of women to men.

Female "circumcision"—probably better termed female genital mutilation—leads to a heavy toll of pain, permanent injury, and death, just as do such other male-regulated practices as the denial of legal abortion and forced prostitution. It has become the subject of considerable international attention, in part because of the migration of many Africans to countries where custom—and in some cases laws—preclude the practice. The term in fact covers a range of practices, ranging from removing the tip of the clitoris to infibulation, which involves the removal of the clitoris, the labia minora, and even some flesh from either side of the labia minora.[72] Similar practices were used by western doctors in the past to control female sexual "deviance." Some African feminists have campaigned against it, and the more severe practice of infibulation was outlawed in the Sudan in 1946 and in Kenya in 1982. The 1994 International Conference on Population and Development opposed female genital mutilation. Since then more African countries, including Ghana, Senegal, and Togo, have criminalized the practice. However, it has been argued that this is largely in response to pressure from western governments, and has had the effect, not of stopping the practices, but of forcing them to be more covert. In Guinea genital mutilation carries the death penalty, but the law remains unenforced.[73] Starting with Sweden in 1982 a number of European countries have outlawed excision, and French courts have ruled that it is forbidden under laws dealing with violence against minors.[74] In a much publicized case at the beginning of 1999 a Malian immigrant in Paris was imprisoned for performing a number of excisions. Several Australian states have made the practice illegal, but have tried to combine this with the provision of adequate counseling within the communities affected.

Despite the apparent rise in commitment to human rights and gender equality, the overall global position of women remains one of clear inequality on almost all measurements. The triumph of neoliberalism has been particularly bad for most women, as it removes traditional social supports and weakens governmental welfare, often leaving women disproportionately responsible for caring for children, the old, and the sick. This is not to ignore the destructive impact of globalization and contemporary capitalism on millions of men; there are too many cases where class privilege is more significant than gender in allowing access to the goodies of the consumer world. But as Zillah Eisenstein puts it, patriarchy has been *re*privatized in first-world countries, while the consolidation of global capital has added considerably to the burden on women who are less likely to be educated or to have access to modern technologies.[75]

Five

Imagining AIDS:
And the New Surveillance

By overwhelming [Africa's] health and social services, by creating millions of orphans, and by decimating health workers and teachers, AIDS is causing social and economic crises which in turn threaten political stability . . . This cocktail of disasters is a sure recipe for more conflict. And conflict, in turn, provides fertile ground for further infections.

—*Kofi Annan, 2000*

By the beginning of this century the number of people infected with HIV was approaching 35 million, with infections increasing rapidly in much of Africa, south Asia, and the Caribbean. Responsible UN officials have compared AIDS to the great plagues of history, with some countries close to an adult infection rate of 25%,[1] and the UN Population Division estimates that life expectancy is falling in twenty-nine African countries due to AIDS.[2] By the turn of the century AIDS had become the number one cause of death in Africa, imposing a particularly heavy burden because it is most heavily concentrated among the most productive sectors of the population. In some ways the epidemic had become a metaphor for the potential struggle between life and death within sexuality at the beginning of the new millennium.

The politics of AIDS encompass its regulation through state and international organizations, the development of a vast range of community responses, the political economy of health, and widespread cultural manifestations. As Richard Parker wrote: "In little more than a decade the rapid spread of the international AIDS pandemic has profoundly changed the ways in which we live and understand the world. Never has a common, global problem so clearly drawn attention to the important differences that shape the experience of diverse cultures and societies. And nowhere is this more true than in relation to our understanding of human sexuality."[3] AIDS has entered the global imaginary, using this term in Appadurai's sense of "a constructed landscape of collective aspirations . . . the imagination as a social practice."[4]

The urgency of HIV/AIDS and the mobilization, interventions, and research generated by the epidemic introduced a new dimension to debates about sexuality. For moral conservatives AIDS seemed almost tailor-made as a rebuke to those who argued that it was possible to regard sex as recreation, and in many parts of the world—in Africa and the Caribbean as much as within the Catholic Church and the U.S. Senate—it was argued that the only meaningful response to AIDS was abstinence, celibacy, or at best mutual monogamy. In KwaZulu-Natal (South Africa), King Goodwill Zwelithini has sought to restore a commitment to celibacy before marriage to help curb the spread of HIV, using the traditional "reed dance" to reemphasize the tradition.[5] Even in Australia, generally agreed to have had one of the most progressive official responses to the epidemic anywhere, the first chair of the National Advisory Committee on AIDS, Ita Buttrose, gained considerable notoriety when she spoke of her own "radical celibacy." Buttrose was a strong supporter of widespread condom use and empowering gay community education, but she also typified a dominant attitude when she wrote: "Woodstock could never happen again after the arrival of AIDS. 'Free love' was now a dirty word [sic] because everyone knew it was not necessarily love or free. Indeed, it could come at a great cost. Free love had meant sex with anyone you chose, with no complications and no strings attached. The problem was, free love could not take account of someone's sexual past—his or her history."[6]

As we shall see, some gay men in particular opposed this view of the implications of the epidemic, but certainly the explosion of HIV from the early 1980s has changed both the discourses and practices of sexuality. As Mark Merlis, one of the most original contemporary gay writers, put it: "No one will ever go that way again, not even if the cure is found. Partly because we will never own our bodies again, as they did. We are vectors now, or vessels, sources of transmission; our bodies belong to the unseen."[7]

AIDS fits the common understanding of "globalization" in a number of ways, including its epidemiology, the mobilization against its spread, and the dominance of certain discourses in the understandings of the epidemic. Note that I follow the accepted usage which increasingly conflates HIV (the virus which weakens the immune system) and AIDS (the medical condition which results from such weakening) despite the fact that there are significant differences in practice between the two. As Anthony Smith has pointed out: "While arguably they are simply cause and effect separated by a significant although variable period of time, they are in fact produced in two, largely distinct, cultural fields, the treatment of AIDS being mainly—almost exclusively—within the purview of clinical biomedicine and the prevention of HIV infection being within the province of the social and behavioral sciences, although the ownership of HIV by these disciplines has been under sustained attack from biomedicine."[8]

Reports of a new infectious and potentially fatal disease date from 1981, when young men were diagnosed as suffering from severe immune deficiency on both coasts of the United States. It is almost certain that some version of HIV/AIDS had long existed in Africa; unfortunately this claim has sometimes been read as racist, though it is no more than an attempt to understand the etiology of the disease. It is possible that HIV mutated in the recent past, so as to become far more harmful to humans, and its rapid spread in the past two decades is closely related to the forces of "development," and to global population movements. It is even possible that the spread of the virus resulted from experiments with a potential polio vaccine in the 1950s.[9] It is probable that the virus was spread beyond its original home through urbanization and population shifts, and that its rapid dispersion across the world is closely related to the nature of a global economy. HIV followed the huge population movements of the contemporary world, whether these are truckers moving across Zaire and India,[10] women taking up sex work as a means of survival as old communities and social order crumbled, men seeking work on the minefields of South Africa and Zimbabwe, or tourists (for example Americans in Haiti), refugees (Haitians fleeing to the United States), and soldiers (Cubans serving in Angola; UN troops in Cambodia or the former Yugoslavia) moving across national boundaries.[11] To take one example almost at random, the early spread of HIV in Honduras, which has the highest AIDS figures in Central America, has been attributed to the interaction of prostitutes and American soldiers at the U.S. base at Comayagua.[12] The involvement of armies from seven African countries in the civil strife at the end of the 1990s in the Congo seemed tailor-made for a rapid spread of HIV.[13]

AIDS is both a product and a cause of globalization, linking the least developed and the most developed regions of the world.[14] Despite attempts to close borders to its spread, as in the restrictions on entry of HIV-positive people applied by many countries, the spread of the virus made a mockery of national sovereignty. Speaking of the greater Mekong region—which straddles China, Burma, Thailand, and Laos—Doug Porter has written: "The nexus of HIV transmission across this territory is a metaphor for the globalisation of investment, trade and cultural identity. Although the dominant realist tradition in international relations studies conceives national territorial spaces as homogenous and exclusive, what is referred to as the 'new global cultural economy' has to be seen as a complex, overlapping, disjunctive order, which cannot be adequately understood in terms of centre-periphery, inner-outer, state border models of the past."[15]

The growing internationalization of trade in both sex and drugs has played a major role in the diffusion of HIV, and its rapid spread into almost every corner of the world. It has been argued that "patterns of use of illicit drugs are becoming globalized and 'standardized,'"[16] leading to the rapid spread of HIV in countries in both Southeast Asia and South America where the U.S.-led "war on drugs" has meant injecting practices have partly replaced traditional opium smoking. The United Nations Drug Control Program estimates that the international trade in illegal drugs amounts to some $400 billion a year, and touches virtually every part of the world. We are used to hearing of the drug trade from Colombia and Burma, but other parts of the world—Nigeria, ex-Soviet Central Asia—are also major exporters. In the same way injecting drugs, with the concomitant risks from shared needles, is a practice found in increasing numbers of countries and populations.

While it is often said that HIV is "spread through prostitution" (a formulation which repeats the usual demonization of the sex worker while ignoring the client), it is also true that fear of AIDS itself changes the nature of the international sex trade. It is well established that AIDS has played a role in increasing demand for younger, presumably uninfected, prostitutes, often from rural areas, which has meant an increased demand for young Burmese women in Thailand and Nepali girls in India, and so on.[17] (There are estimates that nearly half the prostitutes in India are less than eighteen years old, and 20% less than fifteen.)[18] Of course the demand for young girls—above all virgins—is an old tradition, and one which has long fueled a great deal of the trade in prostitution.[19]

In some ways the very policies urged by international bodies and economic theorists to promote faster development have added to the conditions which make people vulnerable to HIV infection. There is now some litera-

ture which discusses the vexed relationship between HIV infection and development;[20] one example I like to cite is the Thai-Lao Friendship Bridge
across the Mekong, which was opened with some fanfare in 1994. By increasing traffic across the river the bridge has also increased the vulnerability of
Laotians, particularly in the border city of Nong Khai, to infection.[21] Similar
connections have been established between globalization and the spread of
cholera in the past twenty years. Lee and Dodgson speak of the adverse im-
pacts of globalization on health systems in Latin America, including "increased national debt, rapid urbanisation, environmental degradation, ineq-
uitable access to health services, and reduced public expenditure on public
health infrastructure. Cholera then arrived in 1991, spreading rapidly across
the continent in an epidemic of 1.4 million cases and more than ten thousand deaths in nineteen countries."[22] This account goes on to point to similar
outbreaks in the former Soviet Union, linked to related conditions. Although
the means of transmission are different, similar conditions of social dislocation, poverty, and the absence of health services mean HIV will spread much
faster (other untreated sexually transmissible diseases increase susceptibility
to infection). As Gita Sen points out: "Globalization itself, in the sense of
unregulated privatization, [means] open season for pharmaceutical companies, health sector cutbacks, and a weakening of concern for health equity
poses enormous barriers to the fledgling reproductive and sexual rights
agenda"[23]—to which one might add the prevention of HIV and other sexually transmissible diseases.

There is an irony in the World Bank's putting increasing sums of
money into AIDS work in countries such as Brazil and India where the
Bank's own policies had helped weaken the health structures which might
have helped prevent the spread of HIV. (One of the most telling examples of
how structural adjustment affected the spread of AIDS is data from Kenya,
which showed a steep drop in attendance at STI clinics after the World Bank
enforced charges for such visits.)[24] Moreover part of the impact of an epidemic linked to social and economic upheavals has been to effectively increase the vulnerability of women, who are more likely to be unable to protect themselves against infection, to carry a greater share of the burden of
care for those who are sick, and to have less access themselves to treatments.[25]
Violence and rape (usually, but not exclusively, directed at women) are a major cause of HIV transmission which increases dramatically in situations of

social and political dislocation. Yet in some countries women who ask their rapists to use condoms are deemed to have given consent.[26]

The development of various international responses to HIV/AIDS forms part of the globalization of human welfare, one of the six "vectors" identified by Hopkins and Wallerstein in their discussion of the developing world system. The formation of the World Health Organization in 1948 could be seen as the beginnings of a so far very slow movement toward recognizing the need to establish certain basic standards of "health for all," a program of global preventive and primary care endorsed by the World Health Organization and UNICEF in 1978.[27] Equally the international response has implications for the globalization of certain biomedical and sociobehavioral paradigms, which are often ignored in discussions of globalization. Global mobilization around the demands of a biomedical emergency has inevitably meant the further entrenchment of western concepts of disease, treatments, and the body. I happen to believe that the western rationalist view of AIDS as essentially caused through infection by a retrovirus is correct, but to recognize this as the basis for global programs is also to recognize that this further undermines other and different ways of viewing medicine and the body. In some societies there has been resistance to western conceptions of AIDS, often linked to the interests of traditional healers, but such resistance has been comparatively weak in the face of the homogenizing impact of global biomedical science. The frequent calls to involve traditional healers in HIV programs too often overlook the problem of integrating very different epistemological frameworks and understandings of illness.

The first significant international response to the new epidemic came in 1986 when the World Health Organization established the Global Program on AIDS (GPA), based in its Geneva headquarters. GPA can be seen as having had three clear achievements: the establishment of an international discourse about HIV/AIDS which stressed the language of empowerment and participation; technical support for a number of developing countries in a range of policy and program areas; and mobilization of donor countries to support a multilateral response to the epidemic.[28] A decade later GPA was replaced by a broader response through the creation of UNAIDS, a joint and cosponsored program of seven major UN agencies under the aegis of the Economic and Social Council.[29]

For the purposes of this book most significant is the impact of the epidemic on regimes of sex and gender. Different cultural understandings of the meanings humans give to their bodies are constantly being challenged and remade by the impact of particular western notions, imported via economic, cultural, and professional influences; the AIDS epidemic has created "experts" who in turn influence perceptions of sex and gender through HIV education and prevention programs. Such programs further the diffusion of a particular language around sexuality and sexual identities which depend upon particular, largely western, assumptions. As Carol Jenkins has pointed out: "Conceiving of a sexual domain which requires taxonomic efforts is rather new, and decidedly Western. The traditional peoples of Papua New Guinea generally did not have specific terms to designate one type of sexual orientation as opposed to another, although a term suggestive of an altered gender identity can be found in at least a few of the nation's 868 or more languages."[30]

Programs around HIV/AIDS have often made use of identities such as "sex worker" or "gay/bisexual men"/"men who have sex with men," and thus play a part in the further globalization of movements based on such identities. (Ironically the term "men who have sex with men" was coined to reach men who rejected any sense of identity based upon their sexual practices, but fairly quickly became used in ways which just repeated the old confusions between behavior and identity.) Most interesting perhaps is the growth of the concept of the "person living with HIV/AIDS" (PLWHA). The creation of the "person with AIDS" as a specific identity clearly drew on earlier gay models of "coming out" and has been a significant factor in breaking down the medical dominance of the epidemic. While there is some disquiet about the relevance of this model in nonwestern societies—I have heard Africans argue that to emphasize positive identity leads to divisions within families and communities—it is a term which has been taken up in most of the official responses to the epidemic and was given international status at the 1994 Paris summit when the governments present committed themselves to "the greater involvement of People with AIDS." It is also an identity which carries grave risks when it is asserted; as one Israeli PLWHA put it: "I understood that people would kill me before the virus [did]."[31] There are cases of people identified as HIV-positive being beaten and killed in a number of countries, the best-known example being that of Gugu Dlamini, who was killed for "bringing shame" on her community after coming out as positive in a South African campaign in 1998 to increase acceptance and disclosure of PLWHAs. It has been claimed that her slaying was part of a contemporary witch-hunting, with HIV serving as the new marker for witchcraft.[32]

Even while recognizing the diversity of sexualities, and the fact that for most people behavior does not necessarily match neat categories, there is a gradual shift toward conceptualizing sexuality as a central basis for identity in most parts of the world in which HIV programs have played a significant role.[33] The next chapter takes up some of the problems inherent in the export of western classifications of sexuality into other cultures. For the moment let me note the close connection between the surveillance and prevention strategies associated with HIV/AIDS and the rapid growth of certain sorts of identity politics in many parts of the world. To quote from one example, a report from Proyecto Girasol, an HIV-prevention program in El Salvador: "When the work started in 1994, few people imagined that this kind of organizing would be accepted or could have an impact. But the space was opened and defended with organization and visibility, and the project built self-esteem within the sex-workers and gay community, 'changing their self-destructive image into a constructive one.' For the first time a positive self-identified gay community was established in El Salvador."[34]

Allowing for the inevitable self-promotion of such a report, it does however point to something which has been remarked upon across the world over the past ten years, namely the development of a sense of identity and assertion among people who come together through a common sexuality or (as in the case of sex workers) a shared relationship to the economy of sex. This does not deny that such developments can be read as either emancipatory or neocolonial; for the moment I am concerned only to recognize these changes.

But AIDS has also changed and broadened sexual experiences. In many societies more open discussion of sex is itself an enormously significant change. It is common to hear HIV workers from African, Asian, or Pacific countries explain the changes in social expectations which are required to even broach the discussion of sexual behavior. Ignorance about basic sexual and reproductive possibilities remains a huge obstacle to safe behavior in probably most parts of the world. Beyond this, the range of preventive programs brought into existence by the threat of the epidemic has meant, at least in some limited arenas, that there have been real changes in behavior. The ongoing campaign to incorporate condoms into sexual intercourse has

forced a new awareness of and discussion about sexuality, and in turn produced other changes in sexual practices, with examples ranging from a new
interest in massage and "nonpenetrative" sex in the rich world, to discussions
in parts of Africa about the risks of "dry sex" practices (the use of herbs etc.
to dry the vagina before or during intercourse).[35] Reports from the meetings
of the Society for Women and AIDS in Africa show a high degree of concern
and interest in changing sexual norms and behaviors to better empower
women in the face of sexually transmitted diseases. In Uganda and possibly
other African countries, the imperatives of HIV prevention have led to a
critical appraisal of the practice of polygamy,[36] and in late 1999 President
Moi of Kenya spoke of raising the minimum age for marriage from fourteen
to eighteen—while still refusing to promote condom use. Probably the most
successful example of behavioral change came through the "100% condom"
campaign in Thailand, whereby the government distributed millions of condoms to all sex venues, encouraging the use of the slogan "No condom, no
refund, no service."[37] There is some evidence that the economic slump at
the end of the 1990s partly undermined this program.

     The use of condoms is part of a wider revolution in sexual mores, one
linked to the idea that it is possible to maintain sexual pleasure and adventure, while preventing the transmission of disease. Gay communities in various countries invented the term "safe(r) sex," which first appeared in literature produced by gay AIDS-prevention groups in San Francisco and Houston
in 1982.[38] These were quickly followed by similar groups across the western
world—early in the epidemic the new messages were dramatized through
groups such as the Safe Sex Sluts in Melbourne and the Safe Sex Corps in
Toronto. Similar messages are now being disseminated through prevention
programs targeting a broader public across the world, often through imaginative use of theater, puppetry, and cartoons.[39] Equally it was the threat of
HIV which ended taboos on advertising condoms on television in countries
such as Australia and France, if not yet the United States.[40] In other countries, such as Mexico and the Philippines, condom advertising has been a
bitterly contested issue, bringing church and state into direct conflict. (In
Mexico the police have used laws prohibiting "offenses against public morality" to prevent AIDS education efforts,[41] although condom promotion is now
fairly widespread.) Condoms are now regularly used in pornographic films,
thus normalizing and perhaps eroticizing them.

     The general belief in the first years of the epidemic was that AIDS

would mean a new conservatism in matters sexual. Bisexual chic was replaced by a new discourse of monogamy, and for a few years there was a
quite serious belief that many men would relinquish homosexual sex; in a
1987 short story Brendan Lemon wrote: "Somewhere toward the end of the
AIDS decade Paul decided to go straight."[42] This shift was described by
Linda Singer as "a move from an inflationary economy of optimism toward
an economy of erotic recession or stagflation."[43] Frank Mort quotes an unnamed writer in the British magazine *Arena* in 1987: "In the wake of AIDS
hysteria bachelors are doing it for themselves . . . one suspects that more and
more are coming out [as masturbators]."[44] The best example of Mort's point
is the growth within gay communities of jerk-off parties, attempts to combine
the celebration of male sexuality with rigid restrictions on any "exchange of
bodily fluids."[45] From the late 1980s on such parties became common in
many western cities, and commercial J/O venues were established in cities
(e.g., New York and San Francisco) whose authorities had closed gay bathhouses. For a time it seemed as if the J/O parties organized by Santé et
Plaisir Gai were the only form of prevention activities in the Paris gay world.
Early in the epidemic there was discussion among some feminists of the possibilities for developing equivalent forms of nonpenetrative heterosexual sex,
but this discussion seemed to have largely disappeared, although the threat
of HIV has led to more open discussion of masturbation not only in the west
but also as part of HIV prevention in countries such as Uganda.

During the past decade it has become clear that the changes brought
about by HIV/AIDS are more nuanced than early predictions suggested.
While condom use has certainly increased, evidence from most western
countries indicates that this has not been accompanied by major reductions in partners or frequency.[46] Indeed in some cases the late 1990s saw
something of a return to the celebration of sexual adventure linked to the
seventies, either through the nostalgic revival of seventies disco music or in
mixed sex clubs which seemed to be opening with some frequency in major cities, sometimes allowing, as has long been the case for gay clubs, for
consu[ma][p]tion on the spot. (While discos may represent nostalgia in the
west, for many in poorer countries they represent both modernity and cos-
mopolitanism, opening up space for experimentation in both self-presenta-
tion and sexuality.)

Nonetheless it is likely that AIDS has transformed the ways in which
we understand sex, linking it once again to concepts of danger, disease, and

death. I say "once again" because the idea of sex as threatening as much as pleasurable has probably been the dominant experience of most women through history; only with the advent of relatively safe and effective contraception, and the ability to cure venereal diseases, could sex be decoupled from danger. This was the real meaning of the "sexual revolution" of the 1960s, and the advent of AIDS has undermined it to some extent, if not to the extent that conservatives might hope.

In countries where the major spread of HIV is through heterosexual intercourse—meaning the great majority of the poor world—the conflict between risk of infection and the desire for children poses the greatest challenge to sexual mores. "Safe(r) sex" is far easier when reproduction is not an issue, even more so when it can be combined with prevention of pregnancy. But in many societies women's worth is measured by their fertility, and HIV poses a life-threatening dilemma between risking pregnancy and denying the strongest social expectations of women. Thus Molara Ogundipe-Leslie noted of Nigeria that "[a] childless woman is considered a monstrosity—as is an unmarried woman (spinster or divorcee) who becomes the butt of jokes and scandal and the quarry of every passing man, married or not."[47] Certain traditional practices—in some African societies a widow is expected to become a second wife to her husband's brother—can compound the dilemma if either one is HIV-positive. While it is increasingly possible to minimize the risk of infection from mother to baby, the resources required are often not available, and the consequence is a growing number of orphans, many of them HIV-positive. (In Zambia it is estimated that *half* the country's children have lost at least one parent to AIDS.) In Zimbabwe some women's organizations argue that the obligation on doctors and counselors to protect confidentiality further disempowers women and confirms existing sexual inequalities. Among Zimbabweans aged less than twenty more than 80% of those infected are women.[48]

REPRESENTATIONS OF SEX AND DEATH

Most of the scholarly/scientific discourse on AIDS ignores its impact on popular culture and the vast creative response the epidemic has created. When I sought to include a session on "writing AIDS" in the program of the Eleventh International Conference on AIDS in Vancouver 1996, it was met with disinterest by social scientists and community organizations, both of whom seemed to see "culture" as what you did after the serious business of the conference was over.[49] Yet creative responses are the best measure we have of the ways in which AIDS has affected our imagination and perception of the world. Norman Spinrad has written that he became aware by 1986 that AIDS "would create, in fact had already created, a baleful new existential equation between sex and death, and that could not fail to alter our psyches and our society on the most intimate and ultimate of levels."[50] His *Journals of the Plague Years*, originally seen as unpublishable because of its AIDS theme, attempts to explore this through a mix of future horror and political fantasy.[51]

Of course the dominant literary and cinematic response is gay and North Atlantic—in late 1980s I met a young man in Kuala Lumpur who told me he "knew all about AIDS" from the American telemovie *An Early Frost*. In Nicaragua the death of Rock Hudson is said to have opened up public discussion about the epidemic.[52] Such examples shows the extent to which AIDS can be understood as both product and cause of globalization. Indeed responses to AIDS provide rich examples of the thesis that globalization is just another word for Americanization—think for example of the widespread international use of the red ribbon,[53] of the AIDS Memorial Quilt, of films such as *Philadelphia* or plays like *Rent* or *Angels in America*. In 1999 Romanian orthodox religious groups were reported as attempting to prevent the production of *Angels in America* in Bucharest.

There exists now a huge literature reflecting the relatively short history of the epidemic, though largely confined to the experience of gay men.[54] Almost at random I quote one example from a novel by Christopher Bram:

> Peter wearily folded up the arts pages. "All I know is that death is boring. It's no fun anymore."
>
> I glanced nervously at Nick. "Was it ever fun?" I asked.
>
> Peter arched his eyebrows, surprised himself by what he'd said. "It didn't feel like it at the time" he admitted. "But now, in comparison, it was certainly new and exciting. The emotions it touched were new and exciting. So dramatic."
>
> "Now it skips over emotion" I said.
>
> He nodded. "And eats right into your soul."[55]

I might as easily have quoted from Alan Hollinghurst, Edmund White, Paul Monette, Armistead Maupin (to cite four of the best-known writers working in English).[56] Over the past decade AIDS has come to haunt much contemporary literature, even if, as Jewelle Gomez claims, it has also made

"queer" writers more marketable.[57] Some of the most effective AIDS literature barely mentions the disease (I think for example of Robert Dessaix's
Night Letters [58] in which the narrator's positivity is acknowledged but unnamed),
but its ubiquity is evidence both of the prominence of gay writers and of their
impact on the larger world. "He is dead of the Illness, just a square in the
quilt now," Rushdie writes in *The Ground beneath Her Feet*,[59] and we all know of
what Illness he writes. As Don DeLillo wrote in *Underworld:* "Retroviruses in
the bloodstream, acronyms in the air. Edgar knew what all the letters stood
for. AZidoThymidine. Human Immunodeficiency Virus. Acquired Immune
Deficiency Syndrome. Komitet Gosudartsvennoi Bezopasnosi. Yes, the KGB
was part of the multiplying swarm, the cell-blast of reality that has to be
distilled and initialled in order to be seen."[60]

Suzanne Poirier has written that "all writing today is AIDS writing in
that it must consciously choose how to respond to the epidemic, whether by
direct involvement or evasion."[61] Even if one confines that comment to gay
writing (which Poirier seems not to do) it is, I think, too prescriptive, though
it is echoed in Gregory Woods's criticism of "some established gay writers
who did not pay sufficient attention to the epidemic"[62] as if it were self-
evident that AIDS needed to replace all other concerns.

If AIDS writing is heavily American, there is more of a response elsewhere than we might recognize, often interwoven with a new gay assertion.
This is most obvious in Latin America, where there has been a considerable
amount of literary and theatrical responses to the epidemic.[63] Indeed the
growing prominence of gay writing as a specific genre is closely linked to the
specter of AIDS: it haunts the background of Boris Davidovich's diaries of
living through the breakup of Yugoslavia, and it becomes the central theme
of Colm Toibin's imagined story of a young man growing up in contemporary Argentina, of E. Lynn Harris's novels of gay African Americans, of the
Maori writer Witi Ihimaera's novel *Nights in the Gardens of Spain,* and of the
South African play, Peter Hayes's *To Have/To Hold.* One of the earlier "AIDS
novels" was Nigel Krauth's *JF Was Here,* set largely in Papua New Guinea,[64]
and AIDS is a theme in a growing body of African writing.[65]

These works often go unrecorded by the AIDS industry, or are reduced
to interesting methods of prevention education. Yet the larger question is
how AIDS has entered the global imaginary as a kind of overacting postmodern symbol: AIDS reminds us of the fragility of political borders, the
limits of modern biomedical control, the vulnerability of the human body,

but it also becomes a new reason for increased surveillance of the most private of human activities, whether through campaigns to link monogamy to health, or more benignly in the multitude of programs aimed at developing peer education and empowerment among sex workers, drug users, men who have sex with men, whose identities are thereby reinforced,[66] recalling the patrolling of female sex workers through the Contagious Diseases Acts a century ago.[67] I have some sympathy with Susan Sontag's warning against seeing AIDS "as metaphor,"[68] but the demand for rationality runs counter to some very powerful forces which imbue AIDS, with its link to the exotic and the proscribed, its routes of transmission through blood and semen, with particular symbolic weight. It is not surprising that James Nicola of the New York Theater Workshop believes plays like *Angels in America* and *Rent* reflect fin de siècle anxiety in America,[69] which may explain why it has allowed for quite extravagant claims, such as Larry Kramer's insensitive comparison of AIDS to the Holocaust.

AIDS has provided the text for a vast amount of cultural work over the past decade. Part of the current nostalgia for the 1970s involves a sometimes exaggerated sense of a pre-AIDS sexual freedom and a recognition of how much of seventies culture died with AIDS, at least as defined in the "fast lane" and chic circles of New York and Los Angeles fashion and show biz.[70] AIDS has been a theme in plays and novels from across the western world and beyond, as well as drama,[71] visual art,[72] music, and dance. At least in the United States notoriety surrounded Bill T. Jones's dance piece—*Still/Here*—inspired by the death of his lover/partner Arnie Zane, which Arlene Croce refused to review for the *New Yorker* on the grounds that this was "victim art."[73] But probably the largest popular impact of the epidemic is through film and television, which insofar as they aim for a mass market are also more affected by the stigma surrounding the disease.

There are of course a number of interesting underground movies with AIDS themes—examples include Gregg Araki's *Living End* and, especially, John Greyson's *Zero Patience*, which plays with the caricature of the "first" person with AIDS in Randy Shilts's book, *And the Band Played On*.[74] Cyril Collard's 1993 *Les nuits fauves* is perhaps an intermediate case—a popular success in France, an art-house movie elsewhere.[75] The French musical *Jeanne et le garçon formidable* made use of HIV in a heterosexual love story which is both bitter and very kitsch. Less interesting than the specific AIDS films, which are usually maudlin (e.g., *Longtime Companion*) or evasive (e.g., *Philadelphia*), is the way in which HIV/AIDS has become background noise to modern life, whether through the invocation of unspecified plagues (e.g., *Dune, Twelve Monkeys, Outbreak*), the emphasis on blood as dangerous, and the link of AIDS to interests in the Gothic and horror.[76] AIDS has been consistently linked with the contemporary interest in vampires and Gothic stories, and the huge popularity of writers such as Anne Rice and Poppy Z. Brite. Thus the critic Mark Edmundson claims that the fear of AIDS "prompts our major public occasion for indulgence in apocalyptic Gothic."[77] (The most specific link may be in Nancy Baker's *Kiss of the Vampire*,[78] where a woman seeks the vampire's kiss to cure her of AIDS.) In an *X-Files* episode made in 1994 Fox Mulder meets a woman in a bar who imagines herself to be—and might be—a vampire. When she offers Mulder blood from a thumb prick he asks isn't she scared of AIDS. Others have linked the specter of AIDS to the interest in cybersex, with its avoidance of any actual physical exchanges.[79]

Of all these products *Philadelphia* remains the best known, and the most explicit attempt to confront AIDS in Hollywood cinema (at least until the long-promised film version of Larry Kramer's play *The Normal Heart*). I regard the confrontation as evasive for the same reasons as Sarah Schulman, who wrote:

> Today we see that the only publicly acceptable presentation of the AIDS crisis is one created by a straight man. What was it about gay-produced films about AIDS that was unacceptable and that was not present in a work such as *Philadelphia*? A short list would include gay anger, gay sexuality, the abandonment of gays and lesbians and people with AIDS by their families, the impact of mass death on the individual, and the dimensions and reach of the gay and lesbian community. Now, with the advent of a fake public homosexuality constructed for heterosexual consumption, we have *Philadelphia* saying it is heterosexuals who have defended and protected gay people with AIDS while other gays lurked meekly in the background.[80]

The political flaw of *Philadelphia*, which postulated that a successful HIV-positive lawyer dismissed from his job would have trouble finding someone to defend him, is that it had to ignore the vast plethora of community-based AIDS organizations which exist in a city like Philadelphia. (On the other hand if one sees *Philadelphia* as the story of the lawyer forced to confront his own homophobia rather than that of the central character with AIDS it becomes a stronger film.) In this the film echoes much of the literary responses, at least in English, which usually center on very private worlds—though Felice Picano does invoke the HIV activist group ACT UP in his novel *Like People in History* (1995) as does Christopher Bram in *Gossip* (1997). More typical is the pathos and fear of almost totally isolated gay men caught in several of the works of David Leavitt which touch on the epidemic.[81]

Most interesting perhaps is the cultural reflection of mourning and loss, which unites the experiences of AIDS in inner-city San Francisco and Newark with that of Kenyan and Zambian villages. Again we are most aware of the particular ceremonies and rituals which have been invented in the western world: the AIDS Memorial Quilt, the candlelight vigils, and so forth.[82] The gay community has been particularly inventive in integrating AIDS into its festivities, so that something like the annual Gay and Lesbian Mardi Gras in Sydney, one of the largest street parades in the world, becomes a means of simultaneously grieving for those gone and reaffirming a commitment to those living.[83] Those of us working in rich English-speaking countries are far less aware of how other cultures have developed ways of commemorating AIDS deaths,[84] although the Quilt and certain photographic exhibitions have sought to encompass the global epidemic.

By 1999 the annual Candlelight Memorial, which began in San Francisco in 1983, involved participants in more than fifty countries, and provided a forum for highlighting the particular issues around the epidemic in the poor world. In 1999 participants took part in ceremonies in seventy towns and cities across Indonesia, and issued a declaration of "solidarity against injustice and fear for a world without AIDS." Similarly, World AIDS Day (December 1) tends to have far greater resonance in a number of poor countries than it does in the west. As the experience of AIDS becomes increasingly linked to poverty and inequality I would expect this to be reflected in artistic responses from other parts of the world. Whether they become widely available outside their own environment will have more to do with the global cultural marketplace than with their intrinsic value.

Both official and unofficial responses to AIDS have required new ways of thinking about the links between "private" behavior and public health, and the often huge discrepancies between actual behavior and official ideology. The epidemic has revealed similar sexual hypocrisies in countries as apparently dissimilar as India, Russia, Argentina, and the United States. Nor is the sort of behavioral surveillance involved in AIDS prevention morally unambiguous; there are risks in encouraging the state to learn more about

behaviors—prostitution, needle use, homosexuality—which might be regarded as criminal, even if the knowledge is central to any successful prevention strategy. If David Halperin's claim for the influence of Foucault on
American AIDS activists is correct,[85] it might be because the politics of AIDS
illustrate so clearly the ways in which the discourses of governmental surveillance and identity politics reinforce each other. There was a bizarre example
of this at the opening of the Fifth International Congress on AIDS in Asia
and the Pacific in Kuala Lumpur in 1999, where Prime Minister Mahathir
was introduced by a self-identified transgender sex worker who has herself
been arrested for cross-dressing.

Ironically the new behavioral surveillance required by AIDS comes
while there is a retreat from state responsibility in other areas. Successful
AIDS work implies both the strengthening and the weakening of the state,
as "the new public health" approach demands the empowerment of nonstate
actors and forces recognition of unpopular groups and behaviors. There are
parallels between the U.S. debates about needle exchange and outreach programs for drug users in countries like Vietnam which matches "the war on
drugs" with its own invocation of "social evils," which are defined as prostitution, drug use, gambling, and alcohol abuse. (Interestingly, homosexuality is
generally ignored by the Vietnamese government, although there is considerable evidence of it, particularly in Ho Chi Minh City.) In both countries
various devices have been found to allow for at least limited programs of
needle-exchange programs.

There is no one AIDS epidemic, but rather a patchwork which has
very different epidemiological patterns and consequences, depending on the
economic and political resources available. The development of highly sophisticated antiviral drugs has reinforced the gap between the epidemic of
those (largely in rich countries) who have access to these therapies, and the
great majority of those infected who do not know their status and would have
little chance of effective treatment if they did. At the turn of the century
governments in the poor world and activists in both rich and poor countries
found themselves grappling with issues of patents and world trade regula-
tions as they sought to make new drugs more accessible to PLWHAs in the
poor world.[86] In both India and South Africa AIDS drugs are produced locally at much lower cost than those controlled by the major international
pharmaceutical companies, and in the latter case there have been consider-

able tensions with the United States, which has accused South Africa of flouting international trade agreements by seeking to produce drugs cheaply.

Within rich countries, above all the United States, AIDS is marked by the significance of gender, class, and race. Yet even those countries which have best contained the epidemic (meaning countries like Australia, Denmark, and the Netherlands, where transmission has been significantly slowed and new therapies are widely available) cannot totally insulate themselves from the outside world. What typifies those countries, and those with far bigger epidemics which are generally regarded as having developed intelligent responses—Uganda and Thailand are the most cited examples—is the commitment by governments to partnership with those communities most affected, and to a public health approach which avoids stigmatization or isolation.

Six

*The Globalization
of Sexual Identities*

Most of the literature about globalization and identity is concerned with the rebirth of nationalist, ethnic, and religious fundamentalism, or the decline of the labor movement.[1] (I am using "identity" to suggest a socially constructed myth about shared characteristics, culture, and history which comes to have real meaning for those who espouse it.)[2] Here I concentrate on the identity politics born of sexuality and gender, and the new social movements which arise from these, already foreshadowed in the previous chapter. These new identities are closely related to the larger changes of globalization: consider the globalization of "youth," and the role of international capitalism in creating a teenage identity in almost every country, with specific music, language, fashion, and mores.[3] In recent years this is expressed in terms of "boy" and "girl" cultures, as in references to "boy bands" or "a booming girl culture worldwide,"[4] which suggests the invention of an intermediate generational identity between "children" and "youth."

Over the past decade I've been researching and thinking about the diffusion of certain sorts of "gay/lesbian" identities, trying to trace the connections between globalization and the preconditions for certain sexual subjectivities.[5] My examples are drawn predominantly from Southeast Asia because this is the part of the "developing" world I know best, but they could even more easily be drawn from Latin America, which has a particularly rich literature exploring these questions.[6] The question is not whether homosexuality exists—it does in almost every society of which we know—but how people incorporate homosexual behavior into their sense of self. Globalization has helped create an international gay/lesbian identity, which is by no means confined to the western world: there are many signs of what we think of as "modern" homosexuality in countries such as Brazil, Costa Rica, Poland, and Taiwan. Indeed the gay world—less obviously the lesbian, largely due to marked differences in women's social and economic status—is a key example of emerging global "subcultures," where members of particular groups have more in common across national and continental boundaries than they do with others in their own geographically defined societies.

It is worth noting that even within the "first world" there is a range of attitudes toward the assertion of gay/lesbian identities. While they have flourished in the English-speaking countries and in parts of northern Europe, there is more resistance to the idea in Italy and France, where ideas of communal rights—expressed through the language of multiculturalism in Australia and Canada, and through a somewhat different tradition of religious pluralism in the Netherlands and Switzerland—seem to run counter to a universalist rhetoric of rights, which are not equated with the recognition of separate group identities.[7] The United States shares both traditions, so that its gay and lesbian movement argues for recognition of "civil rights" on the basis of being just like everyone else, and in some cases deserving of special protection along the lines developed around racial and gender discrimination.

At the same time the United States has gone farthest in the development of geographically based gay and lesbian communities, with defined areas of its large cities—the Castro in San Francisco, West Hollywood, Halsted in Chicago, the West Village in New York—becoming urban "ghettos," often providing a base to develop the political clout of the community. (In almost all large American cities politicians now recognize the importance of the gay vote.) This model has been replicated in a number of western countries, whether it is the Marais in Paris or Darlinghurst in Sydney. There is some irony in the fact that, while homosexual rights have progressed much further in the countries of northern Europe, the United States remains the dominant cultural model for the rest of the world.

This dominance was symbolized in accounts in Europe of "gay pride" events in the summer of 1999, which often ignored national histories and attributed the origins of gay political activism to the Stonewall riots of 1969, ignoring the existence of earlier groups in countries such as Germany, the Netherlands, Switzerland, and France, and the radical gay groups which grew out of the 1968 student movements in both France and Italy. (Stonewall was a gay bar in New York City which was raided by the police, leading to riots by angry homosexuals and the birth of the New York Gay Liberation Front.) In cities as diverse as Paris, Hamburg, and Warsaw the anniversary of Stonewall was celebrated with Christopher Street Day, and the dominance of American culture is summed up by the press release from the Lisbon Gay, Lesbian, Bisexual, and Transgender Pride committee boasting of the performances of a "renowned DJ from New York City" and "Celeda—the Diva Queen from Chicago."

Thinking and writing about these questions, it became clear to me that observers, indigenous and foreign alike, bring strong personal investments to how they understand what is going on, in particular whether (in words suggested to me by Michael Tan) we are speaking of "ruptures" or "continuities." For some there is a strong desire to trace a continuity between precolonial forms of homosexual desire and its contemporary emergence, even where the latter might draw on the language of (West) Hollywood rather than indigenous culture. Such views are argued strenuously by those who cling to an identity based on traditional assumptions about the links between gender performance and sexuality, and deny the relevance of an imported "gay" or "lesbian" identity for themselves. Thus the effeminate *bakkla* in the Philippines or the *kathoey* in Thailand might see those who call themselves "gay" as hypocrites, in part because they insist on their right to behave as men, and to desire others like them.[8] For others there is a perception that contemporary middle-class self-proclaimed gay men and lesbians in, say, New Delhi, Lima, or Jakarta have less in common with "traditional" homosexuality than they do with their counterparts in western countries. As Sri Lankan author Shaym Selvadurai said of his novel *Funny Boy*, which is in part about "coming out" as gay: "The people in the novel are in a place that has been colonized by Western powers for 400 years. A lot of Western ideas—bourgeois respectability, Victorian morality—have become incorporated into the society, and are very much part of the Sri Lankan society."[9]

"Modern" ways of being homosexual threaten not only the custodians of "traditional" morality, they also threaten the position of "traditional" forms of homosexuality, those which are centered around gender nonconformity and transvestism. The title of the Indonesian gay/lesbian journal *Gaya Nusantara*, which literally means "Indonesian style," captures this ambivalence nicely with its echoes of both "traditional" and "modern" concepts of nation and sexuality, but at the same time it is clearly aimed at "modern" homosexuals rather than the "traditional" transvestite *waria*.[10]

It is often assumed that homosexuals are defined in most "traditional" societies as a third sex, but that too is too schematic to be universally useful. As Peter Jackson points out, the same terms in Thailand can be gender *and*

sexual categories.[11] Here, again, we are confronted by considerable confusion, where similar phenomena can be viewed as either culturally specific or
as universal. Insofar as there is a confusion between sexuality and gender in
the "traditional" view that the "real" homosexual is the man who behaves
like a woman (or, more rarely, vice versa) this is consistent with the dominant
understanding of homosexuality in western countries during the hundred
years or so before the birth of the contemporary gay movement. The idea of a
"third sex" was adopted by people like Ulrichs and Krafft-Ebing as part of an
apologia for homosexuality (giving rise to Carpenter's "intermediate sex").[12]
In the 1918 novel *Despised and Rejected* the hero laments: "What had nature
been about, in giving him the soul of a woman in the body of a man?"[13]
Similar views can be found in Radclyffe Hall's novel *The Well of Loneliness*
(1928), whose female hero calls herself Stephen. Today many people who
experience homosexual desires in societies which do not allow space for them
will see themselves as "men trapped in women's bodies" or vice versa.

    In popular perceptions something of this confusion remains today—
and persists in much popular humor, such as the remarkably successful play/
film *La cage aux folles* (*The Birdcage*) or the film *Priscilla, Queen of the Desert*. George
Chauncey argues that the very idea of a homosexual/heterosexual divide
became dominant in the United States only in the mid–twentieth century:
"The most striking difference between the dominant sexual culture of the
early twentieth century and that of our own era is the degree to which the
earlier culture permitted men to engage in sexual relations with other men,
often on a regular basis, without requiring them to regard themselves—or
be regarded by others—as gay ... Many men ... neither understood nor
organised their sexual practices along a hetero-homosexual axis."[14] John
Rechy's landmark novel *City of Night* (1963) captures the transition to "modern" concepts: his world is full of "hustlers," "queens," "masculine" or
"butch" homosexuals," whom he sometimes calls "gay."[15]

    If one reads or views contemporary accounts of homosexual life in, say,
Central America, Thailand, and Côte d'Ivoire,[16] one is immediately struck by
the parallels. It is of course possible that the observers, all of whom are trained
in particular ethnographic and sociological methods, even where, as in the
case of Schifter, they are indigenous to the country of study, are bringing
similar—and one assumes unconscious—preconceptions with them. Even
so, it is unlikely that this itself would explain the degree of similarity they
identify. In the same way, the Dutch anthropologist Saskia Wieringa has

pointed to the similarities of butch-femme role-playing in Jakarta and Lima, and how they echo that of preliberation western lesbian worlds.[17] In many "traditional" societies there were complex variations across gender and sex lines, with "transgender" people (Indonesian *waria*, Thai *kathoey*, Moroccan *hassas*, Turkish *kocek*, Filipino *bayot*, Luban *kitesha* in parts of Congo) characterized by both transvestite and homosexual behavior. These terns are usually—not always—applied to men, but there are other terms sometimes used of women, such as *mati* in Suriname, which also disrupt simplistic assumptions about sex and gender.[18] As Gilbert Herdt says: "Sexual orientation and identity are not the keys to conceptualizing a third sex and gender across time and space."[19] In many societies there is confusion around the terms—for example the *hijras* of India, who were literally castrated, are sometimes considered equivalent to homosexuals even though the reality is more complex.[20]

Different people use terms such as *bayot* or *waria* in different ways, depending on whether the emphasis is on gender—these are men who wish in some way to be women—or on sexuality—these are men attracted to other men. Anthropology teaches us the need to be cautious about any sort of binary system of sex/gender; Niko Besnier uses the term "gender liminality" to avoid this trap[21] and it should also alert us against the sort of romanticized assumptions that some Americans have brought to understanding the Native American *bedarche*.[22] Besnier also stresses that such "liminality" is not the same as homosexuality: "Sexual relations with men are seen as an optional consequence of gender liminality, rather than its determiner, prerequisite or primary attribute."[23] The other side of this distinction is that there are strong pressures to define *fa'afafine* (the Samoan term) or other such groups in Pacific countries as asexual, thus leading to a particular denial in which both Samoans and outsiders are complicit.[24]

Certainly most of the literature about Latin America stresses that a homosexual *identity* (as distinct from homosexual practices) is related to rejection of dominant gender expectations, so that "a real man" can have sex with other men and not risk his heterosexual identity. As Roger Lancaster put it: "Whatever else a *cochon* might or might not do, he is tacitly understood as one who assumes the receptive role in anal intercourse. His partner, defined as 'active' in the terms of their engagement, is not stigmatized, nor does he acquire a special identity of any sort."[25] Thus the *nature* rather than the *object* of the sexual act becomes the key factor. However, there is also evidence that this is changing, and a more western concept of homosexual identity is establishing itself, especially among the middle classes.

Sexuality becomes an important arena for the production of modernity, with "gay" and "lesbian" identities acting as markers for modernity.[26] There is an ironic echo of this in the Singapore government's bulldozing of Bugis Street, once the center of transvestite prostitution in the city—and its replacement by a Disneyland-like simulacrum where a few years ago I was taken to see a rather sanitized drag show presented to a distinctly yuppie audience.[27] There is an equal irony in seeing the decline of a homosexuality defined by gender nonconformity as a "modern" trend just when transsexuals and some theorists in western countries are increasingly attracted by concepts of the malleability of gender.[28] From one perspective the fashionable replica of the stylized "lipstick lesbian" or "macho" gay man is less "postmodern" than the *waria* or the Tongan *fakaleiti*.[29]

Perhaps the reality is that androgyny is postmodern when it is understood as performance, not when it represents the only available way of acting out certain deep-seated beliefs about one's sexual and gender identity. Even so, I remain unsure just why "drag," and its female equivalents, remains a strong part of the contemporary homosexual world, even where there is increasing space for open homosexuality and a range of acceptable ways of "being" male or female. Indeed there is evidence that in some places there is a simultaneous increase in both gay/lesbian identities *and* in transgender performance, as in recent developments in Taiwan where drag shows have become very fashionable, and some of the performers, known as "third sex public relations officers," insist that they are not homosexual even when their behavior would seem to contradict this.[30] Similar comments could probably be made about *onnabe,* Japanese women who dress as men and act as the equivalent of geishas for apparently heterosexual women, and Jennifer Robertson describes the incorporation of androgyny into the "'libidinal' economy of the capitalist market" as "gender-bending" performers are turned into marketable commodities.[31] In the west it has become increasingly fashionable to depict transvestism in unmistakably heterosexual terms; what was daring (and possibly ambiguous) in the 1959 film *Some Like It Hot* becomes farce in the 1993 film *Mrs. Doubtfire.*[32] But at the same time there is, particularly in the United States, the emergence of a somewhat new form of transgender politics, in which the concern of an older generation to be accepted as the woman or man they "really" are is replaced by an assertion of a transgender identity and the malleability of gender.[33] (Western writers tend to be reasonably careful to distinguish between *transsexual* and *transvestite*. However, this distinction is often not made in parts of Asia and, I assume, other parts of the world.)

Speaking openly of homosexuality and transvestism, which is often the consequence of western influence, can unsettle what is accepted but not acknowledged. Indeed there is some evidence in a number of societies that those who proclaim themselves "gay" or "lesbian," that is, seek a public identity based on their sexuality, encounter a hostility which may not have been previously apparent. But there is a great deal of mythology around the acceptance of gender/sexual nonconformity outside the west, a mythology to which for different reasons both westerners and nonwesterners contribute. Romanticized views about homoeroticism in many nonwestern cultures, often based on travel experiences, disguise the reality of persecution, discrimination, and violence, sometimes in unfamiliar forms. Firsthand accounts make it clear that homosexuality is far from being universally accepted—or even tolerated—in such apparent "paradises" as Morocco, the Philippines, Thailand, or Brazil: "Lurking behind the Brazilians' pride of their flamboyant drag queens, their recent adulation of a transvestite chosen as a model of Brazilian beauty, their acceptance of gays and lesbians as leaders of the country's most widely practised religion and the constitutional protection of homosexuality, lies a different truth. Gay men, lesbians and transvestites face widespread discrimination, oppression and extreme violence."[34]

Just as the most interesting postmodern architecture is found in cities like Shanghai or Bangkok, so too the emphasis of postmodern theory on pastiche, parody, hybridity, and so forth is played out in a real way by women and men who move, often with considerable comfort, from apparent obedience to official norms to their own sense of gay community. The dutiful Confucian or Islamic Malaysian son one weekend might appear in drag at Blueboy, Kuala Lumpur's gay bar, the next—and who is to say which is "the real" person? Just as many Malaysians can move easily from one language to another, so most urban homosexuals can move from one style to another, from camping it up with full awareness of the latest fashion trends from Castro Street to playing the dutiful son at a family celebration.

To western gay liberationists these strategies might seem hypocritical, even cowardly (and some westerners expressed surprise at the apparent silence from Malaysian gay men after the arrest of Anwar on sodomy charges).

But even the most politically aware Malaysians may insist that there is no need to "come out" to their family, while explaining that in any case their lover is accepted as one of the family—though not so identified. (The Malaysian situation is further complicated by the fact that Muslims are subject to both civil and *sharia* laws, and the latter have been used quite severely, against transvestites in particular.) Some people have suggested that everything is possible *as long as it is not stated,* but it is probably more complex than that. For many men I have met in Southeast Asia being gay does mean a sense of communal identity, and even a sense of "gay pride," but this is not necessarily experienced in the vocabulary of the west.

Middle-class English-speaking homosexuals in places like Mexico City, Istanbul, and Mumbai will speak of themselves as part of a gay (sometimes "gay and lesbian") community, but the institutions of such a community will vary considerably depending on both economic resources and political space. Thus in Kuala Lumpur, one of the richer cities of the "developing" world, there are no gay or lesbian bookstores, restaurants, newspapers, or businesses—at least not in the open way we would expect them in comparable American or European cities. There is, however, a strong sense of gay identity around the AIDS organization Pink Triangle—its name is emblematic—and sufficient networks for a gay sauna to open and attract customers. Yet when a couple of years ago I gave some copies of the Australian gay magazine *Outrage* to the manager of the Kuala Lumpur sauna, I was told firmly there could be no display of something as overtly homosexual as these magazines—which are routinely sold by most Australian newsagents. In the same way there is also a strong lesbian network in the city, and many women use office faxes and email to arrange meetings and parties.

At that same sauna I met one man who told me he had heard of the place through a friend now living in Sydney. In conversations I have had with middle-class gay men in Southeast Asia there are frequent references to bars in Paris and San Francisco, to Sydney's Gay and Lesbian Mardi Gras, to American gay writers. Those who take on gay identities often aspire to be part of global culture in all its forms, as suggested by this quote from a Filipino anthology of gay writing: "I met someone in a bar last Saturday . . . He's a bank executive. He's mestizo (your type) and . . . loves Barbra Streisand, Gabriel Garcia Marquez, Dame Margot Fonteyn, Pat Conroy, Isabel Allende, John Williams, Meryl Streep, Armistead Maupin, k. d. lang, Jim Chappell, Margaret Atwood and Luciano Pavarotti."[35]

Similarly magazines like *G & L* in Taiwan—a "lifestyle" magazine launched in 1996—mixes local news and features with stories on international, largely American, gay and lesbian icons. As mobility increases, more and more people are traveling abroad and meeting foreigners at home. It is as impossible to prevent new identities and categories traveling as it is to prevent pornography traveling across the Internet.

As part of the economic growth of south and east Asia the possibilities of computer-based communications have been grasped with enormous enthusiasm, and have created a new set of possibilities for the diffusion of information and the creation of (virtual) communities. Whereas the gay movements of the 1970s in the west depended heavily on the creation of a gay/lesbian press, in countries such as Malaysia, Thailand, and Japan the Internet offers the same possibilities, with the added attraction of anonymity and instant contact with overseas, thus fostering the links with the diaspora already discussed. Work by Chris Berry and Fran Martin suggests that the Internet has become a crucial way for young homosexuals to meet each other in Taiwan and Korea—and in the process to develop a certain, if privatized, form of community.[36] In Japan the Internet has become a central aid to homosexual cruising.

It is precisely this constant dissemination of images and ways of being, moving disproportionately from north to south, which leads some to savagely criticize the spread of sexual identities as a new step in neocolonialism: "The very constitution of a subject entitled to rights involves the violent capture of the disenfranchised by an institutional discourse which inseparably weaves them into the textile of global capitalism."[37] This position is argued with splendid hyperbole by Pedro Bustos-Aguilar, who attacks both "the gay ethnographer . . . [who] kills a native with the charm of his camera" and "the union of the New World Order and Transnational Feminism" which asserts neocolonialism and western hegemony in the name of supposed universalisms.[38]

Bustos-Aguilar's argument is supported by the universalist rhetoric which surrounded the celebration of the twenty-fifth anniversary of Stonewall, but he could have had great fun with a 1993 brochure from San Francisco which offered "your chance to make history . . . [at] the first ever gay & lesbian film festival in India & parallel queer tour"—and even more with the reporter from the *Washington Blade* who wrote of Anwar's "ostensibly being gay."[39] It finds a troubling echo in the story of an American, Tim Wright, who founded a gay movement in Bolivia, and after four years was found badly beaten and amnesiac: "And things have gone back to being what they were."[40]

A more measured critique comes from Ann Ferguson, who has warned that the very concept of an international lesbian *culture* is politically problematic, because it would almost certainly be based upon western assumptions, even though she is somewhat more optimistic about the creation of an international *movement*, which would allow for self-determination of local lesbian communities.[41] While western influences were clearly present, it is as true to see the emergence of groups in much of Latin America, in Southeast Asia, and among South African blacks as driven primarily by local forces.

It is certainly true that the assertion of gay/lesbian identity can have neocolonial implications, but given that many anti/postcolonial movements and governments deny existing homosexual traditions it becomes difficult to know exactly whose values are being imposed on whom. Both the western outsider and the local custodians of national culture are likely to ignore existing realities in the interest of ideological certainty. Those outside the west tend to be more aware of the difference between traditional homosexualities and contemporary gay identity politics, a distinction sometimes lost by the international gay/lesbian movement in its eagerness to claim universality.[42] New sexual identities mean a loss of certain traditional cultural comforts while offering new possibilities to those who adopt them, and activists in non-western countries will consciously draw on both traditions. In this they may be inconsistent, but no more than western gay activists who simultaneously deploy the language of universal rights and special group status.

In practice most people hold contradictory opinions at the same time, reminding us of Freud's dictum that "it is only in logic that contradictions cannot exist." There are large numbers of men and fewer women in non-western countries who will describe themselves as "gay" or "lesbian" in certain circumstances, while sometimes claiming these labels are inappropriate to their situation. It is hardly surprising that people want both to identify with and to distinguish themselves from a particular western form of homosexuality, or that they will call upon their own historical traditions to do so. This ambivalence is caught in this account by a Chinese-Australian: "[Chinese] gays were determined to advance their cause but in an evolutionary rather than revolutionary way. They seized on issues such as gayness, gay culture, gay lifestyle, equal rights for gays and so on. In romantic poems the gay dreams of our ancestors were represented by two boys sharing a peach and the emperor who cut his sleeves of his gown rather than disturb his lover sleeping in his arms. To revive this dream, and enable millions of Chinese-born gays to choose their lifestyle, is a huge task. But it has happened in Taiwan, as it did in Hong Kong, and so it will in China."[43]

There are of course examples of Asian gay groups engaging in political activity of the sort associated with their counterparts in the west. Indonesia has a number of gay and lesbian groups, which have now held three national meetings. The best-known openly gay figure in Indonesia, Dede Oetomo, was a candidate of the fledgling Democratic People's Party in the 1999 elections, which followed the overthrow of Suharto. There have been several small radical gay political groups established in the Philippines in recent years, and gay demonstrations have taken place in Manila. ProGay (the Progressive Organization of Gays in the Philippines), as its name suggests, is concerned to draw links between specifically gay issues and larger questions of social justice.[44] The first lesbian conference was held in Japan in 1985,[45] and there have been lesbian organizations in Taiwan since 1990 and the Philippines since 1992.[46] The international lesbigay press carried reports of a national conference of lesbians in Beijing in late 1998 and in Sri Lanka the following year. There have been several *tongzhi* gatherings in Hong Kong (a term adopted to cover "lesbians, bisexuals, gays and transgendered people"), and a manifesto adopted by the 1996 meeting argued that "[c]ertain characteristics of confrontational politics, such as through coming out and mass protests and parades may not be the best way of achieving *tongzhi* liberation in the family-centred, community-oriented Chinese societies which stress the importance of social harmony."[47] (An odd myth, given the revolutionary upheavals in twentieth-century China.) None of these groups have the history or the reach of gay/lesbian movements in Latin America, where Brazil, Argentina, Chile, and Mexico all have significant histories of a politicized homosexuality.

In many cases homosexual identities are asserted without an apparent gay/lesbian movement. In 1998 there was a move by bar owners in Kuala Lumpur to organize a gay-pride party which was canceled after a protest by the Malaysian Youth Council. The best example of a nonpolitical gay world can probably be found in Thailand, where there is a growing middle-class gay world, based neither on prostitution nor on traditional forms of gender non-conformity (as in the person of the *kathoey*), but only a small lesbian group, Anjaree, and no gay male groups at all since the collapse of a couple of attempts to organize around HIV in the late 1980s.[48] In late 1996 controversy erupted in Thailand after the governing body of the country's teacher-training colleges decreed that "sexual deviants" would be barred from entering the colleges. While there was considerable opposition to the ban (subsequently dropped), other than Anjaree most of this came from nongay sources. In the ensuing public debate one could see contradictory outside influences at work—both an imported fear of homosexuals and a more modern emphasis on how such a ban infringed human rights. As Peter Jackson concluded: "A dynamic gay scene has emerged . . . in the complete absence of a gay rights movement."[49]

Indeed it may be that a political movement is the least likely part of western concepts of homosexual identity to be adopted in many parts of the world, even as some activists enthusiastically embrace the mores and imagery of western queerdom. The particular form of identity politics which allowed for the mobilization of a gay/lesbian electoral pressure in countries like the United States, the Netherlands, and even France may not be appropriate elsewhere, even if western-style liberal democracy triumphs. The need of western lesbian/gays to engage in identity politics as a means of enhancing self-esteem may not be felt in other societies. Even so, one should read Jackson's comment about Thailand with some caution. Already when he wrote it there was an embryonic group in Bangkok around an American-owned and -run gay bookstore. At the end of 1999 one of the country's gay papers organized a gay festival and twilight parade in the heart of Bangkok, announcing it as "the first and biggest gay parade in Asia where Asian gay men have a basic human right to be who they want to be and love who they want to love."[50] Similarly, accounts of homosexual life in Japan alternate between assuming a high degree of acceptance—and therefore no reason for a political movement—and severe restrictions on the space to assert homosexual identity, though the gay group OCCUR has recently gained a certain degree of visibility.

The western gay/lesbian movement emerged in conditions of affluence and liberal democracy, where despite other large social issues it was possible to develop a politics around sexuality, which is more difficult in countries where the basic structures of political life are constantly contested.[51] Writing of contemporary South Africa Mark Gevisser notes: "Race-identification overpowers everything else—class, gender and sexuality."[52] In the same way basic questions of political economy and democratization will impact the future development of gay/lesbian movements in much of Asia and Africa. Yet in Latin America and eastern Europe gay/lesbian movements have grown considerably in the past decade, and there are signs of their emergence in some parts of Africa, for example in Botswana and in Zimbabwe, where President Mugabe has consistently attacked homosexuality as the product of colonialism.[53] Similar rhetoric has come from the leaders of Kenya,[54] Namibia, and Uganda, whose President Museveni has denounced homosexuality as "western"—using the rhetoric of the Christian right to do so.[55] Anglican bishops from Africa—though not South Africa—were crucial in defeating moves to change the Church of England's attitudes toward homosexuality at the 1998 decennial Lambeth Conference. South Africa is a crucial exception, perhaps because apartheid's denunciation of homosexuality made it easier for the African National Congress to develop a policy of acceptance as part of their general support for "a rainbow nation." Even so, some elements of the ANC are strongly homophobic, revealed in the rhetoric of many of Winnie Mandela's supporters.[56]

While many African officials and clergy maintain that homosexuality is not part of precolonial African culture, the evidence for its existence—and the slow acknowledgment of its role in African life—is emerging across the continent. One might speculate that the strong hostility from some African political and religious leaders toward homosexuality as a "western import" is an example of psychoanalytic displacement, whereby anxieties about sexuality are redirected to continuing resentment against colonialism and the subordinate position of Africa within the global economy. Western-derived identities can easily become markers of those aspects of globalization which are feared and opposed. Similarly, a 1994 conference for gay/MSMs (men who have sex with men) in Bombay was opposed by the National Federation of Indian Women, an affiliate of the Communist party of India, as "an invasion of India by decadent western cultures and a direct fallout of our signing the GATT agreement."[57] Whether the federation was aware of how close its rhetoric was to right-wing Americans such as Patrick Buchanan is unknown.

Part of the appearance of modernity is the use of western languages. Rodney Jones has noted the importance of English as part of the cultural capital of Hong Kong homosexuals,[58] and when I attended an AIDS conference in Morocco in 1996 participants complained that despite an attempt to ensure equal use of Arabic it was "easier" to talk about sexuality in French. A similar emphasis on English is noted by James Farrar in presumably hetero- sexual discos in Shanghai, where ironically the Village People song "YMCA" has now become "a globalized dance ritual in which the dancers are encour- aged to use their hands to make shapes of the English letters, identifying themselves momentarily with a boundless global ecumene of sexy happy youth 'at the YMCA.'"[59] One assumes the Shanghai dancers are unaware of the clearly gay overtones to both the song and the group. I admit to partic- ular pleasure in reading this piece; an early proposal for my book *The Homo- sexualization of America* was rejected by an editor who complained (this was in 1982) that in a year no one would remember the Village People, the image with which I began that book.

A common language is essential for networking, and the past twenty years have seen a rapid expansion of networks among lesbian and gay groups across the world. In 1978 the International Lesbian and Gay Association (ILGA) was formed at a conference in Coventry, England.[60] While ILGA has largely been driven by northern Europeans, it now has member groups in more than seventy countries and has organized international meetings in several southern cities. Other networks, often linked to feminist and AIDS organizing, have been created in the past two decades, and emerging lesbian and gay movements are increasingly likely to be in constant contact with groups across the world. The inspiration from meeting with other lesbians at international women's conferences has been a powerful factor in the cre- ation of lesbian groups in a number of countries. Thus the Asian Lesbian Network, which now includes women from twelve or thirteen countries, be- gan at an International Lesbian Information Service conference in Geneva in 1986.[61]

In recent years there has been some attempt to promote international networking among transgendered people—or, as Americans now call them, transfolk—with both the British-based International Gender Transient Affinity and the U.S.-based Gender Freedom International lobbying to pro- tect transgendered people across the world from what seems to be routine harassment and persecution. The paradox of globalization is played out in constructions of sex/gender which combine the premodern with the mod- ern, so that people identifying with "traditional" forms of transgender iden- tity will employ modern techniques of surgery and hormone therapy to alter their bodies.

The two largest international gay/lesbian institutions are probably those based around the Metropolitan Community Church and the Gay Games. The MCC is a Protestant sect founded by the Reverend Troy Perry in Los Angeles in 1968, whose congregations and ministers are largely homosexual, with an estimated congregation of more than 40,000 in some sixteen countries. Similar gay churches have emerged somewhat independently in several other societies such as South Africa and Mexico.[62] The Gay Games, modeled on the Olympics, which refused the use of its name, were first held in San Francisco in 1982, and have since become a major international event every four years, for which cities contend very bitterly. They also generate considerable international publicity, much of it of a somewhat voyeuristic nature.[63] Both of these "networks," it is worth stressing, originated in the United States.

Homosexuality becomes a particularly obvious measure of globalization, for the transformation of local regimes of sexuality and gender is often most apparent in the emergence of new sorts of apparently "gay" and "lesbian," even "queer," identities. Yet we must beware reading too much into these scripts. What is happening in Bangkok, Rio, and Nairobi is the creation of new forms of understanding and regulating the sexual self, but it is unlikely that they will merely repeat those forms which were developed in the Atlantic world. Walking through the "gay" area of Tokyo's Shinjuku you will see large numbers of young men in sneakers and baseball caps (or whatever happens to be the current "gay" look) but this does not mean they will behave or view themselves in the same way as equivalent young men in North America or northern Europe.

PROSTITUTE VERSUS SEX WORKER

A growing globalization of both identities and human rights is reflected in the growth of sex-worker groups and the regulation of prostitution. In recent years there have been legislative attempts in a number of first-world countries to decriminalize prostitution and at the same time to control certain forms of sex work, especially that involving enforced prostitution or children.[64] There is a bitter division between those who argue that human rights should mean the end of prostitution (understood as "sex-slavery" to use Kathleen Barry's phrase)[65] and those who argue that adults should have the right to use their bodies to make money, and should be protected from exploitation and danger in making use of that right. Indeed the use of the term "sex worker" is a deliberate ploy to demystify the category of "prostitute," and the terms "sex work" and "sex worker" "have been coined by sex-workers themselves to redefine commercial sex, not as the social or psychological characteristic of a class of women, but as an income-generating activity or form of employment for women and men."[66] One of the most eloquent statements comes from the Indian group Durbar Mahila Samanwaya Committee, even if the language clearly reflects western academic discourse.

> The "prostitute" is rarely used to refer to an occupational group of women earning their livelihood through providing sexual services, rather it is deployed as a descriptive term denoting a homogenised category, usually of women, which poses threats to public health, sexual morality, social stability and civic order. Within this discursive boundary we systematically find ourselves to be targets of moralising impulses of dominant social groups through missions of cleansing and sanitising both materially and symbolically. If and when we figure in political or development agenda we are enmeshed in discursive practices and practical projects which aim to rescue, rehabilitate, improve, discipline, control or police us.[67]

The first sex-worker organization seems to have been COYOTE (standing for Call Off Your Old Tired Ethics), which was established by Margo St. James in San Francisco in 1973 with support from the Glide Memorial Church and the Playboy Foundation.[68] Apparently unconnected to this a group emerged in France in the mid-1970s, following the murder of several prostitutes in Lyons in which the police showed little interest. Out of this group, and the subsequent English Collective of Prostitutes, came the formation of the International Committee for Prostitutes' Rights. COYOTE organized the First World Meeting of Prostitutes in Washington in 1976, following which other groups emerged, such as Red Thread in the Netherlands. At the Second World Whores' Congress in Brussels in 1986 delegates demanded that "[p]rostitution should be redefined as legitimate work and the prostitutes should be redefined as legitimate citizens."[69]

This shift toward seeing prostitution as work is reflected in the development of "sex-work" organizations in some developing countries, the first of which seems to have been in Ecuador, followed by groups in a number of other Latin American countries[70] and a couple in Southeast Asia such as Talikala in Davao City, the Philippines. The women who founded Talikala were concerned from the outset to empower sex workers, and were attacked by conservative Catholics for "promoting prostitution," ironic as the initial funding for the project came from the Maryknoll Fathers. In 1995 sex workers in the Sonagachi area of Calcutta organized the Durbar Mahila Samanwaya Committee, which claims to be the registered organization of more than 40,000 female, male, and transsexual sex workers of West Bengal[71] and with the Usha Co-operative runs its own STI clinics, a cooperative credit union, literacy classes, and a crèche. One report suggested 3,000 people attended the first national prostitution conference in India in 1997.[72] Even if this sort of organizing was in part inspired by western ideas, does that make it less significant? One might remember that the Indian independence movement was also influenced by western concepts of nation and democracy— and itself became a major inspiration for the American and South African civil rights movements. In the same way the Durbar Mahila Samanwaya Committee has taken the mobilization of sex workers to a scale beyond that reached in any western country.

During the 1990s an international network of sex-work projects (NSWP) has sought to link sex-worker groups in both rich and poor countries, often organizing around international HIV/AIDS conferences. By the end of the decade the network linked groups in forty countries, but was limited by huge difficulty in getting resources, and the dependence on a handful of dedicated volunteers.[73] Gaining acceptance for sex-worker groups has been a tough ongoing struggle, with only a few governments being willing to accord any recognition at all. In both Australia and New Zealand the national organizations have at times played a role in national AIDS advisory bodies, but this is rare, nor have better-established community AIDS organizations always been particularly supportive. Guenter Frankenberg's comment about Germany applies elsewhere: "The gay dominated AIDS-Hilfen have effectively colonized junkies, prostitutes and prisoners, speaking for them instead of enabling them to be their own advocates."[74] The recognition of representatives of both sex workers and lesbians in the 1998 Indonesian Women's Congress which followed the downfall of Suharto was therefore particularly significant,[75] as was the inclusion of lesbianism on the official agenda of the 1998 All National Women's Conference in India.

Most people who engage in sex for money have no sense of this comprising their central identity, and they may well be repelled by attempts to organize around an identity they would strongly reject. It is a fact that money will be involved in a great many sexual encounters in almost any cash economy, and that the great majority of such transactions will not involve people who identify themselves as professional sex workers, but see it rather as one among a number of strategies to survive.[76] This is true of young African girls who find "sugar daddies" (sometimes known as "spare tyres") to help with their school fees, as it is of American beach bums who accept hospitality and gifts in exchange for sexual favors. We should be skeptical of those studies which claim to tell us that 36% of sex workers are positive/negative/use condoms or whatever: this assumes a fixed population, which is a dangerous fiction. It seems useful to think of prostitution not as a fixed state or identity, but rather as a continuum ranging from organized prostitution, through brothels, escort agencies, and so forth, to unpremeditated transactions resulting from chance encounters.

This does not mean that organization around conditions of employment and protection from abuse may not be successful. Speaking of drug users, Chris Jones suggested the idea of a "pragmatic community . . . a community in action affected by various forces producing potentially pro-active responses to various situations."[77] We need to know more about organizations which may well include sex workers without making this a central definition, as in the example of the Ghana Widows' Association, which according to at least one account includes large numbers of women in Accra working in commercial sex.[78] In early 1998 a group known as the Henao Sisters was established in Port Moresby (Papua New Guinea) for women known as *raun-raun* girls, those who move in and out of prostitution. While the group grew out of a peer-education program established by a government-supported program for HIV-prevention education, the initiative for its development appears to have come from the women themselves ·who are faced with ongoing issues of survival, violence, and police harassment.

As both the examples of gay/lesbian and sex-worker identities show, socioeconomic change will produce new ways of understanding ourselves and our place in the world. The breakdown of the extended family household as both an economic and social unit was one of the most important consequences of industrialization in the western world. In turn the growth of affluence, and the shifting emphasis from production to consumption, has meant a steady shrinking in households as even the nuclear family is replaced by large numbers of unmarried couples, of single-parent families, of people living large parts of their lives alone or in shared households. With this has come a new range of identities, as people seek to make sense of their lives as divorced, single, unmarried, or sole parents. Both commercial pressures to target specific "demographics" and the personal need to define one's identity in psychological terms means the growth of new sorts of support and social groups for, say, divorcées, single fathers, people living in multiple relationships (for which the word "polyandry" has been revived).

Unlike identities based on sexuality such as "lesbian" or "transvestite," these are identities based on relationship status and can in fact cross over definitions of sexuality. In Harvey Fierstein's play *Torch Song Trilogy* there is an angry argument where Arnold tries to make his mother accept that the loss of his lover is equivalent to her loss of her husband. There are small signs that this emphasis on relationship identities is spreading beyond the rich world, such as a report of an attempt to found "the Divorced Women's Teahouse" in Beijing in 1995. The association foundered on Chinese government restrictions on the creation of nongovernmental organizations.[79]

Underlying all these developments is an increasing stress on ideas of individual identity and satisfaction, and the linking of these concepts to sexuality. One of the dominant themes in post-Freudian western thinking about sex has been to explain why sexuality is so central to our sense of self, and thus the basis of both psychological and political identity. These assumptions about sexuality are far from universal; as Heather Montgomery warned, speaking of children in the sex industry in Thailand: "Sexuality was never identified with personal fulfilment or individual pleasure . . . Prostitution was an incidental way of constructing their identities."[80] Similarly Lenore Manderson wrote, also of Thailand: "For women, commercial sex is the mechanism by which many women today fulfill their obligations as mothers and daughters. For them, the body and its sexual expression in work are a means of production rather than a mirror to the self."[81]

That last phrase is crucial, for it sums up the dominant script by which westerners have interpreted sexuality for the past century, whether they have sought genetic and biological explanations or, like the radical Freudian school derived from thinkers like Wilhelm Reich and Herbert Marcuse, have sought to develop concepts of repression and sublimation to explain political attitudes and behavior.[82] In some ways Frantz Fanon also belongs to this tradition, and the fact that he wrote from the position of a colonized Algerian has made him particularly attractive to postcolonial theorists, who tend to ignore his strong homophobia.[83] This attempt to link sexuality with the political is far less fashionable today, where sexuality is more commonly linked with contemporary capitalism, and we increasingly think of ourselves as consumers rather than citizens. Indeed it is the Right who seem to set the agenda for sexual politics, through attacks on abortion, contraception, and homosexuality, which they link clearly to dissatisfaction with the whole tenor of modern life, yet refusing, except for a small group of religious thinkers, to see the connection between contemporary capitalism and the changes in the sex/ gender order they so abhor.

Seven

The New Commercialization of Sex: From Forced Prostitution to Cybersex

The previous chapter discussed the reconceptualization of prostitution as sex work, and the attempt to create a political movement based on this shift. Here I am more concerned with the dynamics of the commercialization of sex itself, and how this reflects the larger sociopolitical order. Prostitution is only the most dramatic aspect of a sex industry which is increasingly interrelated with the global economy. In part this is associated with the huge increase in tourism since the development of the jumbo jet,[1] but often young women are recruited into sex work through migration, often under conditions which are virtual enslavement. This has now become so commonplace that it is the central theme of the best-selling German thriller *One Man, One Murder*.[2]

PROSTITURISMO

> *The national bourgeoisie will be greatly helped on its way towards decadence by the Western bourgeoisies, who come to it as tourists avid for the exotic, for big-game hunting and for casinos . . . The casinos of Havana and of Mexico, the beaches of Rio, the little Brazilian and Mexican girls, the half-breed thirteen year-olds, the ports of Acapulco and Copacabana—all these are the stigma of this deprivation of the national middle class . . . [which] will in practice set up its country as the brothel of Europe.*
> —*Frantz Fanon*, The Wretched of the Earth, *1961*

Since Fanon wrote those words, tourism has become the most significant and visible arena of global sexual inequality. As Jeremy Seabrook writes: "It is a savage irony that sex tourism should be one symptom of globalization, the 'integration' of the whole world into a single economy, when both the workers in the industry and the clients from abroad are themselves the product of disintegration—of local communities, the dissolution of rootedness and belonging, the breaking of old patterns of labour and traditional livelihoods; and the psychic disintegration of so many people caught up in great epic changes, of which they have little understanding and over which they have less control."[3] Tourism is, of course, a significant factor in globalization, both economic and cultural, and it has become on some measures the largest single employer in the world. In many places it is closely linked to commercial sex, in what Brazilians term "prostiturismo."[4]

The media is full of references to new centers of international prostitution, with cities like Tokyo, Dubai, and Istanbul often identified as centers of a new internationalization of both workers and customers. The net site Club Paradise offers "love trips" to once enemy territory in St. Petersburg, Kiev, and Minsk; Planet Love offers links to sites such as Cuban Affairs and From Russia with Wife.[5] I've already discussed the case of Bangkok, which is often portrayed as more exceptional than is probably the case. Despite the undoubted boom in sex tourism to places such as Bangkok, Pataya, and Phuket, most prostitution in Thailand depends upon local customers. It is conceivable that widespread cross-national prostitution will change both behaviors and emotions. One author has speculated that sexual tourism might lead to greater use of kissing and oral sex in some countries,[6] just as it is claimed that the availability of western pornography has created a demand for (heterosexual) anal sex in China. In many parts of the world it is claimed that the threat of AIDS has increased the demand for underage prostitutes.

Prostitution is hardly new, and it is difficult to distinguish between an actual increase in commercial sex and an increasing openness in acknowledging it. Indeed it is possible that there is far *less* commercial sex in many parts of the rich world now than a century ago, though this has probably been more than compensated for by increases in other parts of the world. Internationally prostitution appears to be increasing rapidly due to the spread of travel, migration, and liberal economic "development" across the globe. Never underestimate the impact of the 747 on rapid population movements; European tourists who once saw the Mediterranean as a distant luxury now holiday in the Seychelles and Phuket, while women and men from Nigeria and Brazil sell themselves on the streets of Rome and Dusseldorf, and many migrants find their jobs as entertainers, maids, and nannies carry with them the expectation of sexual services. In my visits to Europe over the past ten years I have noticed a marked growth in commercial sex in gay saunas, with young men from across the world using saunas as bases for illegal sex work, in the process changing the ground rules on which such saunas have previously rested, namely as sites for casual but noncommercial sex.

It is important to remember that tourism makes up only one part of a vast movement between and within countries as a result of global flows of people which involve the most and the least privileged. Such movements—involving "guest" workers, refugees, immigrants, soldiers, fishermen, and so forth—can have considerable impact on cultural and socioeconomic structures. Neoliberalist policies, by hastening economic "growth" and the destruction of traditional supports, also force more people into what is in effect indentured service (e.g., Filipina or Bangladeshi workers in the Gulf) and prostitution.[7] Thus the economic collapse in Indonesia in 1997/98 was reflected in reports of a growth of commercial sex in Jakarta, where there is some official attempt at regulation through compounds for prostitutes.[8] These compounds are made up of small rooms, big enough only for a bed and wardrobe, where women both sleep and see clients; they are still preferable—and safer—than working the sides of roads (as do *waria* prostitutes in Jakarta) or the old Dutch cemetery in Surabaya.[9]

The collapse of Communism in Soviet/Eastern Europe has opened up huge growth in sex work (as it has in injecting drug use): one estimate in mid-1998 was that half a million women had been brought from the former Soviet states into western Europe for prostitution in the past three years. The same story spoke of huge increase of syphilis in Russia, Ukraine, and Belarus, and drug use has similarly increased.[10] But these figures may be an underestimate: the Ukrainian government believes 400,000 Ukrainian women alone have moved west into various forms of prostitution since the collapse of the Soviet Union.[11] Within Russia itself there is a marked growth of the visibility of prostitution, and, as Lynne Attwood observed, "more than a hint of respect for these self-proclaimed 'independent businesswomen.'"[12] In the last couple of years observers claim that prostitution has reappeared in Cuba, partly to cater for tourists.[13] In the same way relaxation of China's restrictions on emigration have led to a flood of young Chinese women, known as *dalumei*, who move to Taiwan in search of a better life: "Popularized by sensational stories of sexual exploitation in newspapers, the *dalumei* is a woman who in most cases serves as a prostitute, willingly or otherwise, and who in some cases successfully disguises herself as a native and makes money as a singer, waitress, bar hostess or beautician."[14]

The growing commercialization of sex is often the unintended consequence of opening up an economy to the larger world. Critics of free-market economics might observe this is the logical consequence of increasing commodification—this overlaps with the feminist critique of prostitution as reducing all of human interaction to a commodity. In a satirical piece calling for "sustainable prostitution" Thai writer Anita Pleumarom wrote: "We should no longer worry about the commercialisation and commodification of all aspects of life . . . since unfettered capitalism and consumerism are part of the inevitable reality."[15] American attitudes to commercial sex are particularly schizophrenic; it is ironic that the country most committed to the rule of the market is also one of the more censorious about including sexual services. There are of course some notable exceptions, such as the acceptance of brothels in some parts of the country, as the musical and film *The Best Little Whorehouse in Texas* reminds us.

Despite the current emphasis on "sex tourism" it is worth remembering that the military has a long connection with various forms of prostitution, often forced, and that the ready availability of prostitutes has long been a major concern of military commanders as a way of both maintaining the morale of their troops and restricting possible homosexuality among their troops. As Cynthia Enloe asks: "Without sexualized rest and recreation, would the U.S. military command be able to send young men off on long, often tedious sea voyages and ground manoeuvres? Without myths of Asian or Latina women's compliant sexuality, would many American men be able to sustain their own identities, their visions of themselves as manly enough to act as soldiers?"[16] The provision of "rest and recreation" was one of the central features in creating the image of Bangkok discussed in the beginning of this book.

One aspect of the contemporary world is the apparent globalization of what would have once been localized conflicts, with the growing use of foreign troops, often as peacekeeping forces. One factor in the rapid growth of a sex trade in Cambodia during the 1990s was the presence of UNTAC soldiers in that country, and Prime Minister Hun Sen has said that AIDS will be the lasting legacy of the UN peacekeeping operation.[17] Even under the Taliban there are reports of underground prostitution in Afghanistan, echoing Rabih Alameddine's comments about Lebanon under civil war, when "[p]oor Shiite girls can make money in two ways, either by becoming prostitutes or by diapering themselves . . . A diapered woman is one who covers her whole body except for her hands and face."[18] (Alameddine claims that Iran paid Lebanese women to wear traditional head covers.)

While prostitution is almost always portrayed in terms of women it also involves a significant number of young men, although the dynamics of male prostitution tend to be somewhat different. As Patrick Larvie commented in respect to Brazil: "For many males the act of prostitution may actually be more akin to a ritualized form of sexual transgression than the kind of sex-for-money transaction which occurs commonly among female and transvestite sex workers."[19] It is not a new observation that many young men will prostitute themselves as a way of enjoying homosexual sex while retaining the illusion that they are not, themselves, "queer." Whereas women are stigmatized by being known as prostitutes, young men will often insist they are really hustlers to avoid being thought of as homosexual.[20]

Culturally, too, the images associated with male and female prostitution are rather different. While the female is seen as either a victim or as glamorous but amoral (and therefore, ultimately, as in *Traviata*, a tragic figure), the male hustler is often depicted as predatory or violent, as in the novels of Genet or the real-life morality tales of famous men (Sal Mineo, Pasolini, Versace) who have been slain by hustlers. Once again the redeemed (female) prostitute has become a media stereotype, as in the film *Pretty Woman* or the character of Megan in the television series *Melrose Place*. Against this there is a tendency to portray male prostitution in poorer countries as involving a certain level of reciprocal "fun," even when the underlying inequalities are recognized.[21]

Male prostitution is probably more widespread than is often recognized. One attempt by government officials in the early stages of the AIDS epidemic to estimate the numbers of male commercial sex workers concluded there were "none" in China or Zambia; of the governments who responded only France, Colombia, and the Czech Republic acknowledged men might make up 10% or more of "commercial workers."[22] This latter figure is likely to be widely duplicated in both rich and poor countries. There is less acknowledgment of men who provide paid services to women, although this is not uncommon in certain tourist destinations such as Bali, Sri Lanka, the Dominican Republic, and the Gambia, where sexual liaisons are often accompanied by expensive presents rather than direct payment. In some cases casual liaisons lead to continuing relationships, possibly to the emigration of the new boyfriend to his partner's country. It is usually assumed that such relationships must end disastrously, but financial advantage is not always a bad reason for embarking upon a relationship.

While there is now a considerable body of relevant research on sex work this is rarely incorporated into wider theories of global political economy. Indeed, despite its economic significance, prostitution remains largely unanalyzed as a business rather than a moral phenomenon, though in those countries in western Europe and Australasia which have decriminalized certain forms of commercial sex the sheer amounts of money involved are changing attitudes. Thus a front-page article in late 1998 in the Melbourne *Age*'s business section reported the growth of the sex industry as "more acceptable and respectable"—and stressed the flow of benefits to hotels, taxis, and condom manufacturers.[23] The article estimated Australia to have 23,000 people employed in the sex industry, with almost a billion-dollar turnover in the 800 legal and 350 illegal brothels, escort agencies, and massage parlors. Britons are estimated to spend roughly three times as much, which is roughly the same on a per capita basis—if only one-eighth of their expenditure on illegal drugs.[24]

In many poor countries the sex industry is proportionately more important. The largest brothel in Bangladesh, in the port city of Narayanganj outside Dhaka, is said to have 1,600 workers who live there with their families.[25] In 1998 the International Labour Organisation published a study of prostitution in four Southeast Asian countries, estimating that in Indonesia, Malaysia, the Philippines, and Thailand:

> the number of workers earning a living directly or indirectly from prostitution would be several millions . . . The sex sector in the four countries is estimated to account for anywhere from 2 to 14 per cent of Gross Domestic Product, and the revenues it generates are crucial to the livelihoods and earnings potential of millions of workers beyond the prostitutes themselves. Government authorities also collect substantial revenues in areas where prostitution thrives, illegally from bribes and corruption, but legally from licensing fees and taxes on the many hotels, bars, restaurants and game rooms that flourish in its wake.[26]

This report was very significant in that it suggested a move within the UN system toward recognizing sex work as an industry to be regulated, rather than a scourge to be eliminated. (Even so, the report carefully avoids any recommendations on the legal status of prostitution.) Not surprisingly, the report created acrimonious debate with some governments, particularly from Catholic Latin America, expressing considerable hostility to this shift.

In both rich and poor countries the rapidity of economic change is increasing the sex trade. From the copious literature available take this example from Nepal: "To the dismay of activists and citizens' groups, brothels have proliferated in the capital and other urban areas, keeping pace with the sudden demand of [*sic*] sex-workers in Nepal. Says NGO activist Rana: 'Sex has begun to play a major role in Nepal's tourism earnings, which is unfortunate.' Another facet of the sex trade is trafficking in women and girls, a huge business in Nepal . . . According to a recent estimate by UNICEF, more than 300,000 Nepali women are reported to have been sold to Indian brothels."[27] On a smaller scale there is now a similar trade in young women from Mozambique into the brothels of Cape Town and Johannesburg. The collapse of downtown Johannesburg has seen sex work along with drugs become a major industry in the inner-city area of Hillbrow, once a chic bohemian quarter of the city.[28]

Even in rich countries, sex work is often the most available means of survival for those who are marginalized because of deindustrialization, migration, family breakdowns, the collapse of welfare, and so forth, although there are more middle-class sex workers, often working as "masseurs" and "escorts" out of private apartments in the ritzy areas of large cities, than is sometimes acknowledged. (There have been a number of high-class call girls in movies, and the murder of the fashion designer Versace by Andrew Cunanan led to a flurry of media stories about "gay gigolos.")[29] Indeed the class divide is very obvious in sex work, with a growing gap between the legitimate and luxurious brothels now operating in many western cities and the realities of street work in most cities, rich or poor. Because of globalization the class divide often overlaps with a racial one, with migrant workers from poor countries heavily overrepresented among the most marginalized parts of the industry. One of the arguments often made against sex-work organizations is that they hugely overestimate the element of choice available to most of those who work in prostitution.

Prostitution is central to any analysis of the sexual order—as is more generally the relationship of money and sex. There is a need for some exploration of the erotic charge of paying and being paid, suggested in the common term "to spend" for male orgasm. Edmund White has written that "[j]ohns [customers] resent having to pay. Even if the idea of paying (and controlling) someone excites them in advance, after they come they feel insulted."[30] Some "johns" like to believe that sex work involves mutual exploitation and reciprocity, claiming that the workers either "really" enjoy the sex, or alternatively complaining that they are always ready to "rip off" the client—or indeed both at once. In general it is one of the deepest illusions of the client that he is special, and one which any successful worker will encourage. Yes, clients and workers may fall in love, but less often than the myths would suggest.

I do not wish to avoid the moral issues raised by prostitution: while some feminist analyses seem to conflate all forms of sex for money in ways which deny any agency on the part of the worker, it also seems likely that most of those who "choose" prostitution do so under conditions of considerable constraint. At the same time we should avoid stereotypes which see prostitution as the refuge of the most marginalized and self-hating: "To sell oneself implies one has a value (sexual in nature) and often a considerable value . . . Through the view of morality the young prostitute finds himself valued sexually and devalued socially."[31] This is not to deny the very real abuses and exploitation which surround the sex industry; it is to recognize that moral indignation is inadequate when people are forced into selling their bodies to survive and uncalled for when people enjoy a real choice. In affluent societies there are not inconsiderable numbers of porn actors and prostitutes who have chosen the business as a rational way of doing well in the world; in most parts of the world those who sell their bodies do so for survival, and often under appalling conditions. As Shivananda Khan wrote: "For the vast majority of people, sex work or whatever name you give it, is a survival strategy . . . The term sex work appears to imply some form of equality in economic and negotiating power, a labor contract between the customer and the provider. But can this be true in a city like Calcutta, Mumbai or Dhaka, or in any city in a developing country where poverty, hunger, homelessness and family deprivation are rife, and where significant numbers of such 'workers' below the age of 14 are primary wage-earners for their family?"[32]

Prostitution is regulated very differently across the globe, with the only common element seeming to be hypocrisy, except perhaps in the case of Sweden, which has now legislated to make the *purchase* of sexual services illegal, a welcome change from the usual tendency to blame the worker and ignore the customer. Many jurisdictions do of course criminalize procurement and pimping, the most famous example being the American Mann Act (1910), which prohibits the "knowing transportation or enticement or coercion to go from one place to another of a female for the purpose of prostitution in interstate or foreign commerce." Since the first international conference on the prevention of trafficking in women in Paris in 1885 there have been international moves to restrict the trading of women for sexual purposes, and both the League of Nations and the United Nations addressed the issue. Arguments around trafficking (and not least the meaning of the word) continue today.[33] Thailand retains the legal fiction that prostitution is illegal but generally tolerates it;[34] on the other hand in many countries where there are limited legal restrictions sex workers are consistently harassed. In Turkey, for example, the state licenses brothels, and places considerable restrictions on women registered to work in them. Brothel owners are not required to pay social security contributions for their employees, as are other employers, and the children of registered sex workers are debarred from certain ranks in the military or police.[35] Many women now work outside the legal system, but face considerable police harassment.

The one generalization that is probably true is that prohibition—as in the case of alcohol and drugs—does not work. More than that, prohibition increases the risks to the health and security of workers, and benefits organized crime. When the mayor of Manila closed down the city's brothels a few years ago he succeeded only in pushing the trade into adjoining cities— or farther underground. The criminalization of prostitution—and the denial of basic civil rights to sex workers—is a significant factor in the perpetuation of a whole set of practices which amount to sexual slavery. In view of some of the extreme statements from feminist antiprostitution campaigners it is important to note that sex-work organizations are active in campaigning against these abuses, which include forcible imprisonment, rape, beatings, and denial of earnings.

I am sympathetic to the views of Hoigard and Finstad who argue: "One should, in every way possible, try to make it as easy as possible for the women while they are in prostitution. One should simultaneously work to provide them with better alternatives to prostitution."[36] I remain deeply skeptical that the latter is realistic without changes in the socioeconomic structures of almost all societies which go beyond even my utopian hopes for a radical politics. In one of the best overviews of this debate Ryan Bishop and Lillian Robinson suggest that only major global social and economic restructuring could remove the exploitation implicit in most sex work.[37] Unfortunately—as is true of much feminist theorizing—they are almost totally ignorant of gay male theory, though they suggest there may be some significant differences between heterosexual and homosexual prostitution without saying what these may be.

Are there different moral traditions which view prostitution differently across societies? Certainly there appear to be different attitudes, ranging from religious practices where young women enter into something equivalent to prostitution under the control of priests, to societies which brand any woman who has sex outside marriage as a whore. But we need to be skeptical of claims such as this from one development report: "Prostitution is accepted as a traditional way of life among women of many of Rajasthan's tribal communities . . . with the income derived from sex work supporting entire communities."[38] (The very reference to "income" suggests we might read the word "traditional" with some skepticism.) Sex work can be both oppressive and liberating. But it is hard to argue that for most of those involved the latter outweighs the former.

The contradictions of the globalized sexual order are caught in the phenomenon of "mail-order brides," so common a term that a Singapore writer used the phrase for a play exploring the phenomenon.[39] There is a portrayal of one such woman in *Priscilla, Queen of the Desert*, which many Australians criticized as unnecessarily racist. Unfortunately this is not an isolated phenomenon; by 1998 there were almost 50,000 Filipina women in Australia, many of whom had moved there to marry Australians. Many such marriages pair older and uneducated white Australians with young women desperate to emigrate, and research suggests that violence and in extreme cases murder can result from these marriages.[40] There are, of course, many other examples of successful and happy marriages, but too many of them are the product of structural inequalities which set up unfortunate expectations from the beginning. I recall meeting a young man outside a gay bar in Manila— he was too poor to afford the drink which would allow him to go inside— who told me his sister had married an Australian and he wanted to follow her by finding a rich man who would take him away from the Philippines. His counterparts are found in the many ads from young men in developing countries looking for friendship that one finds in western gay newspapers, a surprising number from Ghana. (Why Ghana I am not sure but I have no-

ticed the phenomenon in both Australian and Swiss papers.) In the economic
collapse of Russia in the late 1990s many women signed up with marriage
agencies, hoping to find a way of escape to the west.[41]

THE NEW RESPECTABILITY OF PORNOGRAPHY

> *[He] controlled a maze of one hundred and fifty corporations which numbered among their ac-*
> *tivities and holdings a chain of bookstores, strip joints and peep movies coast to coast; mas-*
> *sage parlors and nude-encounter studios in southwest U.S. and western Canada; outlets for*
> *leather goods and mechanical devices west of the Mississippi; sex boutiques, topless bars, top-*
> *less billiard parlors across the Sunbelt; a New Orleans car rental firm with topless chauffeurs.*
> —Don DeLillo, Running Dog, *1978*

Over the past two decades there has been an explosion in the open discussion
and depiction of sex, so that what was once pornographic is now commonplace. This is most obvious in the case of the United States, where the existence of the First Amendment proscribing any restrictions on "freedom of
expression" means the courts have struggled to keep up with changes in publishing, film, and video (as we are reminded in the film *The People versus Larry
Flynt*), but changes in open depiction of sexuality have affected most of the
world. From the perspective of the 1990s, with its adult videos in hotels and
near naked advertisements, the battles of the 1960s over *Lady Chatterley's Lover*
and Henry Miller seem extraordinarily old-fashioned; in today's far more
visual culture the Disney studios produce films which would have been in-
conceivable in the days when courts and governments struggled to preserve
decency. As late as 1969 I was involved in a court case in Australia over
importing the unexpurgated version of Gore Vidal's *Myra Breckenridge;*[42] today
Australian governments are seen as unnecessarily conservative when they
seek to enforce restrictions on "adult movies."

This is not the place for a long discussion of the debate on pornography
and its various definitions—as with prostitution I am more concerned here
with the economics than the morality of the industry.[43] It is clear that one
person's pornography is another's erotica—I personally find the average
Hollywood movie depiction of violence far more offensive than much restricted "pornography," while what is commonplace in most western countries is totally banned (that is, forced underground) in other parts of the
world. The famous comment of one U.S. Supreme Court Justice that he

knew pornography when he saw it, hardly covers the emergence of explicit sex from under the counter to smart bookshops, and publishers such as X-listed (owned by Little, Brown) and Black Lace (owned by Virgin).[44] There are increasing moves to both mainstream and glamorize commercial sex. Laurence O'Toole describes what he calls "the future of adult retail," the Fairvilla Megastore in Cape Canaveral, Florida.

> A 14,000 square-foot, two storey, one-stop shopping experience, tapping into the still underexploited single women and couples market for sex in America. Here people come and buy videos, sex toys, magazines, T-shirts, lingerie, greeting cards—the whole range. Owned and operated by husband-and-wife team Bill and Shari Murphy, Fairville provides a new kind of up-scale porn-buying experience, more like shopping at Gap or Virgin than the traditional adult bookshop, with hardwood floors, a forty foot domed ceiling with a galleried mezzanine floor and an adjoining open-air palm court with waterfalls and a coffee shop.[45]

It is interesting to compare his hype with the reaction of the journalist Andrew Masterson to Sexpo, a sex-trade industry fair in Melbourne: "For all of its purported democratisation and openness, much of the sex industry present at Sexpo still evinces the values of a 19th-century circus freak show. It's not about sexuality, much less sensuality, but about the profitable objectification of women and the exploitation of men. It offers, not freedom, but commercial exchange, and in the ribbed, knobbed, rotating, vibrating, expanding, brutally penetrative apparatus of sex 'play,' a sadism all the more deceitful because of its guise of pleasure-giving."[46]

With little attention from economists or the business press, pornography has become big business. One 1997 estimate for the United States claimed, "At $4.2 billion it's a business twice as large as major league baseball, three times as large as Disney's theme park division, eight times as large as Broadway."[47] It is estimated that 8,000 to 9,000 porno films are made each year in the States.[48] Most of the U.S. pornography industry is centered in Los Angeles's San Fernando Valley north of Hollywood, so much so that one area is known locally as Silicone Valley. There is less material available on the development of the porn industry outside the United States. It is clearly significant in Europe: in respectable hotels, in the Calvinist city of Geneva, I have watched twenty-four-hour television channels advertising both pornography and escort services featuring anatomically improbable young women with call-back numbers across Europe and the Middle East.

There is clearly a huge market for pornography in east Asia and a large Japanese industry, which one estimate claims generates perhaps $10 billion a year[49]—which if accurate is more than twice the U.S. figure.

Certainly pornography is very widely available in Japan, which Ian Buruma sought to explain by reference to the particular repressions of Japanese society, though with uncharacteristically sufficient rigor in his analysis to be fully convincing.[50] Japan also appears to place fewer restrictions on child pornography (more accurately teenage pornography) than almost anywhere else—one estimate claimed that Japan produces four-fifths of all child pornography.[51] Active porn industries emerged in Hungary and Slovakia after the fall of the Wall—according to one German film producer eastern European actors "cost less and do more."[52] And, as if to illustrate the sometimes bizarre circuits of globalization, a Russian television channel, TB-6, is allegedly a significant source for "adult" movies in Bangladesh.[53]

A study by Hebditch and Anning in 1988 spoke of the international nature of the porn business and claimed there were a dozen or so "porn barons" who dominated the industry, controlling more than 50% of the trade.[54] While they appear to equate "international" with transatlantic (no mention in their book of the Japanese industry), they do offer some insight into the increasingly legitimate business of pornography, and the existence of firms which produce multiple magazines and videos. Among their "barons" is the German Beate Uhse, who when Hebditch and Anning wrote ran a large business involving sex shops across Germany, with 550 staff and an annual turnover of DM90 million: "Set in spacious grounds"—clearly writers about the porn business are keen observers of architecture—"the Uhse building is more like a combination of a modern theatre and an art gallery than an office."[55] There are now Beate Uhse shops across Germany, including a very large one at Frankfurt Airport, and in 1999 the company was floated, with 8 million shares being offered on Frankfurt's secondary stock exchange.

The moves to mainstream pornography can be traced back to Hugh Hefner's launch of *Playboy* magazine in 1953 with its combination of softcore images of naked women and its appeal to upwardly mobile male consumerism, a sort of under-the-counter version of the *New Yorker*.[56] As Bernard Arcand has remarked: "*Playboy* is without question a product of American society . . . it is enough to draw attention to the typically modern character of Hugh Hefner."[57] *Playboy* was followed by a slew of imitations, including

Penthouse and *Hustler,* and an attempt to create similar magazines for women (whose main readership is probably homosexual men). By the following decade standards of censorship were beginning to be relaxed across the western world, making acceptable words and images which had previously been banned. Almost too symbolically the deputy chief film censor in Australia resigned in 1994 to become the country's first X-rated moviemaker.[58] Nonetheless, *Playboy* remained in business at the turn of the century, though with declining readership.[59] Perhaps its publishers should take heart from reports that the Dutch government provided copies of the magazine to its peacekeepers in the former Yugoslavia.[60]

Among its other effects pornography helps spread certain sexual assumptions—note the particular narrowness of U.S. gay porn which fetishizes muscular and tanned bodies to the exclusion of any other type. To look back at the gay porn films of the 1970s is to recognize how gyms have literally reshaped the male body in the past two decades. Note too the nostalgia for the 1970s as the "golden age" of porn—as depicted in films like *Boogie Nights* and *The People versus Larry Flynt*[61]—a period which probably began with the film *Deep Throat* (1972), the first porn movie to reach a mass audience. (It is claimed that it grossed $100 million worldwide, and made its main actors, Linda Lovelace and Harry Reems, the first widely recognized porn stars.)[62] Films became more sophisticated with plot lines and recognized stars, and there developed both an academic interest in and a bitter feminist debate about pornography, which caused deep rifts in the women's movement, particularly in the United States.

Increasingly the line between pornography and mainstream entertainment has collapsed. "Over the past decade," Barbara Creed has written, "the cinema's life-long flirtation with sexuality and eroticism reached a high point when Sharon Stone uncrossed her legs in *Basic Instinct,* revealing a brief glimpse of skin and pubic hair. With the first above-ground beaver shot the dividing line between mainstream and pornographic cinema collapsed."[63] In the late 1980s a number of European television channels started broadcasting soft-core pornography, leading to attempts by British authorities to restrict them in the name of "good taste and decency."[64] But increasingly pornography was establishing itself as a semilegitimate (and significant) industry, with its main outlets through cable television and suburban video stores (more than a quarter of the American home video industry's revenue was estimated to come from pornography).[65] However, these outlets in turn were under threat from the possibilities of using the Internet to deliver pornography, and there is currently a continuing race between the technology, which is increasing the speed and accuracy with which one can download images, and those who would control the content of the net.[66]

New technologies, especially video, have transformed pornography by reducing the cost of production and making movies available for home use. Most video stores feature an "adult section," and increasingly hotels and motels offer pornography as part of "in-room entertainment" (with sometimes elaborate precautions against use by minors). In the same way the development of chatrooms and porn sites on the Internet means that sexual desires can be globalized despite attempts to control them by governments and families. In 1998 joint police action in a number of countries closed down an Internet group known as wOnderland which facilitated the exchange of sexual images of children, claimed to have members in over forty countries, and was protected by codes which allegedly came from the former Soviet KGB,[67] and the FBI has been increasing its hunt for "travellers, people who troll the net for impressionable children, trying to persuade them to meet for sex in the real world."[68] In this light the attempts of Canadian customs to prevent the import of pornography from the States or the censorship of "western decadence" by paternalistic governments seems oddly old-fashioned. The Singapore government, for example, banned the films *The First Wives Club* and *Eyes Wide Shut*, allegedly because of lesbian references. But the Singapore authorities have also been leaders in trying to limit access of children to "undesirable" sites on the web. "Your child could be a victim on the net," proclaimed a full-page advertisement for the major Singapore Internet service provider: "The World Wide Web has been a safety haven for social deviants of the world—flesh-traders, hate-mongers, advocators [*sic*] of dissent have all gathered there to give volume to their voices."[69]

Not only pornography seems to be ubiquitous, but there has been a marked increase in the spread of live sex shows to places like downtown Melbourne and Toronto.[70] Phone sex is now an international business which the *Economist* claims "has been a boon of midget countries such as Moldova, Guyana and the Netherlands Antilles. Their short dialling codes mean that the punter may think he is dialling a domestic long-distance number rather than making an expensive international call. In 1993 Guyana's revenue from telecommunications traffic came to a startling 40% of national GNP."[71] The hero of the novel *Tokyo Vanilla* first explores his homosexuality through the phone: "More and more of the advertisements . . . were being devoted to the new telephone services: sex tapes, message banks, dial Q2's, and telephone clubs."[72]

Note as ever the ambiguities of globalization: the west is simultaneously the source of moral strictures and of the commodification which undoes them. Many of the "traditional" taboos invoked as needing defending against globalization are in fact the product of earlier imported ideologies, whether they be Christianity in the Pacific and Africa or Communism in China and Cuba. The attempts by governments such as the Chinese to foster economic growth without the corresponding "freedoms" of the west are unlikely to prevent a growth in sexual consumerism, whether because of the sorts of economic inequality fostered by neoliberal economics, the impact of new styles and tastes brought about through affluence, the influx of tourists, or the greater mobility and access to western ideas through travel and electronic communications.

$\mathscr{E}$IGHT

Sexual Politics and International Relations

Tell me why as a woman
I have all this burden
When God, the Constitution and the
United Nations all tell me
You and I are equal in all respects?

                                —Agnes Dewenis

Following the end of the Cold War there has been a marked increase in concern about human rights, and, as part of this, pressure to see questions of gender and sexuality as central to the study and practice of international relations.[1] Significant networks of transnational social movements have developed, often centering on gender, reproductive rights, and the extension of human rights to include sexuality, whether these be through gay/lesbian networks or antiprostitution movements. As Macintyre suggests in discussing Dewenis's and other poems by Pacific women,[2] the appeal to universal and humanist notions of rights is a meaningful strategy for many in poor countries, even as academics in the rich world devote considerable energy to deconstructing them.

We forget sometimes how recent are these developments; the framers of the 1948 Universal Declaration of Human Rights largely ignored issues of gender, let alone sexuality. The declaration does mention "sex" as one of the criteria which should not be used to deprive one of human rights, and has an explicit reference to the right to marry. It states further that "both partners have equal rights in the marriage and their free and full agreement is needed for the marriage to take place" (Article 16). For many women enforcement of this article would be an important gain.

While there were limited achievements in earlier years—the Hague

Convention of 1907, following the second international peace conference, prohibited rape as an act of war—it is only since the 1980s that violence against women has been widely recognized as a human rights issue. Amnesty International issued its first report on rape as a case of state-sanctioned deprivation of human rights in 1992. The issue has gained considerable attention since, with concurrent debates around restitution for Japan's use of "comfort women" during World War II, and concern over widespread rape within former Yugoslavia.[3] The issue of "comfort women," most of whom were Korean, was a crucial issue in mobilizing the women's movement in Korea and in the development of networking among east Asian feminists.[4] Yet as Enloe points out there are two problems facing feminists who raise the issue of violence against women: many governments are hostile to intervention in what can be defined as matters related to "family," and recognition of the issue can become "a self-serving justification for escalating the militarization of masculinity and for imposing more restrictions on women in the name of their safety."[5] She might have added the resistance within the discipline of international relations, which remains largely male-dominated and resistant to gender analysis.

The attempt to develop such an analysis demonstrates clearly the ambiguities of globalization. Certainly the economic, social, and political dislocations which result from rapid change have probably increased both the vulnerability of women and the resort to state-sanctioned violence as, for example, in the Sudan and Afghanistan under fundamentalist Islamic governments. However, expanding concern for human rights and the increasing use of international forums to pressure governments means a new attention to these abuses. (The language of human rights is itself one of the best examples of epistemological globalization available.) Thus in late 1998 the United Nations Development Fund for Women (UNIFEM) organized a "virtual working group" leading to a global video conference to discuss issues related to violence against women. A cynic might note that violence, unlike conferences, is not virtual.

Most important, however, is the gradual but consistent erosion of the argument that national sovereignty is supreme and that nation-states cannot be called to account for breaches of human rights. This is a difficult principle to achieve; not only do countries like China and Yugoslavia vigorously oppose any interference in domestic matters, but the United States is both a strong supporter of human rights principles and a strong opponent of attempts to create transnational institutions to enforce them. Despite such opposition the combination of international institutions and pressure from transnational social movements is gradually developing mechanisms for universality. I use "universality" as did the former secretary general of the United Nations, Boutros Boutros-Ghali, when he said: "We must remember that forces of repression often cloak their wrongdoing in claims of exceptionalism. But the people themselves time and again make it clear that they seek and need universality. Human dignity within one's culture requires fundamental standards of universality across the lines of culture, faith and state."[6] There are increasing examples of this appeal to universal values, as in the attempt to prosecute military and political figures from Serbia and Rwanda for their role in "crimes against humanity," and the moves to extradite former Chilean president General Pinochet to stand trial in Spain for the same reasons. There is no persuasive culturally relativist defense of torture or murder.

The recognition that state sovereignty should not be used as an excuse to hide human rights abuses is matched by a growing recognition that not only states abuse human rights. Thus the Declaration on the Elimination of Violence against Women, adopted by the UN General Assembly in 1993, included violence in the family and the community as a violation of human rights.[7] Given the realities of oppression and violence based upon "private" arrangements of gender and sexuality, this is an enormously important development. (It is probable that domestic violence is the most common of all crimes against the person.)[8] The assertion that human rights are involved in what many men have defined as a purely private matter can begin to create movements against the abuse of women and children which is routine in many societies. Thus one Japanese feminist attributed considerable importance to the 1995 Beijing conference in forcing Japanese men to consider the issue of domestic violence.[9]

The vast apparatus of international institutions which now attempt to regulate and coordinate almost all aspects of international transactions dates back to the nineteenth century, when organizations such as the Universal Postal Union (1874) and the International Red Cross (1863) laid the beginnings for the creation of the League of Nations after World War I and the United Nations after World War II, as well as the proliferation of international nongovernmental organizations.[10] Increasingly the once firm line between governments and nongovernmental actors is breaking down, as big international conferences open up to the participation of nongovernmental organizations and voices. So far the record is probably the 1995 Fourth World Conference on Women in Beijing, where 3,000 NGOs were accredited—and up to 40,000 people attended the accompanying NGO forum.[11] Pressure from the conference put issues of sexual violence, the right to women's control over reproduction, and lesbianism on the international agenda in ways which would have stunned most of those who drew up the Universal Declaration of Human Rights fifty years earlier. In doing this the women involved were building on the role of NGOs and activists already established at earlier UN conferences, such as that on environment (Rio de Janeiro 1992), human rights (Vienna 1993), and population (Cairo 1994). These developments form part of the larger move to develop a meaningful language of global human rights, which activists are pushing to incorporate via institutions such as the United Nations Commission on Human Rights, the European Court, and other supranational institutions.[12] The statute negotiated in Rome in 1998 to establish an international criminal court, now awaiting sufficient states to ratify it to bring it into existence, defines gender-related crimes as "rape, sexual slavery, enforced prostitution, forced pregnancy, enforced sterilization or any other form of sexual violence of a comparable gravity." It is not yet clear whether the court, should it come into existence, will define "gender" to include persecution on the basis of homosexuality or transvestism.

One of the major globalizing forces of the past two decades has been the move toward gender equality, and the gradual involvement of increasing numbers of international agencies in programs aimed at eradicating the systemic and structural disadvantages experienced by most women. While progress is slow and uneven, the recognition of the empowerment of women as a goal is itself a significant development, and one that grows out of the globalization of certain values and institutions but also, and more importantly, out of the lived experience and struggle of millions of women in shanty towns and villages across the globe. While western ideas and movements have certainly been important influences, their impact depends upon people transforming their messages to fit local conditions and needs, and often western ideas provide a new way of articulating already existing demands and allowing them to find an international audience. The work of groups like DAWN (Development Alternatives with Women for a New Era), which is a network of "women scholars and activists from the economic South," is an example of the new possibilities for global feminist advocacy which is possible in the current world.[13]

Activism itself has become globalized, as is evident in the activities of feminist, peace, environmental, and human rights movements across the globe. Note that in arguing this, I am not denying the extent to which autonomous feminist and environmental movements have emerged out of particular situations and contexts in a variety of states, but rather noting that they will inevitably make links and be influenced by the global environment.[14] Writing of AIDS in Puerto Rico, Grosfoguel, Negron-Muntaner, and Geroas commented:

> The AIDS crisis underlines both Puerto Rico's colonial situation in relation to the United States and the possibility of transferring resources from the United States to Puerto Rico to combat the epidemic. Thus the "air bridge" functioned in multiple ways: migration of HIV-positive Puerto Ricans to the United States in search of better medical treatment and support networks, formation of activist communities linking U.S. and island-based AIDS activists, sharing of resources and information and return migration of People with AIDS from the United States to Puerto Rico.[15]

ACT UP, which began in New York in 1987 as an activist and participatory group largely concerned with access to treatments, is a superb case of the globalization of activism, as the name and methods of direct confrontation were adopted in half a dozen other countries. Often the American inspiration was quite direct: in Montreal and Sydney the founders of ACT UP included a number of expatriate Americans. Because of its direct style and media savvy ACT UP has been able to attract considerable attention, and at recent international AIDS conferences ACT UP groups from France and the United States sought to make global access to treatments a central demand, without much input from those whom this approach was allegedly intended to help.

While ACT UP attracted considerable media coverage at the turn of the decade, there is a longer and more substantial history of international organizing around gay/lesbian and HIV/AIDS issues. As already suggested organizations like the ILGA and the International Gay and Lesbian Human Rights Commission (IGLHRC) promote a universal language of identity politics through their admirable work in promoting support for basic human rights for "gays and lesbians." UNAIDS has quite consciously assisted in the organization of gay groups as part of the strategy of preventing the spread of HIV, setting up MSM/HIV pilot projects in areas of the former Soviet Union, while the Dutch government now explicitly funds gay organizing within its overseas development programs. The first gay-pride event in Belarus, in late 1999, was supported by UNDP.

It was not surprising that when the "leaders of the Americas" met in Santiago in 1998, fifty Latin American lesbian and gay groups demanded that their equal rights be recognized, nor that they used the language of the Universal Declaration of Human Rights to support their claim. In 1994 two gay activists from the Australian state of Tasmania were able to appeal to the United Nations Human Rights Commission to help in overturning that state's antisodomy laws, the last remaining such laws in the country. (This appeal was possible only because the Australian government had legislated to give its citizens the right to take this avenue—a right not available to American citizens.) After a favorable response the Labor federal government introduced the 1994 Human Rights (Sexual Conduct Act), which was intended to overrule Tasmania's remaining sodomy laws and certainly played a role in forcing change through the very conservative Tasmanian Upper House. Under considerable pressure Tasmania finally decriminalized homosexuality in 1997.[16] More recently a Colombian lawyer has sought to use the same route to protest the Colombian government's persecution of homosexuals.

Changes are uneven, but nonetheless significant. In the last few years Amnesty International has accepted that imprisonment for homosexual behavior qualifies as a breach of human rights, and a number of governments have lent their support to protests over such cases. Nor is the shift confined to western countries; one of the most significant changes came in Korea, often described as a deeply conservative country, where President Kim Daejung stated in 1997: "I do not agree to same sex love, but I think we should not unconditionally perceive it as heathenism . . . We need a vision through which we can approach activities of lesbians and gays as a part of security of human rights."[17]

In similar ways the dominance of western discourses around HIV/ AIDS meant the introduction of human rights as a major issue, often linked to the so-called new public health based on ideas of empowerment and community control. In general most observers have seen this as a positive step, although it can be criticized as privileging a certain sort of autonomous liberal individualism which may not apply to many societies. The American anthropologist Nancy Scheper-Hughes has criticized the dominance of this particular paradigm as "founded on a phallocentric sexual universe that ignores the especially vulnerable position of women, children, transvestites and other sexual 'passives' vis-à-vis the dominant, aggressive and active conquistador male sexuality,"[18] and has seen some virtue in the more repressive (or traditional public health) responses essayed by Cuba. While I think she is wrong—and there are examples in Africa of HIV leading to a major questioning of existing practices which maintain the structural inequality of women[19]—it is certainly necessary to interrogate the applicability of American concepts of individual rights in societies with very different social, economic, and cultural resources.[20]

To recognize this is not, emphatically, to subscribe to the sorts of arguments for "traditional Africanness" or "Asian values," which are often invoked by government and religious leaders to argue against the universality of human rights, especially when they affect hegemonic attitudes toward homosexuality, sex work, or male dominance. The concept of "Asian values," in particular, is often used by a whole range of apologists for government actions which infringe human rights in the name of nation building and economic growth, but are more often ideological statements intended to justify a particular sort of rapid economic growth which will not disturb entrenched privilege. Interestingly the need to limit rights to promote economic growth is still used in countries like Singapore which are now richer than most western liberal democracies. In this sense the rhetoric of some Asian governments is reminiscent of Soviet claims for a socialist form of industrialization, and their dismissal of those concerned about the human costs as no more than expressions of their class privilege. Stalinist fellow travelers have been replaced by western economic rationalists—one thinks of the Chicago School in Pinochet's Chile or western investors in China—who today defend assaults on human rights in the interests of rapid economic growth.

The difficulty in challenging claims for "Asian values" is compounded by the colonial legacy, which makes western critics all too aware of the extent to which conservative politicians—Mahathir is a good example–appeal to nationalist pride to disguise their own self-interest.[21] While Mahathir may seem a long way from the (often expatriate Asian) inventors of postcolonial theory, there is a sense in which he and his supporters call on a popular if not always well-articulated resentment of the colonial legacy. Indeed one might suggest that postcolonial theory can become another source to legitimize the assault on "decadent westernization," a phrase used by governments in both Asia and Africa.

As soon as we accept the notion of defending "traditional values" we enter upon slippery ground. Should we therefore defend foot binding, or the ritual deflowering of prepubescent girls, both of which certainly have claims to being part of "traditional" east Asian culture? The crudest examples come from regimes such as Burma's military dictatorship, whose propaganda proclaims: "We are not Caucasians, we are Asians, and we wish to preserve our own national identity. So the Democracy we want is the kind that is most suitable for us and not an imitation of the western model. As a sovereign nation no one should try to force us into a mould that is completely out of character with our people. The same holds true for human and civil rights . . . Freedom for us does not mean licence, and rights bring along in its wake responsibilities and duties."[22]

There are more sophisticated attempts to defend particular Asian cultural values without using them as an alibi to deny basic rights. Tu Wei-ming has argued convincingly that there is a more humanist strand in Confucianism than the official spokesmen of Beijing allow.[23] Equally, a number of Islamic scholars have sought to demonstrate a basic commitment to human rights within that tradition. In what might already have been read as a criticism of the man who would persecute him, Anwar Ibrahim explicitly argued that Asian values are consistent with certain basic universal assumptions about individual dignity: "It is altogether shameful, if ingenious, to cite Asian values as an excuse for autocratic practices and denial of basic rights and civil liberties."[24]

There is considerable strength to the argument that western understandings of human rights place too much emphasis on individual legal and political rights to the exclusion of social, economic, and cultural rights. (Of course one way to protect social and economic rights is through effective and independent trade unions, which are anathema to many of the proponents of an "Asian" concept of human rights.) This argument has recently been worked through in an attempt to reconcile western liberal with certain "Asian" values by joint Australian and Asian "teams" of experts, and has produced some interesting results. It has also produced some very silly arguments, as in the following: "Punishments such as mutilation and stoning under the Islamic penal code, for instance, horrify many Westerners, who put the right to freedom from pain before freedom of religion."[25] In this instance the issue is surely the right to inflict religion upon others, which is a quite different concept from that suggested in the sentence.

To argue that human rights are universal does not lead to some inflexible position which sees the homogenization of cultural and political forms as necessary or inevitable. Recognition of human rights should lead precisely to a recognition of diversity, in which individuals and groups are able to choose from a range of cultural values and forms which will reflect different material and historical circumstances. They should, however, never act as a legitimation of brute force over others. "Culture," wrote Ken Booth, "can be torture, and 'authenticity' the means of maintaining oppressive power structures."[26]

AND INTERNATIONAL RELATIONS

Until very recently the literature of international relations was, as Saskia Sassen characterized it, "a narrative of eviction," which takes "the State as its exclusive subject and has excluded other actors and subjects. These narratives are male: they are centered in a vast array of micro practices and cultural forms enacted, constituted and legitimized by men and/or in male-gendered terms."[27] While there is now a growing literature on gender and international relations,[28] less attention has been paid to the impact of sexuality. Recently a number of anthropologists have "come out" about their own sexual motives, an issue of relevance for the discipline at least as far back as Mead and Malinowski.[29] But while anthropologists have begun to discuss the issue seriously, there is little debate within international relations or development studies about the impact of their work on changing perceptions and understandings of sexuality, though there is an increasing awareness of the gender dimension to development. There is interesting work on the margins of international relations about the sexual implications of military activity, where Cynthia Enloe has been a pioneering figure.[30] As she summarizes some of the possible connections: "Militarism . . . depended upon policies to ensure certain sorts of sexual relations: male bonding that stopped short of sexuality; men's sexual liaisons with foreign women that stopped short of the affection that might reduce militarized racism; misogyny that stopped short of a domestic violence that might undermine discipline and morale; wives' and lovers' sexual fidelity that stopped short of their having any sense of entitlement."[31]

Enloe's account may draw too sharp a distinction between women and men with regard to war. Sara Ruddick has claimed of war that "[y]oung men have been designated a sacrificial class, sent by their fathers to fight other fathers' sons,"[32] but women are more complicit in warfare than this comment suggests, and not only in the ways Enloe suggests. At least Ruddick recognizes the extent to which most soldiers are unwilling conscripts, and does not go the extent of Zillah Eisenstein, who speaks of the "iraqi women [who mourn] the blackened corpses that once were their loved ones"[33] without any apparent compassion for the young men themselves. Despite the image of the women in Aristophanes' play *Lysistrata* who deny sex to their husbands to end war between Athens and Sparta, more commonly women have been actively involved in the promotion of patriotic pressure to force men to fight. When World War I broke out, suffragettes such as Isabella Pankhurst set their struggle for the vote aside to concentrate on supporting the war effort. War is certainly gendered, but this is not the same thing as arguing that women are just passive bystanders, victims of some essentialist male impulse to fight each other. At least one section of feminism argues strongly for the right of women to take an equal part in military combat.

Are there more systematic ways in which we could think about the relationship between international relations and sexuality? There have been a couple of attempts to suggest ways of "queering international relations," though these seem to me little more than elaborate word playing.[34] Nonetheless there are several ways in which we might explore the interconnections between sexuality and international relations.

One is to explore Connell's notion of hegemonic masculinity and its promotion of a dominant heterosexuality which nonetheless allows for powerful homosocial bonds. Such male bonding is essential to the maintenance of particular sorts of gender structures, and has been analyzed both by those such as Lionel Tiger and later sociobiologists who see it as rooted in biology,[35] and by those who attribute far more importance to psychoanalytic and social constructionist arguments. Thus Nancy Hartsock has argued that "[o]ur own political life . . . must be understood to be structured by a masculine *eros* closely associated with violence and death."[36] Here there may well be stronger grounds for seeing war as a particularly masculine construction, albeit one which women may support and enable. In a very interesting reflection on the gendered nature of war Adam Farrar suggested that "[masculinity] is a potential way of assembling the world which can at any time be invoked or retreated from. We can only really capture 'masculinity' in those few moments of unalloyed male desire—pornography, rape, science . . . and war."[37] An interesting assemblage, certainly, but all of them socially constructed.

Do men go to war to defend their masculinity? This does not seem too far fetched an interpretation: after all, blood feuds, duels, and "honor" killings are common in some form to most societies. Yet as the nature of war changes, it is hard to see a clear connection between the sort of hypermasculinity which is exhibited in feuds between individual families and the high technology typical of modern warfare. Indeed, some feminists have made the point that the sort of "masculinity" required of soldiers is far removed from the rational and autonomous model of desirable behavior which dominates most western societies.[38] Rambo, in other words, was hardly a model soldier. This point can be reversed: the modern army is itself a product of rational and bureaucratic forms of control. It is also a primary site of both nation and gender formation, and there is insufficient analysis of the way in which compulsory military service operates to create particular forms of hegemonic masculine nationalisms, particularly in poor countries where the military is often both all-male and a central institution of the state.[39]

Even so, the willingness of men to go to war—even allowing for the large numbers who will flee, bribe officials, or maim themselves to avoid service—needs explanation. One of the best examples of this in recent years is the enormous casualties in the eight-year war between Iran and Iraq in the 1980s, when over a million young men were slaughtered in the name of defending the honor of their nation and their faith.

Yet in the contemporary world most people are not killed by missiles and smart bombs, but by the sort of individual violence which in recent years has seen mass slaughter in Rwanda, Kosovo, and East Timor, and which Mary Kaldor has identified as "new wars," which are closely bound up with globalization.[40] Some of what is involved in "new wars" is a reversion to more "traditional" constructions of masculinity, in part in response to the upheavals of modernity and the sense of disempowerment caused by global shifts. As Barbara Ehrenreich wrote: "War becomes a solution to what Margaret Mead termed 'the recurrent problem of civilization,' which is 'to define the male role satisfactorily enough.'"[41] In Afghanistan, the former Yugoslavia, west and central Africa, and the Caucasus there has been an upsurge of terror and violence, which is less related to old forms of wars between nation-states than to the particularist identity politics of the contemporary era. Nor is this confined to the poor world: there is a parallel between the bands of young men who terrorize populations in the civil wars in Kosovo, Ambon, and Sierra Leone and the worst excesses of inner-city gang warfare in the United States.

There are ways yet to be fully explored of using the insights of psychoanalysis to explain the tensions between new ways of organizing militarily and the apparent reversion to direct violence in so many parts of the world. Connell points to Freud's central role in making possible a social theory of gender: "The point he most insistently made about masculinity was that it never exists in a pure state . . . Though his theoretical language changed, Freud remained convinced of the empirical complexity of gender, and the ways in which femininity is always part of a man's character."[42] I recognize that there are many objections, both from behaviorists and from poststructuralists,[43] to the Freudian notion of a universal libido which can be repressed/sublimated, but it is not necessary to believe all that Freud wrote to find useful his concept of sexual repression being displaced into a range of social behavior. (bell hooks has made a similar call for the uses of psychoanalysis in understanding the legacy of racism and colonialism.)[44] In *Group Psychology and the Analysis of the Ego* Freud suggested that institutions such as the army and the church (we might update his examples) are based upon the sublimation of libidinal energies, thus maintaining the group ties which hold the organizations together while displacing overt sexual feelings outside the group.[45] There are echoes of Freud's work in the ways some feminists have argued that war allows for the expression of a certain sort of repressed homoeroticism, so that in films such as *Rambo* "[w]omen are present as signs that the soldier is not a homosexual, but in every other respect, they are irrelevant."[46] Moreover, the emphasis on male bonding helps make sense of the persistence of the "glass ceiling" against women in so many institutions, and of the hostility to both women and overt homosexuals within the military.

This sort of analysis was carried farther by Wilhelm Reich's "sex-pol" ideology, which saw the roots of authoritarianism and violence in sexual repression. (In 1931 Reich founded the German Association for Proletarian Sex in an attempt to develop a political program out of his analysis.) Though Reich's initiative was firmly ended by the Nazis, and his own views were to become notably more eccentric in his postwar career in the United States, his attempts to synthesize Marx and Freud influenced some of the Frankfurt

School, especially Erich Fromm and Theodor Adorno.[47] There are clear
echoes of this in Marcuse's *Eros and Civilization,* in some strands of 1970s gay
liberationist theory,[48] and in the counterculture's interest in tantric energy
and bodywork. At a commonsense level most people can acknowledge the
extent to which fear of one's own sexual impulses can be distorted into preju-
dice and aggression, often reflected in brutal assaults on transvestites, effeminate men, or women who seem too "masculine."

There is something of a postmodern vogue for elaborate psychoanalytic readings of international relations. In one such piece the author argues
that "the U.S. invasion of Panama suggests both emasculation and feminiza-
tion. That Noriega and Bush lacked phallic power and compensated for this
lack with the excessive miming of masculinity indicates male hysteria."[49] The
article, which goes on to suggest that the invasion of Panama involved two
rape scenarios, the second being that "by a male transvestite of a female," is
an excellent example of a symbolic reading of a clash in which political,
economic, and strategic interests are ignored in the interests of the clever
deployment of psychoanalytic language which risks—I know this will sound
hopelessly old-fashioned—confusing the metaphorical for the real. There is,
however, room for a more materialist psychoanalytic understanding of international relations, particularly in making sense of how disputes around gender and sexuality are displaced into external conflicts. This displacement often appears to have a sexual element, which is reflected in the preoccupation
of many religious fundamentalists with sexuality, and the linkages between
these preoccupations and the use of violence.[50]

A "materialist psychoanalytic" perspective might sound either trendy
or jargonistic, but it is meant to point back to the attempts earlier this century
to reconcile Marx and Freud, and to reassess their value. Without reading
either of these theoretical traditions as canonical, there is an important way
in which the simultaneous exploration of socioeconomic and psychological
structures of power and authority can provide a particular insight into the
understanding of human society which is more profound than the dominant
discourses of either liberal positivism or postmodern relativism. As the American psychoanalyst Joel Kovel reminds us: "By placing Freud within the
framework of historical materialism, we remove the iron hand of biological
determinism from psychoanalysis, while retaining a radical relation to nature
. . . As Marx said in another context: we do not only make our own history;
we make our own nature—but we make neither as we please."[51]

But even without a particular reliance on psychoanalysis we can use the notion of "hegemonic masculinity" to make sense of certain underlying patterns in the interrelationship between the sexual and the political. In terms of gender the test cases are powerful women—from Elizabeth I and Catherine the Great to Golda Meir, Indira Gandhi, Margaret Thatcher, and Madeleine Albright. While such women might seem to question male dominance in arenas almost always regarded as essentially masculine, in practice they are incorporated as "honorary men," whose power does little to change the essential homosocial nature of the military arena. One thinks, as well, of the role of powerful wives, a feature of many recent dictatorial regimes where they have often ruled de facto with their husbands, whether it be Imelda Marcos, Eva Perón, or Elena Ceausescu. It is hard to think of any significant female political figure in recent times who did not feel the need to prove she was "one of the boys," or, unhappily, of one who failed in the attempt.

Homosexual men, too, can be incorporated into hegemonic structures of power *provided they remain closeted:* think of J. Edgar Hoover or the role played by Roy Cohn in the McCarthy hearings of the 1950s. Cohn's hypocrisy is a central theme of the play *Angels in America,* and summed up in the speech, oddly reminiscent of traditional Latin "macho" definitions, where he boasts that "[u]nlike almost every other man of whom this is true, I bring the guy I'm screwing to the White House and Ronald Reagan shakes his hand . . . Roy Cohn is not a homosexual. Roy Cohn is a heterosexual man who fucks around with guys."[52] Yet the precarious place for homosexuals is suggested by the ongoing links between homosexuality, espionage, and treason, whether in the literature of Genet or the infamous Cambridge circle around the spies Burgess and Maclean.[53] The Nazis are only the best known among authoritarian regimes for their combination of strong male bonding and intense homophobia.[54]

One could certainly develop psychoanalytic theories which link "masculine" violence both to fear of "the feminine" and to repressed homosexuality, though few conservatives are as honest about their feelings as Paul Cameron, founder of the Family Research Institute, who justifies his attacks on homosexuals because "[i]f you isolate sexuality as something solely for one's personal amusement, and all you want is the most satisfying orgasm you can get—and that is what homosexuality seems to be—then homosexuality seems too powerful to resist . . . Marital sex tends towards the boring end. Generally it doesn't deliver the kind of sheer sexual pleasure that homosexual sex does."[55] Such analyses do not by themselves explain organized violence, nor the sort of total mobilization involved in state conflicts. Nonetheless they offer insights which supplement more conventional analyses about national interest, whether economic or strategic, or domestic political advantage in explaining why states go to war—and such insights are all the more useful in a world in which war is increasingly associated with the breakdown of the state system and the failure of governments to control internal violence.

Even without too much reliance on psychoanalytic theory, there are certain relationships between state power and particular forms of sexual regulation which are worth exploration. In *1984* George Orwell posited a totalitarianism which sought to restrict sexual pleasure: "Unlike Winston, [Julia] had grasped the inner meaning of the Party's sexual puritanism. It was not merely that the sex interest created a world of its own which was outside the Party's control and which therefore had to be destroyed if possible. What was more important was that sexual privation induced hysteria, which was desirable because it could be transformed into war-fever and leader-worship."[56]

Certainly the major authoritarian regimes of the twentieth century have shared a strong puritanism, whether we are speaking of Nazi Germany, Stalinist Russia, apartheid South Africa, or military regimes in Argentina and Greece, even though dictators themselves have often ignored the rules laid down for others. Mao Tse-tung comes to mind here, and North Korea's Kim Jong-il is said to have a handpicked team of young women bodyguards, referred to as "the joy team."[57] (It is of course common to seek links between sexual perversions and political pathology, as in the various stories which circulated about Hitler and his alleged relationship with his niece.) Where there are exceptions they seem linked to an economic interest in promoting sex tourism, which was true of the Batista government in Cuba and that of Marcos in the Philippines. Writing of the repression of homosexuals in Franco's Spain, Ricardo Llamas and Fefa Vila argue that "[a]ll sexual dissidence was defined as a symbolic space foreign to the values upon which the regime supported itself."[58] This tradition was echoed in the extreme homophobia of Communist Albania and Romania.[59]

Totalitarian governments seem threatened not just by organizations (and orgasms?) they cannot control, but by any sort of free expression which posits satisfaction as possible outside the lines decreed by the state. Thus both the Communist regimes of China and Vietnam and the fundamentalist rulers of Iran and the Sudan seek to impose particular norms of sexual behavior, which they recognize, if only implicitly, are necessary to maintain the total and internalized hold of the state which is the nature of totalitarianism. By and large sexual choices will be greatest in rich liberal democracies, although there are interesting variations: East Germany was far more accepting of abortion than West, while the United States remains unique in the western world in not having fully decriminalized adult homosexual acts.

The arguments for sexual freedom cannot be divorced from broader arguments about individual rights, social obligations, and the need for legitimate government, able to provide both security and relative equality for its citizens. Whereas I would criticize some contemporary western accounts of individual pleasure as the only goal for political activity, I would be equally critical of regimes which allow no space for individual and private satisfaction. The demand of the revolutionary sect, the Weatherpeople, in the 1970s to abolish monogamy, or the angst of some sexual radicals and feminists that fantasies are often inconveniently politically incorrect, serve to underline the fact that there are realms of human behavior which follow different rules, and neither totalitarian governments nor progressive movements should seek to erase these differences.

*N*ine

Squaring the Circle:
The Battle for "Traditional" Morality

Frantic orthodoxy is never rooted in faith but in doubt. It is when we are not sure that we are doubly sure.

—Reinhold Niebuhr

Speaking at the World Economic Forum in Davos at the beginning of 1999, the senior minister of Singapore, Lee Kuan Yew, spoke of his concerns that travel and new technologies threatened to destroy the cohesion of Singapore society. "Once you abandon the responsibility that comes with bringing children into the world," he said, "we become as feckless as some societies elsewhere."[1]

Meanwhile halfway across the world the Republican prosecutors who were beseeching the Senate to impeach President Clinton were struggling with the same paradox that bothered Lee. The social changes wrought by globalization have fundamentally changed the norms around sexual behavior, and in dissolving the divide between "private" and "public" have introduced new issues and tensions into everyday political life. We are constantly struggling to make sense of a shifting global order, in which it is gradually becoming apparent that international capitalism is both capable of unsettling almost all areas of life and of generating huge movements of resistance, the most potent of which are likely to appeal to a yearning to return to an imagined past in which the "traditional" sex/gender order symbolized a society in which the social order was widely understood and slow to change.

When I began this book in 1998 one read stories of women being forced into compulsory segregation by the new fundamentalist Taliban regime in Afghanistan,[2] while in the United States the lynching of a young gay man, Matthew Shepard, came to symbolize the extent to which hatred of homosexuals could go. While almost every country could offer its own stories of sexual hysteria and the politicization of issues around sexual morality, there did seem to be a common element in the concerns expressed about the rapidity of social change and its impact on morality and sexual behavior. Sometimes such politicization has taken the form of explicitly antiwestern attacks, as in criticisms in Russia of sex education as leading to "a violation of the ecology of the soul"[3] or the mob attacks in late 1998 on Indian cinemas showing Deepa Mehta's film *Fire,* about a love affair between two sisters-in-law, led by the Hindu group Shiv Sena, which claimed the film was an affront to national morality. Meanwhile rising divorce rates in China—nationally 13% but over 25% in some of the largest cities—provoked a national debate about whether to criminalize adultery, as increasing numbers of women were abandoned by their husbands.

Perhaps the best way of understanding the links between, say, the Moral Majority in the United States and the Taliban in Afghanistan, is to see them as both reactions to rapid social and economic change—in other words to globalization itself. Both cases represent a retreat from and attack upon secularism and rationality, and a determination to break down the divide between the religious and the political. Fundamentalism is itself gendered, and while it may be backed by some women it usually displays itself as a form of masculine assertion in the face of discomfort due to social change.[4] Discussing the tendency of fundamentalists to concentrate on the control of women's bodies, Karen Brown argues that "fundamentalism is born in times and places where, for a variety of reasons, the world suddenly seems too complex to comprehend" and often arises "where social, cultural and economic power is up for grabs."[5] Under such conditions, appealing to sexual fears and insecurities is a likely response from both government and nongovernmental sectors, as breakdowns in the old gender/sexual order, often a direct product of globalization, become a target for both Right and Left. This is most obvious in fundamentalist movements, whether in Algeria or in North America, but huge confusion around these issues is reflected almost everywhere. There is a rich symbolism to the story about the first-ever beauty contest in Rabat, Morocco, where opposition from fundamentalists led, not to the canceling of the event, but to contestants parading in ankle-length caftans, their hoods serving as veils.[6]

This sort of fundamentalism is often expressed as a desire to exclude the rest of the world, and reaches its apogee in the horrific killings of the Khmer Rouge or today's Algerian terrorist attacks on anyone who disagrees with them. The juxtaposition of these two examples reminds us that fundamentalism need not rest upon religious beliefs; the political fundamentalism of Pol Pot or the Nazis shared with religious fundamentalism the desire to exterminate, quite literally, all divergence within society. As the world becomes more and more subject to the influence and images of consumer capitalism the attempts to reject globalization may well become more savage, whether in the name of religion, tradition, or national sovereignty (as in Burma and North Korea). V. S. Naipaul suggested that the strengthening of Islam in Malaysia is in part to create a bulwark against the forces of globalization,[7] and ultra-Orthodox Jews in Israel warn against the Internet because of its links to the outside world.[8]

There seems to be a remarkably widespread belief that we are living through a period of collapsing moral values. In terms which would apply equally to many rich countries, Carol Jenkins wrote of Papua New Guinea: "The myth of the golden age of sexual restraint circulates among Papua New Guinea's elders (as elsewhere) and almost every man and woman in an opportunistic sample of over 400 persons interviewed throughout the nation in 1991 believed that sexual behavior had increased in licentiousness."[9] In Laos government officials bemoan the declining morality of "youth," ignoring the fact that it is largely a consequence of their own economic policies. Similar beliefs and contradictions seem to underlie calls for a return to moral conservatism in the United States from the Christian right and movements such as True Love Waits, which since 1993 has sought to pledge teenagers to abstain from premarital sex.

Central to all these forms of fundamentalism is a view of the world in which there is no room for uncertainty or ambiguity, and a hostility to what is seen as foreign and cosmopolitan threats to an imagined national or ethnic identity. As Lynn Freedman put it: "While the fundamentalist's own community is reinvented with a righteous and glorious past, the Other is demonised and vilified, thus lending an apocalyptic quality to the battle that is looming."[10] Often national and religious identities are linked to a particular view of women, who are both venerated as the defenders of moral purity and feared for their sexuality, which risks escaping total male control. While this sort of analysis is common to the western perception of fundamentalist Islam, very similar factors existed in the creation of the myth of white Southern womanhood, or in the contemporary rhetoric of the "profamily" religious right. This is most apparent when we consider the role of organized religion, probably the most powerful force in opposing the changes in morality and the sex/gender order brought about by global markets and neoliberal economics. (Pope John Paul II, for all his anti-Communism, has been also critical of what he regards as the excesses of capitalism.) After the Clinton administration reversed the hard line against abortion adopted by the United States under Reagan and Bush, the Vatican became the leading international exponent of this position, and lobbied strenuously at the 1994 Cairo conference to prevent any acceptance of abortion in the final document, with support from some Islamic countries.[11]

Through the century movements for equality for women have often been depicted by their opponents in exclusively sexual terms, with feminism often equated with promiscuity and lesbianism in an attempt to discredit it. Thus the proposed Equal Rights Amendment to the U.S. Constitution was attacked as leading to unisex toilets, the use of women in combat, and the legalization of gay marriage, and was defeated after a failure to win ratification in enough state legislatures.[12] Equally fear of pregnancy and venereal disease were major factors used in winning women's support for "traditional" morality until biomedical developments made them less persuasive arguments. There were both Left and Right versions of this, with Communists blaming capitalism for prostitution and the degradation of women, and the Right speaking of radical leftists undermining morality with subversive ideas of female equality and free love.

It is hardly surprising that sexual panics are so central to many of the angry reactions against social change, for even non-Freudians can recognize the extent to which fear of change is often based on unconscious fears of rampant sexuality. Think of the sexual scripts underlying the Ku Klux Klan's hatred of blacks or the "redneck" reaction to hippies in the sixties, depicted in the film *Easy Rider.* Only those over fifty can remember the extraordinary fury which greeted the fashion for young men in the 1960s to grow their hair long, a reaction which seemed born of a whole set of sexual and gender anxieties, although for some years immigration officials in some east Asian countries would order instant haircuts for young men whose locks were too long. Despite the largely unconscious homoerotic undertones to much extremist politics, these tend to coexist with passionate hostility toward any acknowledgment of homosexuality, as among contemporary European skinheads or American right-wing groups. Thus crazies like the Phineas Priest-hood oppose the banking system and interracial marriage and "want to root sodomites from the land."[13]

That there is a sexual element to racism is now widely acknowledged, and fears of the exotic "other" are fueled by the increase in migration and population movements which now are an indispensable part of the global economy. In both the pre–Civil Rights South and apartheid South Africa there was an obsession with "racial purity," reflected in stringent laws against "miscegenation." It is hardly surprising that one observer claims that since the end of apartheid "[i]nter-racial and gay sex . . . crop up more frequently in South Africa's advertising than they do in that of most western coun-tries."[14] More recently there have been echoes of fear of sexual mixing across race and religious lines in virulent anti-immigrant feelings in many parts of Europe, while the Ku Klux Klan has added hatred of homosexuals and abor-tionists to its earlier fears of racial mixing.

Scapegoating around sex has a long history, with prostitution and vene-real disease commonly blamed on foreigners—syphilis was commonly asso-ciated with any nationality but the speaker's own. Equally, sexual fears and fantasies have often played a significant role in persecutions, whether it be the medieval crusades against the Albigensians, feared for their vows of chas-tity, or the stereotypes of predatory sexual monsters deployed against the Chinese in nineteenth-century America, or the Jews in Nazi Germany. Such persecutions result from what Stanley Cohen called "moral panics," a condi-tion where "a condition, episode, person or group of persons emerges to become defined as a threat to societal values and interests."[15] In his overview of the concept Kenneth Thompson links the apparent frequency of "moral panics" in the contemporary world to the sorts of structural, technological, cultural, and discursive changes which constitute what is generally regarded as constituting "globalization," though he does not use this term.[16] "Moral panics" need not center on issues of sexuality, though they will usually have some sexual overtones.

In his discussion of the reaction to the growth of pornography and free discussion of sexuality in post-*perestroika* Russia Igor Kon uses the term "moral panic,"[17] and recurring panics over race, drugs, and youth, though often ex-pressed in terms of threats to "law and order," tend to conjure up images of wild and uncontrolled teenage sexuality. The arguments around "trafficking in women," already discussed, can be related to "moral panics" in a number of countries revolving around both fear of sexuality and dislike of the ways in which migration is changing the social order. Interestingly there are examples of such panics both in countries which are the source and in those which are the recipients of immigrant sex workers. Doezema cites mission workers and police in Nigeria and Romania appealing to traditional values and national pride as justifications for denying women permission to leave the country.[18]

"Moral panics" can be understood both as specific populist reactions, and as calculated appeals by political and economic elites to these reactions as ways of winning popular support for other policy shifts. Both Reagan and Thatcher were skillful in combining neoliberal economics with social conservatism, using the rhetoric of "family values" and "traditional morality" to disguise the extent to which their own policies were undermining the social fabric. Thus Reagan adopted a very hard line against abortion, and Thatcher introduced restrictions on the discussion of homosexuality—the infamous section 28, which banned local governments from "intentionally promoting homosexuality,'"[19] which was reversed by the Blair government (not without opposition) in 2000. Such measures were calculated to win support from conservative working-class workers who might not be enchanted by the attacks on unions and the dismantling of welfare problems which were central to both leaders' programs.[20]

Both Reagan and Thatcher understood the possibility of displacing the very real fears and anxieties brought about through rapid economic change onto the alleged social disintegration represented by rising divorce, single mothers, lesbian and gay assertion, and other symbols of a changing sex/gender order. Both also understood the need for the Right at the end of the Cold War to replace the external enemy of Communism with one closer to home. (Of course other sorts of issues and groups, most notably immigrants and ethnic minorities, have been seized on as scapegoats in many industrialized countries to explain the casualties of neoliberal economics.) And both probably believed the arguments of such capitalist triumphalists as George Gilder and Charles Murray, who argued that reducing welfare and strengthening the free market would enhance family stability, despite the considerable evidence around them to the contrary.[21]

One of the justifications of conservative politicians in the United States for "getting tough on welfare" was quite explicitly to link new welfare restrictions to fears of the alleged sexual degeneracy of the poor, as in attacks on women who, it was claimed, sought to become pregnant in order to qualify for single-parent benefits. Weighing in on the side of the welfare "reform" espoused by conservative Republicans in the 1990s, Murray declared that "[i]llegitimacy is the most important social problem of our time . . . because it drives everything else."[22] Symbolically the welfare reforms finally enacted in 1996 were known as the Personal Responsibility and Work Opportunity Reconciliation Act, which stated in its preamble that the Congress finds "1: marriage is the foundation of a successful society; 2: marriage is an essential institution of a successful society which promotes the interests of children." Similarly, highly publicized campaigns to close brothels have been a frequent device of politicians seeking, as Ian Buruma wrote of one such campaign in Taipei, to establish "public probity and private virtue."[23]

In the contemporary world AIDS has become a central focus around which all sorts of sex panics can be generated.[24] Rather like syphilis the initial stages of AIDS are frequently blamed on foreigners. Early in the epidemic Japanese officials claimed they would avoid AIDS because they had "no homos," and gay bars banned foreigners on the grounds that they might carry infection.[25] In his remarkable study of Japanese denial of HIV, John Treat suggests that it was fueled by both fear of the foreign and a particular sort of voyeurism, allowing for a displacement onto others, especially Americans.[26] An Egyptian film, *Love in Taba*, shown on television in 1992, tells of the seduction of three Egyptian men by western women, who leave them a note saying "Welcome to the world of AIDS"[27] (in other versions of this story the women are explicitly Israeli). As late as 1998, reports from Pakistan suggested that HIV was being still linked with "the impact of western society."[28] In one sense, as the argument of this book illustrates, there is some truth to this, but one fears the stereotyping of western decadence is being used as an excuse to avoid honesty about both sexual behavior and needle use in Pakistan. In the same way I have met Vietnamese officials who claim their prostitutes come from Cambodia and their drug users from China. In all these cases the metaphor of contamination is clear: fear of HIV merges with a larger and more amorphous fear of being infected by foreigners.

Many of these panics are about creating AIDS as the domain of "the other," through the demonization of "foreigners," of the bisexual man, of the promiscuous black stud, of the sex worker, and so forth. Examples of all of these abound in the twenty-year history of the epidemic, when it has been common for particular individuals who could be defined as "AIDS carriers" to become convenient scapegoats for a whole set of unexamined fears and phobias. In western countries such scapegoating has not infrequently been linked to racial stereotyping, with particular hysteria around positive African men which plays on existing myths about hypersexuality and fears of AIDS as particularly linked to Africa.[29] Fear of infection has become a new urban myth, as in stories of people holding up banks by threatening to use infected needles on the tellers. Other cases are more serious; there is at least one apparently accurate report of a man being burned to death in a village in India because he was suspected of "spreading AIDS through a syringe needle and . . . molesting women."[30]

Beyond the stereotyping of AIDS as "a foreign disease," the implementation of prevention programs leads to larger moral arguments about sexual (and injecting) behavior. Thus after at least ten years of HIV-prevention work in the Philippines a spokesman for the Catholic Bishops' Conference could say that "[t]he solution is that husbands should remain faithful to their wives and then there is no AIDS."[31] Monsignor Quitorio's statement ignored one of the real dilemmas in HIV work, namely that those at risk are often themselves monogamous and yet, as is true for women in most cultures, not in a position to demand monogamy from their partners. The larger point is that the epidemic has created a series of issues around which defenders of "traditional morality" have been forced to make painful choices, involving a recognition that public health measures to prevent transmission of HIV and other sexually transmitted infections often conflict with dominant religious codes. Many countries have seen bitter battles over moves to advertise condoms, to develop sex-education programs in schools, or to openly discuss homosexuality.

Since the 1990s sex tourism/pedophilia scares have served as moral panics which displace real issues of social justice and development. Genuine indignation at horror stories of children being sold into the sex industry are easily inflated, so that absurd claims show up in pamphlets and on the Internet, such as the assertion that "in Thailand 12% of the GDP comes from child prostitution."[32] Partly due to the work of End Child Prostitution, Pornography, and Trafficking (ECPAT) there has been an increase in arrests for pedophilia in Southeast Asia as western nations legislated to criminalize pedophilia, even when it occurs outside national borders. (ECPAT was established in Bangkok in 1990 by a group of NGO workers, and now has chapters in almost thirty countries, both rich and poor. It joined with UNICEF and the Swedish government to organize the first World Congress against Commercial Sexual Exploitation of Children in 1996, which was attended by 122 governments.)

Thailand itself has proscribed paid sex with anyone under the age of eighteen, although it took a long struggle to pass the legislation. One MP who sponsored the 1996 bill said that some had criticized moves to punish those who sold their children into prostitution "as running contrary to norms requiring children to respect, obey and be grateful to their parents."[33] Japan followed suit in 1999, setting the age for paid sex at eighteen, both at home and abroad. While there have already been occasional much-publicized trials of tourists for purchasing the services of underage prostitution in several Asian countries, it is hard to believe that this legislation has more than symbolic importance.

While there is a great deal written about the growth of child prostitution, above all in Southeast Asia, it is extremely difficult to get accurate figures. Part of the problem is definitional: no one would dispute that someone of eight is a child, but what about a girl or boy of fourteen? In 1995 UNICEF published figures defining anyone under the age of eighteen as "a child"; on their estimates India (with 450,000) and the United States (with 300,000) were far ahead of Thailand, the Philippines, and Cambodia in the numbers of children working as prostitutes.[34] Yet given the realities of life in cities such as Calcutta and Manila—or Elizabeth, New Jersey—is it meaningful to include sixteen- and seventeen-year-olds as "children" for these purposes? When the London *Sunday Mirror* ran allegations against science fiction author Arthur Clarke for having sex with boys in Sri Lanka, one of the "boys" whose testimony they quoted was seventeen at the time[35]—in a country where far younger children have been conscripted as soldiers into the ongoing civil war. Moreover how reliable can such figures be, when the very definition of prostitution is vague and often law enforcement authorities have a stake in existing arrangements?

It becomes convenient for both local governments and western morals campaigners to portray pedophilia as the product of an expanding international sex trade, even though evidence suggests the foreign pedophile, prowling the beaches and bars of Sri Lanka or the Dominican Republic, is only a minor figure either in maintaining prostitution or in child abuse. (A 1998 UNICEF study in the Philippines suggested 80% of child sexual abuse was by locals.)[36] There are growing reports of police uncovering "international rings" of child pornography and prostitution, and such reports commonly blur such vital distinctions as that between six- and fifteen-year-olds. The pedophile is almost always cast as male, but ECPAT has also claimed that some western women are sexually abusing "boys" at the Vietnamese coastal city of Hoi An.[37]

In some ways the panic about sex with children is a displacement of earlier panics about homosexuality, revealed in the emphasis on protecting children in antihomosexual campaigns and the disproportionate emphasis on homosexual pederasty, even though it makes up only a minority of "sex abuse" of children.[38] It appears that the hostility which could be displayed in attacks on homosexuals in the recent past, but which is now both ideologically politically incorrect and likely to upset significant interest groups, is increasingly displaced into a new mythology of the omnipresent figure of the child molester, who can be painted as unproblematically evil and often protected by powerful friends. This was a feature of the hysteria around pedophilia which accompanied a highly publicized series of investigations in the Australian state of New South Wales in the late 1990s,[39] which led to several suicides of people named as pedophiles.

Equivalent panics can be found in the past, but globalization allows for their internationalization, so that stories of pederasty around public figures like Michael Jackson spark off panics across the world. Michael Jackson's prominence from the mid-1980s on as a global superstar—100,000 concert tickets were sold when he appeared in Bangkok in 1993, a record for Thailand—meant global media attention to the allegations of child sexual molestation that same year.[40] Such allegations allow a display of self-righteous indignation which appears to transcend any divisions of nation, class, or race, and permit the media and politicians in both rich and poor countries to avoid facing up to far more difficult issues like the systemic abuse and exploitation of children as a result of structural adjustment and global economics.

The question of pedophilia is a particular problem for gay men, who are often caught between two conflicting pressures. On the one hand there is a constant tendency in the media to conflate pederasty with homosexuality, despite the fact that the most common form of child molestation is of girls by older men; on the other many gay men know from their own experience that teenage boys are often the initiators of sexual contact with adult men, and are aware of the hypocrisy which often sets the age of legal consent at a higher level for homosexual sex. Some of the most interesting contemporary

gay literature grows out of these conflicts—in recent years I think of Scott
Heim's *Mysterious Skin,* Neal Drinnan's *Glove Puppet,* and Matthew Stadler's
Allan Stein, all of which can be read as somewhat ambivalent about the issue
of sex between adults and "children"[41] but nonetheless concerned to interrogate the issues seriously. More common of course are sensationalist novels
such as Andrew Vachss's *Batman: The Ultimate Evil,* whose cover speaks of "the
most vicious and remorseless enemies he has ever faced . . . those who traffic
in the flesh of children."[42] The novel is set in a disguised version of Thailand,
and Vachss subsequently called for a total boycott of Thai products in protest
at alleged government encouragement for "the sexual exploitation of children as a tourist attraction."[43] There is at least one recent literary exploration
of female pedophilia, in A. M. Homes's tour de force *The End of Alice,* which
is far more ghoulish than the gay writings mentioned.[44]

IN THE HEART OF THE GLOBAL: THE PARADOX OF THE UNITED STATES

> *Sex. In America an obsession. In other parts of the world a fact.*
> —*Rabih Alameddine*, Koolaids, *1998*

While Communists and fundamentalists alike in nonwestern countries can
blame the rapid shifts in the gender/sexual order on foreign influences, it is
more difficult for those who share their fears within the United States, itself
the source of many of the globalizing changes responsible for these shifts.
Yet moral panics seem particularly apparent in the United States, which is
characterized by the constant tension between hugely successful consumerism and deeply entrenched puritan values—the contrast which so bewil-
dered foreigners when it was played out in the Clinton trials. As Steven Seidman put it: "Americans are divided between a romantic and a libertarian
sexual ethic, two constructions which serve as master frameworks through
which Americans think about sexuality."[45] This is symbolized by the dual
myths of America's foundation, as a place for individual freedom and as a
refuge for those whose religious beliefs were so strong they were unable to
find a peaceful home in Europe. Needless to say neither myth has much to
say to the indigenous population who were displaced in the name of "freedom," nor to the descendants of those brought to America as slaves.

The United States has always been caught between its dual heritage of religious puritanism and liberal capitalism. As Richard Hofstadter pointed out in his classic essay "The Paranoid Style in American Politics":

> The sexual freedom often attributed to [the enemy], his lack of moral inhibition, his possession of especially effective techniques for fulfilling his desires, give exponents of the paranoid style an opportunity to project and freely express unacceptable aspects of their own minds. Priests and Mormon patriarchs were commonly thought to have especial attraction for women, and hence licentious privilege. Thus Catholics and Mormons—later Negroes and Jews—lent themselves to a preoccupation with illicit sex. Very often the fantasies of true believers serve as strong sado-masochistic outlets, vividly expressed, for example, in the concern of anti-Masons with the alleged cruelty of Masonic punishments.[46]

This was written in 1963, but the contradictions have never been as sharp as in the past twenty years.[47] Changes in the nature of the economy, the emergence of a society dependent on mass consumption, and the relentless colonization of almost all areas of life by huge corporations make it increasingly difficult to maintain simultaneously the market economy and the puritan ethos. Thus religious conservatives have boycotted the Walt Disney Company (owner of the ABC network) over several of its shows, such as the television series *Ellen,* and Republican House leader Newt Gingrich pointed to what he saw as the "degeneracy" of contemporary popular culture: "Look at the sick signals we are now sending through the entertainment industry and popular culture. Is it any wonder that society is so confused if not downright degenerate?"[48]

Gilbert Herdt has argued that certain economic and political changes, caused by globalization, are helping produce new anxieties and responses around sexuality in the United States.[49] The question is why do similar anxieties in other rich western countries not produce the same fixation on sexuality, and the same polarization around issues of sex and gender? While some issues of sexual regulation have produced great anxieties in other western countries—abortion in Germany, Ireland, and Poland; homosexuality in Britain—there is far less evidence of the passions which have produced bombings of abortion clinics and lynchings of gay men in the United States.[50] Even Ireland, with its deeply Catholic culture, has considerably relaxed prescriptions against abortion, though not without very bitter debates which have stressed the identification between Catholic doctrines and "Irishness."[51] The reason for the passions around sexuality in America would seem to lie in the peculiar emphasis on sexual morality in American history, combined with the absence of the more disciplined class-based politics found in Europe. Yet Canada, which shares at least the latter with the United States, has experienced less of a mobilization around a right-wing moral agenda in recent years. The most significant variable is probably the high degree of religious belief in the United States (almost all studies find a much higher degree of fundamentalist beliefs in the United States than in any other liberal democracy) and the political mobilization around religious beliefs over the past several decades.[52]

Soon after the liberationist movements of the 1960s people began speaking of a moral "backlash," largely in relation to race, feminism, and sexuality in the United States, so that opposition to issues such as school desegregation, abortion, and the Equal Rights Amendment was depicted as the reaction of those who supported the status quo to rapid change. The breakdown of the distinctions between "public" and "private" for the past thirty years has involved bitter debates about the balance between "liberation" and "responsibility," as part of which increasing areas of social life have become arenas for political contestation. Susan Faludi quotes Dr. Jean Baker Miller as saying "A backlash may be an indication that women really have had an effect, but backlashes occur when advances have been small, before changes are sufficient to help many people . . . It is almost as if the leaders of backlashes use the fear of change as a threat before major change has occurred."[53] Yet the danger of using the term "backlash" is that it underestimates the extent to which moral conservatism is itself a social movement, with its own vision for change and a desirable future.[54]

The first contemporary examples of such sexually motivated "backlash" are found in the reactions to the feminist and gay movements of the 1960s and the broader shifts around gender and sexuality, often fought over issues like abortion, divorce, homosexuality, and pornography.[55] Richard Nixon campaigned for the presidency in 1972 as a champion of traditional values, painting George McGovern as the candidate of "acid, amnesty and abortion," and his vice president Spiro Agnew was fond of attacking his opponents as "effete intellectuals," echoing the implicit homophobia of McCarthyism. After the 1973 Supreme Court decision (*Roe versus Wade*) that abortion was a constitutional right, debate over abortion became central to mainstream American politics. Traditionally fundamentalist Christians had kept away from mainstream politics, but there was a significant change as increasing numbers of "born again" Christians became political activists, symbolized by the Moral Majority, which was founded by the Reverend Jerry Falwell in 1979.[56] In abortion they found an issue which allowed for alliances with their traditional enemy, the Catholic Church, and which became pivotal to the religious right's growing influence within the Republican party.

By the time of Reagan's presidency abortion had became a touchstone against which all national Republican candidates were judged, and Reagan vowed to appoint only known anti-abortionists as federal judges. The 1984 election saw a common front between Catholic and evangelical Protestant leaders in attacking the Democratic vice-presidential nominee, Geraldine Ferraro, a pro-choice Catholic, particularly vulnerable because she was a woman. Under pressure from the Right, George Bush abandoned his some-what more liberal attitudes, and had he won the 1992 election it is conceivable that his appointments to the Supreme Court could have led to the over-turning of *Roe versus Wade*. As it was, the Court did impose a number of restrictions on abortion during the late 1980s, in practice limiting the availability of abortion to poor women.[57] Political passion about abortion far exceeded that in other western countries other than those, such as Ireland or post-Communist Poland, with a particularly strong Catholic Church. At the same time the charged language around "illegitimacy" and "births out of wedlock" has largely disappeared in the richer countries of Europe, a language which combines appeals to "traditional" mortality and fear of the (largely nonwhite) "underclass." Ironically that side of American conservatism which prevents effective sex education in schools and the provision of contraceptives to teenagers is responsible in large part for the illegitimate mothers whom conservatives condemn.

In the 1990s abortion was less clearly a vote winner for the Right. In 1996 Bob Dole won the Republican nomination despite being lukewarm about much of the religious right's agenda, and pro-choice Mary Landrieu was elected to the Senate from Louisiana, a state which might be expected to combine strong Catholic and fundamentalist Protestant voters. Yet despite this, the Right has sought to use other issues—pornography, homosexuality, creationism—to rally support from groups whose economic interests might lead them away from the Republican party. The hatred of the Right toward Clinton, so apparent in the determination of the Republicans to remove him from office despite his popular support, is a reflection of the rise of politics built around the rhetoric of "traditional morality." That Clinton adopted much of the conservative rhetoric about issues such as welfare reform and a balanced budget just increased right-wing passions about his positions on issues such as abortion rights and allowing homosexuals to serve in the military. That he was forced into an uncomfortable compromise on the latter—the "don't ask, don't tell" formula, which still allowed the military to discharge personnel for homosexuality[58]—once again set the United States aside from most other western countries. Even Israel, where the military is a central institution and where Orthodox pressure is significant, lifted most such restrictions in 1993.

From the late 1970s, when Anita Bryant led a very well publicized campaign to repeal an antidiscrimination ordinance in Dade County, Florida, using the name Save Our Children, homophobia was central in American political debate. Again, the United States is a peculiar anomaly. Despite other rulings implying a constitutional right to privacy, the Supreme Court in 1986 in *Hardwick versus Bowers* refused to overturn state antisodomy laws, which still remain in a number of states, the last such examples in the western world. At the same time the United States has by far the largest and best-organized gay/lesbian movement in the world, and one which has become a significant donor to many liberal political campaigns.[59] Despite the Supreme Court's ruling, many U.S. states and cities have enacted antidiscrimination ordinances on the basis of sexuality, and in a few cases have recognized domestic partnerships. Perhaps in the Court's ruling on sodomy there is a parallel to the American commitment to capital punishment, also outlawed in most other western democracies, and also linked to a peculiar religiosity which sees no contradiction between preaching respect for life and executing large numbers of criminals. It is not accidental that capital punishment and gun ownership are heaviest in those areas, mainly in the South and West, where fundamentalist Protestantism most thrives.

The hypocrisies of the American approach to sex is a perennial punching bag, and it is nowhere clearer than around adolescent sex. When the PLWHA magazine *Poz* included three condoms in a special issue on youth and HIV in 1998, a number of distributors, including the big bookstore chain Barnes and Noble, refused to carry the issue. While the sexual attraction of adolescents is assiduously promoted by media and advertising, in real life it is either criminalized or medicalized. Note the case of the American school teacher and her thirteen-year-old lover, which was treated as both, with the teacher sentenced to jail after pleading guilty to second-degree rape, then rearrested after seeking out the boy on her release—while the media, having acknowledged that the boy "looked and acted older than his years," explained her acts as the product of "bipolar disorder, also known as manic-depressive illness."[60] Note, too, the difficulties in finding an American distributor for the 1997 film *Lolita*, finally released in the States a year later after various cuts. Here the film followed the path of the novel, which was rejected by four American publishers before being accepted by Olympia Press in Paris. That, however, was in 1955 and three years later Putnam published it in the United States.[61] There were similar problems in Australia, where a decision to release the film for restricted viewing led to a storm of protest, orchestrated by right-wing parliamentarians, but in much of Europe the film was released without protest. Presumably what was most disturbing to its critics was the depiction of a fourteen-year-old girl as knowingly seeking the attention of an older man, thus unsettling the image of the passive victim which is central to the conventional way of understanding pedophilia.

In 1994 legislation known as Megan's Law (after a particularly notorious case of child molestation), requiring the compulsory—and public—registration of pedophiles even after their release from prison, was introduced in New Jersey. Subsequently similar laws were adopted across the country, a requirement for federal crime-fighting funds. The status of these laws is now in doubt after a ruling by the Pennsylvania Supreme Court in July 1999 finding its state's law "constitutionally repugnant," but this has not prevented arguments for similar laws in other countries.[62] And it was largely pressure from the United States which led to the ILGA's losing its observer status at the Economic and Social Council of the United Nations because some of its member organizations refused to condemn "man-boy love."[63]

The peculiarly American combination of free-market economics with restrictive sexual morality means that sex panics are not always easily internationalized. Indeed the U.S. moral right, despite considerable efforts, has had at best a patchy influence on the rest of the world, despite their intervention in disputes such as the New Zealand debates around the decriminalization of homosexuality in the mid-1980s (when American evangelists linked the alleged "soft" line of the government on moral issues to their prohibition of visiting nuclear warships). In the late 1990s there were reports of U.S.-based groups funding campaigns against moves in Britain to lower the age of consent for homosexual acts and more general antihomosexual campaigns in both Australia and New Zealand. Since the end of apartheid several avowed Christian parties have emerged in South Africa, whose rhetoric echoes closely that of the American religious right, combining appeals to "traditional" morality with support for capital punishment and "the free market" (justified by appropriate biblical quotes).[64] Considerable American money has flowed into various overseas antiabortion campaigns.

Reagan's position on abortion had a global impact as it came to be imposed as a condition of American assistance to reproductive health programs abroad, and at times his administration went beyond this to question support for any type of family planning. At the 1984 International Population Conference in Mexico City the U.S. delegation, headed by right-wing Republican Senator James Buckley, not only opposed any mention of abortion but questioned the assumption that rapid population growth was necessarily a problem.[65] While the Clinton administration reversed this stance and returned to the earlier American position of enthusiastic support for birth-control programs, the issue became enmeshed in conflict between Congress and President Clinton over payment of dues to the United Nations—and led to the decision of the United States in 1998 to cease all funding for the United Nations Population Fund (UNFPA).

The problem which faces American moral conservatives wishing to export their values is that they are undermined by the very pleasures of consumption which represent the American way of life to much of the world—and often find themselves in an uneasy alliance with governments (such as those of China, Cuba, and Iran) they most detest. Similarly the internal arguments of American feminists and homosexuals often seem largely irrelevant outside the United States. By the 1990s gay communities in urban America were bitterly divided between those who argued for a culture of sexual adventure and those who saw in this a necessarily irresponsible attitude to HIV. In 1996 the group Sex Panic emerged in New York in protest at closures of various sex venues, claiming a major backlash against sexual freedoms. These claims were probably exaggerated, but they pointed to a particular form of moralism which was now coming from *within* the gay community and created extremely explosive divisions in which prominent writers and activists clashed over the extent to which the gay movement should promote particular forms of sexuality, rather as feminists still clash over pornography;[66] indeed Sex Panic included several women who had been prominent in the pornography debates of the 1980s. The clashes were complex, involving as they did radical differences about appropriate strategies for HIV prevention and arguments about how far the gay/lesbian/queer movement should embrace the call for recognition of same-sex marriage. Both the proponents and opponents of the new morality showed that particular disinterest in either history or geography—other times, other places—which so characterizes New York intellectual provincialism.

But if Sex Panic was disinterested in the rest of the world this disinterest was not reciprocated, and it is the nature of the global media that millions of us outside the United States will know far more about you than you do about us. American influence helps export its anxieties to the rest of the world, as in the spread of American evangelism. (Billy Graham's crusade in the 1960s was an important influence on the best-known Australian Protestant crusader, Fred Nile, who since 1981 has held a seat in the upper house of New South Wales.) There are a few examples of evangelism coming from elsewhere, most notably Sun Myung Moon's Unification Church, which from its base in Korea has made some inroads into the United States, and supported right-wing political causes, in particular through control of the *Washington Star* newspaper. Its clout is suggested in the support of such influential Americans as former Nixon and Reagan adviser General Alexander Haig.[67] One might see some parallels in the influence of Indian gurus, such as Krishnamurti, in California since the 1920s, and more recently the spread of Buddhism in some western countries, but in neither case is the same sort of political mobilization involved.

Mormon missionaries, sent abroad in pairs to promote their particular version of the word of God, have been joined by a powerful evangelical Pentecostalism, which is important in South Korea and parts of Africa. (American televangelists are often seen on South African television.) In particular this sort of evangelism has been making significant converts in Catholic Latin America. In Guatemala up to 40% of the population are now Protestants, as are around 30% of the population of Chiapas state in Mexico, site of bitter protests against the central government. In Brazil the Protestant vote has become significant, and shares with the American right a preoccupation with defending traditional morality and the family, even while not necessarily more conservative on economic issues.[68] Yet while there are significant similarities with the American religious right on some issues, it would be misleading to see the growth of evangelical Protestantism in Latin America as simply another example of American imperialism, as David Martin hints at in questioning whether Latin American religion has been "americanized."

As he points out, it is also true that Protestantism is being "latin american-ized."[69] Equally the rigid orthodoxy of some American Jews has had an enor-mous impact in Israel, and has been one of the largest stumbling block to any reconciliation with the Palestinians. Alongside Disney movies and Amer-ican pop music the particular apocalyptic vein of American religiosity is be-ing exported, with, I would argue, potentially far more serious consequences.

Ten

Conclusion:
A Global Sexual Politics?

Suggestions that the sexual is political can be found in a range of nineteenth-century philosophical writings, but became central for a number of twentieth-century thinkers, whether like Reich and Marcuse they drew on the theories of Freud, or, as in the case of many second-wave feminists, they were consciously hostile to psychoanalysis. In a globalizing world there is a need to rethink these connections, both practically and theoretically.

A sexual politics for this century will need to draw on various theories of sexuality but also on recent developments in the study of international relations, and conceptualizations of both the state and the global. We badly need a political economy of sexuality, one which recognizes the interrelationship of political, economic, and cultural structures, and avoids the tendency to see sexuality as private and the political and economic as public. Such a political economy, as the term suggests, is more concerned with material conditions and political action than it is with theories of discourse and representation, but it is also concerned with the ways in which the state is being undermined by a combination of global economic forces and particularist political movements. Globalization implies the decline of state sovereignty and allows the rise of transnational social movements as political actors. Thus Manuel Castells argues:

> The growing incapacity of states to tackle the global problems that make an impact on public opinion . . . leads civil society to increasingly take into their own hands the responsibilities of global citizenship. Thus Amnesty International, Greenpeace, *Medecins sans Frontieres*, Oxfam, and so many other humanitarian non-government organizations have become a major force in the international arena in the 1990s, often attracting more funding, performing more effectively, and receiving greater legitimacy than government-sponsored international efforts. The "privatization"

of global humanitarianism is gradually undermining one of the last rationales for the necessity of the nation state.[1]

Yet there can be major traps in both the rhetoric and the reality of the retreat from the state, as any genuine system of social justice depends upon the distributive and welfare role of government. Partly influenced by Foucault's notions of "micropolitics," it has become fashionable to stress the role of grassroots activism without any corresponding attention to the macrosources of power, corporations, the state, and the military (to paraphrase C. Wright Mills's notion of the "power elite"). I am sympathetic to R. W. Connell's call for a fresh politics of masculinity around, "for instance, the politics of the curriculum, work around HIV/AIDS and anti-racist policies . . . far more internationalist than masculinity politics has been so far, contesting globalization-from-above."[2] But we must also recognize that nation-states and governments, like the body, remain insurmountable and material realities. Political institutions matter, just as do corporations and the religious and educational institutions which maintain particular cultural regimes of power. Moreover the rise of civil-society organizations, as North Americans term them, is not an unambiguous good. Powerful nationalist and sexist forces, legitimized by religious teachings and drawing their support from repressed angers and frustrations, are as much part of civil society as are the liberal internationalists to whom Castells refers.

A practical politics for major social change must simultaneously engage with the conventional sources of political and economic power, as well as with the far more disparate and interwoven ways in which hegemonic beliefs and practices are constituted and perpetuated. Such an approach includes a recognition of the interconnections between different forms of power, and of the ways in which the state can both repress and protect. It also needs to take account of the ambivalent nature of the nongovernmental sphere, which includes the Ku Klux Klan and the National Front just as it includes women's and environmental groups.

Postmodern feminist and queer theories are relatively unhelpful in constructing this sort of politics because of their lack of emphasis on political institutions as distinct from discourse, their first-world centrism, and their lack of interest in social movements.[3] (Anyone who doubts the Atlantic centrism of postmodern theorists should look at the editorial boards of their journals, which are typically a long list of people in prestigious northern universities, with a token Indian or Argentinean thrown in to justify the claim to being "international.") There are two major problems in the postmodern turn in sexual theory, as well as a minor one, namely a belief that the more impenetrable the language the deeper the thought. The first objection is that the emphasis on discourse, performance, and play too often means a disinterest in material realities and inequalities. As Connell argued: "This approach is stimulating for the players, and it does involve a certain personal risk to simulate being queer in the streets. If the streets are patrolled by homophobes. It does not involve much more . . . Indeed, absorption in the game, on the part of players who are greatly privileged in global terms, might be considered the semiotic equivalent of what Marcuse called 'repressive desublimation'—as we might now call it: Getting lost in sexual cyberspace."[4]

Second, the emphasis on discourse tends to deny the role of social movements and political work in creating the conditions in which queer theory is able to flourish. As Lisa Duggan, by no means unsympathetic to queer theory, wrote: "There is a tendency among some queer theorists to engage in academic debates at a high level of intellectual sophistication, while erasing the political and activist roots of their theoretical insights and concerns. Such theorists cite, modify or dispute Foucault, Lacan, and Derrida, while feminist, lesbian, and gay innovations and political figures disappear from sight."[5] Reading work by young queer scholars in Australia I am struck by how often they will invoke Butler and Foucault, while ignoring the particular his/her/stories of the Australian movements.

The queer and postmodern feminist desire to escape from the limitations of identity politics is commendable. The resistance of much contemporary theory to any Marxist analysis—which becomes equated with "grand narratives" and "old-fashioned leftism"—means they have nothing useful with which to replace the limited politics of identity. Thus the attraction of more and more convoluted theories of desire which evade questions of social and economic power and inequality—and indeed ignore the inconvenient reality that sex occurs because of a lust for power or revenge or cruelty as often as it is an expression of desire.

Yet postmodern theorists are correct when they insist upon the symbolic importance of sex. "Traditional" societies tended to use sexuality as part of the rites of passage, whether through ritualized intercourse, as in Gilbert Herdt's famous example of the Sambia,[6] or through the sacrifice of virgins, as in a number of religious ceremonies. Such symbolic uses of sex might seem bizarre, even "primitive," to contemporary westerners, yet we in turn tend to expect too much of sex, to see it as central to relationships, social cohesion, and our sense of identity. It plays a role in all those things, but insofar as it is expected to provide both our greatest pleasures and our most authentic sense of self, we also load sex with more than it is able to carry. As globalization extends western concepts of identity, consumerism, and self-fulfillment to other societies, so too it replaces existing scripts about sex with those of Hollywood and the romance novel (widely read, if their profusion on the shelves of most secondhand bookshops in the world means anything). The questions posed by the small free-love circles of interwar Bohemia, or the student movements of 1968, are increasingly being raised across the world.

The idea of sexual liberation as integral to larger social and political liberation was an underlying theme in radical and romantic theories since the early nineteenth century, and became central to both the counterculture and New Left movements of the 1970s. While this idea has largely disappeared in the rich countries of the north, it still influences feminist and gay activists in Latin America, and was a reality in South Africa, where gay supporters of the African National Congress were instrumental in having protection against discrimination on the basis of sexuality incorporated into the postapartheid constitution. The liberationism of the 1970s currently has a bad name though there are also signs of nostalgia for it, as in films such as *Boogie Nights, 54,* and the Singapore film *That's the Way I Like It.*[7] The very large Love Parades each summer in Berlin since 1989 also appear to be echoes of the countercultural celebrations of the 1960s.

There are two major problems (at least) with the liberationist project: it assumed a link between sexual and other freedom which was naive (note Marcuse's reading of Freud in *Eros and Civilization*); and in practice it was largely male-oriented. In the former case those of us caught up in the radical enthusiasms of the period underestimated the extent to which sexual "liberation" could be successfully co-opted by commercial consumerism. As mainstream publishers produce glossy erotica and sex toys are sold in mall-like sex emporiums, the hope that freedom from sexual restraints will lead to revolutionary change seems increasingly utopian. Matthew Stadler paints one possible future: "If the terrific gains of gay liberation continue apace we'll soon be joining these straight potbellied swingles on the margins of those twelve lane highways that seem to go on forever . . . The bright light of sexual liberation will shine out of the cities to reach the towns and sprawl, and everything will shift so that perversity will be allowed to thrive in that purgatory too, where we can join our brothers, the drunk ex-husbands, at R. U. O'Bliterated Ale House, Blande Woode Towne Center Branch, 250550 Blande Parkway (old Highway 3)."[8]

For gay men, who could benefit most easily from the new sexual freedom and the short period when sexual adventure seemed chic—in the 1970s Bette Midler drew both straight and gay audiences to her performances in New York gay bathhouses—the benefits of liberation have become particularly problematic because of the links with AIDS. The debates over sexual adventure within the gay community predate the epidemic to some extent. Larry Kramer was already critical of promiscuity in his 1978 novel *Faggots,* a position he restated with far greater urgency in his play *The Normal Heart* eight years later. But even those of us more enthusiastic about sexual freedom than Kramer could question the limits to sex without emotion—when I wrote *Homosexual: Oppression and Liberation* at the start of the 1970s I quoted the lines from the rock musical *Salvation:*

If you let me make love to you
Then why can't I touch you?[9]

It is worth recognizing that sexual liberation can imply a recognition of the overimportance modern societies attribute to sexuality. In Jeffrey Weeks's words: "The road away from moral authoritarianism lies not with the elevation of King Sex, whether in the sacred form of puritanism or in the profane form of permissiveness, but rather in his dethronement."[10]

As to the second criticism, Julie Burchill could write in 1998: "Ironically the sex-rev failed because, Freudian or not, it failed to ask what women want."[11] But against this was the recognition by some feminists that not all sex without commitment was undesirable, as in Erica Jong's invocation of the "zipless fuck" in her novel *Fear of Flying* or Rita Mae Brown's account of crashing a gay bathhouse, disguised as a man.[12] (This view of the potential for enjoying casual sex lives on in many subsequent female private-eye stories.) Linda Grant argues that Jong's celebration of sex was reborn in the 1990s, and quotes Madonna's book *Sex* and Annie Sprinkle's *Post Porn Modernist Manifesto:* "Post Porn Modernists celebrate sex as the nourishing life-giving force. We utilize our genitals as part, not separate from, our spirits . . . We empower ourselves by this attitude of sex-positivism. And with this love of our sexual selves we have fun, heal the world and endure."[13] What Grant does not recognize is that this view of liberation has lost the commitment to larger social change which fueled liberationist movements of the 1970s.

In the rich world sex is increasingly seen as a form of recreation. "We need to wake everyone up," says one of the characters in J. C. Ballard's ironic novel *Cocaine Nights*. "The people . . . are desperate for new vices."[14] For most people in the world, certainly for most women, the real vices of poverty, hunger, disease, and war are problems enough. Even in the rich world the divorce of ideas of sexual pleasure from any larger social concern has sad consequences. When the thirtieth anniversary of Woodstock was celebrated by a massive concert at the same site, there were reports of gang rapes of young women.[15] Does this capture the danger of modern consumer society in which individual gratification has been elevated to the dominant principle?

Even so, it is too easy to dismiss the search for pleasure as purely the luxury of the rich. There are growing testaments from women in many societies that, once they are able to speak, sexual pleasure becomes significant. Elizabeth Jelin writes of Latin America: "Concealed and forbidden in words, but real and everyday in practice, to make sexuality visible and to expose the sexual oppression suffered by most women has been one of the feminist movement's significant achievements."[16] And studies of young people in a number of countries reveal a growing awareness and desire among women to take pleasure in the exercise of their sexuality.[17]

Maybe the pseudo-Reichianism of sexual liberation is now suspect, but there is something in its project worth saving, especially the stress on the interconnection between sexual and social justice.[18] If there really is none, then why is sexual repression so central to both organized religion and most authoritarian regimes? Neoliberal capitalism seems to escape the moralism of both of these, allowing private satisfactions to compensate for the erosion of the public sphere: are X-rated videos and stripper clubs the contemporary equivalents of Roman gladiatorial displays? On one level these are at best temporary evasions, at worst new forms of exploitation, and it is easy to argue that questions of sexual liberation are irrelevant to people struggling to survive. Yet all too often people experience real and violent oppression and exploitation because of certain regimes of sexuality, and the violence which is used to maintain their hegemony. Sexual liberation may be an inappropriate term, but it is hard to argue it is irrelevant to women stoned for adultery in Iran or disfigured with acid in Bangladesh for choosing the wrong husband. From a rather different perspective than mine, Robin Morgan argued:

"What if we never again apologized for emphasizing 'sexual politics,' but realized that, as both Jain of India and Lugo of Mexico point out, the subjects of contraception, abortion, sexual violence and battery *are* conscious concerns of even the poorest rural woman struggling for daily survival?"[19]

Perhaps we should turn the precepts of the seventies around, and recognize not just that sexual freedom is connected to other struggles, but that it is meaningless in the absence of other forms of freedom and equality. Only if women are empowered in the economic and social sphere can they engage equally with men in the sexual arena, and for this to happen does require, as we claimed in those distant halcyon days of liberation politics, revolutionary change. Without access to the basic necessities of survival it is likely that sex will be nasty, brutish, and short, and that it will be constructed entirely to suit the convenience of powerful men. Violence against women may exist in all societies, but it is less likely where there is sufficient wealth, education, and sense of personal integrity to allow women to leave abusive relationships.

Drawing on my earlier discussion of Nancy Fraser's distinction between the politics of *redistribution* and the politics of *recognition*, I would argue that a meaningful sexual politics in a globalizing world must involve both the inequities of the larger socioeconomic order, and those implicated in the broader structures of sex and gender, which are constantly being remade through the very processes of globalization. Implicit in the spread of neoliberal capitalism through more and more of the world is the growing disjunction between "traditional values" and (post)modern consumerism. But this is not merely a debate about values or an academic struggle over discourses. Social structures which provided at least a modicum of security and welfare are being destroyed by the relentless march of the market, the massive growth in urbanization, the atomization of social relationships, and the decline of government services. Globalization is creating enormous wealth and enormous dislocations: the richest three men in the world are said to control more assets than the forty poorest countries. At the same time the social structures which are being destroyed are themselves often based on assumptions of deep inequality around gender, race, and class, as in the caste systems of south Asia or the gender structures of most orthodox religions. This is the dilemma Penny Andrews points to: "What became increasingly obvious in South Africa was that the metamorphosis from a European to an African country required that its Africanness be reflected in the legal system and that it incorporate certain aspects of traditional law. But this reality had to recognise that the strictures of traditional law kept women in perpetual tutelage."[20]

In the struggle to make sense of the disjunctures and inequalities of the contemporary world we should avoid both the triumphalist rhetoric of neoliberalism and the romantic nostalgia of traditionalists. The market cannot deliver human happiness, but equally there is no imagined past to which we can return which will abolish injustice and inequality. Appeals to religion, tradition, and culture are often no more than justifications to perpetuate the worst kinds of institutionalized subordination and barbarism. In the end, ideas of human rights, social justice, acceptance of diversity, and the empowerment of those who are marginalized and deprived are universal goals which remain important no matter the particular culture. Moreover they will require both strengthened global order *and* effective national governments: ironically the ravages of globalization are worst when the state cannot—or will not—provide means to help its populations benefit from socioeconomic change.

The central lesson that I have learned from a decade of working in the international HIV/AIDS world is that the interconnectedness of the world is both a threat and an opportunity. The sexual politics which burst upon western countries in the late 1960s spoke a vague language of internationalism, but its preoccupations were largely with the immediate and the nation-state. Three decades later the world is very different. Much of what we fought for then has been at least partially achieved in the west, but equally the triumph of liberal capitalism to a degree unforeseen by either its boosters or its detractors has created new challenges and new sorts of oppression. Those of us who are part of the privileged elite whose lives are being enriched by the processes of globalization must never forget just how precarious and dangerous the world is for most people.

There is no preordained certainty that we will be successful in achieving the goals of a more just and equitable world, and it is already clear that the struggle to attain them has extensive casualties. But how we adjust to these disjunctions will say a great deal about the prospects for human dignity and happiness in the coming decades. In that struggle sexuality is both a battlefield and a legitimate area for political action.

Acknowledgments

Because this book draws on various research projects over the last decade, the number of people who have contributed to it is quite considerable. Some have made quite specific contributions to the development of the book itself: Doug Mitchell at the University of Chicago Press, always a responsive and supportive editor; Richard Parker, whose initial and continuing support for the proposal was very significant; David Stephens, both a good friend and a good research assistant; and the staff of the La Trobe University Library, especially Eva Fisch, who were always helpful in tracking down elusive sources. Many other people also contributed through their assistance with associated projects over the past decade: I want to thank particularly Peter Aggleton, Niko Besnier, R. W. Connell, Michael Connors, Peter Drucker, Stephen Gill, Mark Heywood, Jeff O'Malley, Maila Stivins, and John Treat. The book began during a six-week stay at the University of Chicago in 1997, and Jacqueline Bhaba, the staff of the Humanities Research Center, and Neville Hoad deserve thanks for helping make that stay a productive one.

Books are written in particular contexts, and special thanks are due to my colleagues in the School of Sociology, Politics, and Anthropology at La Trobe University, above all to the administrative staff, Liz Byrne, Barbara Matthews, Nella Mete, and Mary Reilly, without whom my time there would be far less productive. Special thanks to particular colleagues and students, especially Tony Jarvis, Brendon O'Connor, Sanjay Seth, and Geoff Woolcock, and my fourth-year honors class of 1999, with all of whom I discussed aspects of this book. The book also draws on my particular involvement in international HIV/AIDS politics, and thanks go to the members of the various community networks, the staff of UNAIDS, and the International Forum of Montreal, with whom many of these ideas were rehearsed. Hard as it is to single out individuals, I do want to mention Calle Almedal, Bai Bagasao,

Stef Bertozzi, Roy Chan, Sally Cowal, Marina Mahathir, Shawn Mellors, Dede Oetomo, Shane Petzer, Peter Piot, Malu Quintos, Werasit Sittitrai, and Paul Toh.

For generous funding of my research I am grateful to the Australian Research Council, the Evans Grawmeyer Foundation (and former foreign minister Gareth Evans), and the MacArthur Foundation. Once again particular thanks have to go to Anthony Smith, who not only read many versions of the manuscript, but put up with me during the writing of it.

Notes

PREFACE

1. Russell Baker, "The Great Meltdown," *International Herald Tribune*, September 23, 1998.
2. See interview with Mahathir, *International Herald Tribune*, September 23, 1998.
3. "10 Years for Presidential Sodomy," *Australian,* January 20, 1999.
4. Jeremy Seabrook, *In the Cities of the South* (London: Verso, 1996), 24.
5. John MacInnes, *The End of Masculinity* (Buckingham: Open University Press, 1998), 134–35.
6. Thomas Friedman, *The Lexus and the Olive Tree* (New York: Farrar, Straus, 1999), 26–27.
7. Mary Kaldor, *New and Old Wars* (Cambridge: Polity, 1999), 4.
8. E. L. Doctorow, *The Waterworks* (New York: Macmillan, 1994), 26–27.

ONE

1. Roland Robertson, *Globalization* (London: Sage, 1992), 8.
2. Gilbert Herdt, *Third Sex, Third Gender* (New York: Zone Books, 1994), 12.
3. Alison Murray, "Femme on the Streets, Butch in the Sheets," in D. Bell and G. Valentine, eds., *Mapping Desire* (London: Routledge, 1995), 70.
4. Nancy Fraser, *Justice Interruptus* (New York: Routledge, 1996), esp. chap. 1, "From Redistribution to Recognition?" 11–39.
5. On social constructionist debates see David Greenberg, *The Construction of Homosexuality* (Chicago: University of Chicago Press, 1988); Carole Vance, "Social Construction Theory: Problems in the History of Sexuality," in A. van Kooten Niekerk and T. van der Meer, eds., *Homosexuality, Which Homosexuality?* (London: Gay Men's Press, 1989), 13–34.
6. The same sense of the bathhouse as a zone of pleasure is found in Ferzon Ospetek's 1988 film *Hammam,* an Italian-Turkish coproduction. Other cultures have created similar erotic spaces out of communal bathhouses. See, e.g., Scott Clark, "The Japanese Bath: Extraordinarily Ordinary," in J. Tobin, ed., *Re-Made in Japan* (New Haven: Yale University Press, 1992).
7. Michael Ignatieff, "The Temple of Pleasure," *Time Magazine.*

8. Beryl Langer, "The Body in the Library," in L. Dale and S. Ryan, eds., *Cross/ Cultures: Readings in the Post/Colonial Literatures in English* (Amsterdam: Rodopi, 1994), 15–34.

9. *New York Times,* July 21, 1962, quoted in Charles Kaiser, *The Gay Metropolis, 1940– 1996* (Boston: Houghton Mifflin, 1997), 80.

10. Gayle Rubin, "The Traffic in Women: Notes on the Political Economy of Sex," in R. Reiter, ed., *Toward an Anthropology of Women* (New York: Monthly Review Press, 1975). This and her later article "Thinking Sex: Notes for a Radical Theory of the Politics of Sexuality," in C. Vance, ed., *Pleasure and Danger* (Boston: Routledge & Kegan Paul, 1984), 267–319, have had a huge influence on continuing feminist and gay theorizing about sexuality.

11. "Looking for Love," *Far Eastern Economic Review,* January 20, 2000, 32.

12. In the 1990s the highest divorce rates were found in European countries in the former Soviet Union (Estonia, Latvia, and Russia). See Joni Seager, *The State of Women in the World Atlas* (London: Penguin, 1997), 23.

13. And compare Eduardo Archetti, "Playing Styles and Masculine Virtues in Argentine Football," in M. Melhuus and K. A. Stolen, eds., *Machos, Mistresses, Madonnas* (London: Verso, 1996), 34–55.

14. Brian Pronger, *The Arena of Masculinity: Sports, Homosexuality, and the Meaning of Sex* (New York: St. Martin's Press, 1990).

15. Kim Berman, "Lesbians in South Africa," in M. Krouse, ed., *The Invisible Ghetto: Lesbian and Gay Writing from South Africa* (London: Gay Men's Press, 1995), xviii.

16. V. Spike Petersen and Jacqui True, "'New Times' and New Conversations," in M. Zalewski and J. Parpart, eds., *The "Man" Question in International Relations* (New York: Westview, 1998), 25 n. 11.

17. Gary Dowsett and Peter Aggleton, "Young People and Risk-Taking in Sexual Relations," in *Sex and Youth: Contextual Factors Affecting Risk for HIV/AIDS* (Geneva: UNAIDS, 1999), 36. The seven countries were Cambodia, Cameroon, Chile, Costa Rica, Papua New Guinea, the Philippines, and Zimbabwe.

18. Grace Osakue and Adriane Martin-Hilber, "Women's Sexuality and Fertility in Nigeria," in R. Petchesky and K. Judd, eds., *Negotiating Reproductive Rights* (London: Zed, 1998), 196.

19. Anthony Giddens, "Family," 1999 BBC Reith Lectures, no. 4 (news.bbc.co.uk/hi/ english/static/events/reith_99).

20. Gail Pheterson, *The Prostitution Prism* (Amsterdam: Amsterdam University Press, 1996), 24.

21. R. W. Connell, *Masculinities* (Sydney: Allen & Unwin, 1995), 77.

22. Marta Lamas, "Scenes from a Mexican Battlefield," *NACLA Report on the Americas,* January–February 1998, 17.

23. David Landes, *The Wealth and Poverty of Nations* (New York: Norton, 1998), 414.

24. Silvana Paternostro, *In the Land of God and Man* (New York: Dutton, 1998), 308.

25. There is a brief discussion of the meanings of machismo in Marit Melhuus, "Power, Value, and the Ambiguous Meanings of Gender," in Melhuus and Stolen, *Machos, Mistresses, Madonnas,* 240–44.

26. Sarah Radcliffe, "Women's Place in Latin America," in M. Keith and S. Pile, eds., *Place and the Politics of Identity* (London: Routledge, 1993), 111.

27. Martha Macintyre, "Melanesian Women and Human Rights," in A. M. Hilsdon, M. Macintyre, V. Mackie, and M. Stivens, eds., *Human Rights and Gender Politics: Asia-Pacific Perspectives* (London: Routledge, 2000), 154.

28. Jan Jindy Pettman, *Worlding Women* (Sydney: Allen & Unwin, 1996), 187.

29. Lillian Ng, *Swallowing Clouds* (Melbourne: Penguin Books, 1997), 153–54.

30. Richard Parker, *Beneath the Equator* (New York: Routledge, 1999), 74.

31. Peter Gordon and Kate Crehan, "Dying of Sadness: Gender, Sexual Violence, and the HIV Epidemic," UNDP HIV and Development Program Paper FF964 (New York: UNDP, 1999).

32. "Migration and HIV," *Newspaper of the XII International AIDS Conference*, Geneva, July 2, 1998. See also Vesna Nikolic-Ristanovic, "War and Violence against Women," in J. Turpin and L. Lorentzen, eds., *The Gendered New World Order* (New York: Routledge, 1996); Amnesty International, *Bosnia-Herzegovina: Rape and Sexual Abuse by Armed Forces* (London: Amnesty International, 1993).

33. See Boris Davidovich, *Serbian Diaries* (London: Gay Men's Press, 1996).

34. Linda Grant, *Sexing the Millennium* (New York: Grove, 1994), 5.

35. Nikos Papastergiadis, *Dialogues in the Diasporas* (London: Rivers Oram, 1998), 149.

36. See Penelope Andrews, "Violence against Women in South Africa," *Temple Political and Civil Rights Law Review* 8:2 (1999): 425–57.

37. Graeme Simpson and Gerald Kraak, "The Illusions of Sanctuary and the Weight of the Past: Notes on Violence and Gender in South Africa," *Development Update* (Braamfontein) 2:2 (1998): 8.

38. See Jeffrey Alexander, "Modern, Anti, Post, Neo," *New Left Review*, March–April 1995, 63–101.

TWO

1. Bruce Rich, *Mortgaging the Earth* (Boston: Beacon, 1994), 2.

2. See Thanh-dam Truong, *Sex, Money, and Morality* (London: Zed, 1990); Rita Brock and Susan Thistlethwaite, *Casting Stones: Prostitution and Liberation in Asia and the United States* (Minneapolis: Fortress Press, 1996).

3. I owe this story to Michael Connors, who researched it through issues of the *Nation* (Bangkok) in June–July 1993. See also Annette Hamilton, "Primal Dream: Masculinism, Sin, and Salvation in Thailand's Sex Trade," in L. Manderson and M. Jolly, eds., *Sites of Desire, Economies of Pleasure* (Chicago: University of Chicago Press, 1997), 145.

4. Elliott Kulick and Dick Wilson, *Thailand's Turn* (London: Macmillan, 1992), 121.

5. William Greider, *One World, Ready or Not* (New York: Simon & Schuster, 1997), 348.

6. See Lourdes Arguelles and Ruby Rich, "Homosexuality, Homophobia, and Revolution: Notes towards an Understanding of the Cuban Lesbian and Gay Experience," *Signs* 9:4 (1984): 686–87.

7. See Ryan Bishop and Lillian Robinson, *Night Market: Sexual Cultures and the Thai Economic Miracle* (New York: Routledge, 1998), chap. 2.

8. Albert Goldman, *The Lives of John Lennon* (New York: Bantam, 1988), 683.

9. Stefan Zweig, *The World of Yesterday* (Lincoln: University of Nebraska Press, 1964; originally published 1943), 83. I owe this reference to Judith Brett.

10. See Donna Guy, *Sex and Danger in Buenos Aires* (Lincoln: University of Nebraska Press, 1990), esp. chap. 1.

11. Sueann Caulfield, "The Birth of Mangue," in D. Balderston and D. Guy, eds., *Sex and Sexuality in Latin America* (New York: New York University Press, 1997), 89.

12. Guy, *Sex and Danger,* 34–35.

13. Peter Hall, *Cities in Civilization* (London: Weidenfeld & Nicolson, 1998), esp. 192–200.

14. See Jacques le Rider, "Between Modernism and Postmodernism," in E. Timms and R. Robertson, eds., *Vienna 1990* (Edinburgh: Edinburgh University Press, 1990), 3.

15. Alex Callinicos, *Against Postmodernism* (Cambridge: Polity Press, 1989), 45.

16. John Updike, "Can Genitals Be Beautiful?" *New York Review of Books,* December 4, 1997, 10–12.

17. On the sexual themes of Klimt's art see Carl Schorske, *Fin-de-Siècle Vienna* (New York: Knopf, 1990), 224–25.

18. This title is a French translation of the original German title, *Reigen,* and is the title of a 1950 French film directed by Max Ophüls. It is also known as *The Round Dance* (English version translated by Charles Osborne [Manchester: Carcanet New Press, 1982]), and was the basis for David Hare's *Blue Room,* which achieved considerable success in London and New York at the end of the 1990s. Schnitzler was greatly admired by Freud for his examination of bourgeois sexuality. See Bruce Thompson, *Schnitzler's Vienna* (New York: Routledge, 1990), esp. chap. 3.

19. See Seabrook, *In the Cities of the South,* chap. 10.

20. See Schorske, *Fin-de-Siècle Vienna,* chap. 2.

21. For two recent fictional attempts to come to grips with contemporary Bangkok see Lawrence Chua, *Gold by the Inch* (New York: Grove, 1998), and Gregory Bracken, *Unusual Wealth* (Bangkok: Asia Books, 1998).

22. E.g., Bryan Turner, *Orientalism, Postmodernism, and Globalism* (London: Routledge, 1994), 108.

23. Peter Beinart, "An Illusion for Our Time," *New Republic,* October 20, 1997, 21; "The Century the Earth Stood Still," *Economist,* December 20, 1997.

24. Karl Marx, "Manifesto of the Communist Party," in Marx, *The Revolutions of 1848,* ed. D. Fernbach (Harmondsworth: Penguin, 1973), 70.

25. Theo Varlet, *Roc d'Or* (Paris: Serpent de Plumes, 1997; originally published 1927), 15, (my translation).

26. See Pattara Danutra, "A Useful Catchword or Linguistic Lamprey?" *Bangkok Post,* July 8, 1995; Charnvit Kasetsiri, "Siam/Civilization—Thailand/Globalization: Things to Come," paper presented at the International Association of the Historians of Asia Conference, Chulalongkorn University, Bangkok, May 1996.

27. David Held, "Democracy, the Nation-State, and the Global System," *Economy and Society* 20:2 (1991): 145. This argument is expanded in D. Held, A. McGrew,

D. Goldblatt, and J. Perraton, *Global Transformations* (Cambridge: Polity, 1999), 424–35. See also Manuel Castells, *The Information Age*, 3 vols. (Oxford: Blackwell, 1996–98), and the long review article by Peter Waterman, "The Brave New World of Manuel Castells," *Development and Change* 30 (1999): 357–80.

28. Ulrich Beck, *World Risk Society* (Cambridge: Polity, 1999), 1–8. Compare Frederick Jameson, "Postmodernism, or the Cultural Logic of Capitalism," *New Left Review*, July–August 1984, 53–93; Deena Weinstein and Michael Weinstein, *Postmodern(ized) Simmel* (London: Routledge, 1993).

29. See, e.g., David Harvey, *The Condition of Postmodernism* (Oxford: Blackwell, 1989).

30. See, e.g., Kim Dovey, *Framing Places: Mediating Power in Built Form* (London: Routledge, 1999), 158–60.

31. A similar argument is made by Ian Taylor, Karen Evans, and Penny Fraser, *A Tale of Two Cities: Global Change, Local Feeling, and Everyday Life in the North of England* (London: Routledge, 1996), 9–11. There is a very different perspective in Zygmunt Bauman, *Work, Consumerism, and the New Poor* (Buckingham: Open University Press, 1998), chap. 1.

32. Tony Judt, "A la recherche du temps perdu," *New York Review of Books*, December 3, 1998, 52.

33. Julian Barnes, "Always True to France," *New York Review of Books*, August 12, 1999, 29.

34. Shelly Simonds, "Satellite TV Loosens Mid-East Regimes' Grip," *Australian National University Reporter*, April 8, 1998, 8. For an overview of the impact of television on globalization see Philip Carl Salzman, "The Electronic Trojan Horse," in L. Arizpe, ed., *The Cultural Dimensions of Global Change* (Paris: UNESCO, 1996), 197–216.

35. Wang Jiang and Chang Tsan-kuo, "From Class Ideologue to State Manager: TV Programming and Foreign Imports in China, 1970–1990," *Journal of Broadcasting and Electronic Media* 40:2 (1996): 196–207. Thanks to Chris Carroll for this reference.

36. Saskia Sassen has discussed the new patterns of migration, and their relationship to globalization. See her *Globalization and Its Discontents* (New York: New Press, 1998), section 1.

37. Iain Chambers, *Migrancy, Culture, Identity* (London: Routledge, 1994), 3.

38. This description of the Yanaua detention camp is taken from a 1995 report of the United Nations High Commission for Refugees, quoted in MAHA News (mahanews@lists.e-net.ch). MAHA stands for Migrants against HIV/AIDS, and is based in Bagnolet, France.

39. On the new international elite see Christopher Lasch, *The Revolt of the Elites* (New York: Norton, 1995); and Peter Berger, "Globalisation and Culture: Not Simply the West versus the Rest," paper from the Centre for Development and Enterprise, Johannesburg, January 1999.

40. Jane Margold, "Narratives of Masculinity and Transnational Migration," in A. Ong and M. Peletz, eds., *Bewitching Women, Pious Men: Gender and Body Politics in Southeast Asia* (Berkeley: University of California Press, 1995), 292–93. There is a graphic, if picaresque, account of migrant Filipino workers in Timothy Mo, *Renegade or Halo?* (London: Paddlepress, 1999).

41. See Joel Kahn, *Culture, Multiculture, Postculture* (London: Sage, 1995), 106.

42. These figures are taken from a special issue on migration, *New Internationalist*, September 1998, 18–19.

43. In the mid-1990s it was estimated that there were 6 million Filipino workers abroad, one-tenth of the entire population. See *Asia and Pacific Migration Journal* 7:1 (1998).

44. Andrew Kilvert, "Golden Promises," *New Internationalist*, September 1998, 16–17.

45. For background see Richard Lloyd Parry, "What Young Men Do," *Granta* 62 (summer 1998): 85–123.

46. Arjun Appadurai, "Patriotism and Its Futures," *Public Culture* 5:3 (1993): 424.

47. Leila Gandhi, *Postcolonial Theory* (Sydney: Allen & Unwin, 1998), 4.

48. Tony Burke, "Faithful Son Is Primed," *Age* (Melbourne), November 3, 1998, Sports section, 1.

49. There are many examples of this sort of argument. See, e.g., Stephen Gill, "New Constitutionalism, Democratisation, and Global Political Economy," *Pacifica Review* 10:1 (1998): 23–38.

50. For one example of the impact of neoliberalism see Lynne Haney, "'But We Are Still Mothers': Gender, the State, and the Construction of Need in Postsocialist Hungary," in M. Buroway and K. Verdery, eds., *Uncertain Transition* (Lanham, MD: Rowman & Littlefield, 1999), 151–87.

51. Zygmunt Bauman, *Globalization: The Human Consequences* (Cambridge: Polity, 1998), 103–4.

52. See, e.g., Susan George and Sabelli Fabrizio, *Faith and Credit: The World Bank's Secular Empire* (London: Penguin, 1994); D. Ghai, *The IMF and the South* (London: Zed, 1991); Walden Bello, *Dark Victory: The United States, Structural Adjustment, and Global Poverty* (London: Pluto, 1994).

53. Richard Cornwell, "Who Will Control Africa in the Twenty First Century?" unpublished paper, Institute for Security Studies, Johannesburg, 1998.

54. UNDP, *Human Development Report* (New York: Oxford University Press, 1998).

55. Joseph Hanlon, "A Pound of Flesh," *New Internationalist*, March 1999, 27.

56. "Drop the Debt," *New Internationalist*, May 1999, 9.

57. Seabrook, *In the Cities of the South*, 298.

58. Greider, *One World, Ready or Not*, 467.

59. Paul Smith, *Millennial Dreams: Contemporary Culture and Capital in the North* (London: Verso, 1997), 56.

60. I owe this last example to Richard Parker, who discusses it in *Beneath the Equator*, 159–60.

61. The list of such futuristic novels is huge. Perhaps the best known is Phillip Dick, *Do Androids Dream of Electric Sheep?* (London: Grafton, 1972) (filmed as *Blade Runner*). But consider also Philip Kerr, *A Philosophical Investigation* (London: Chatto & Windus, 1992); Paul Johnston, *Body Politic* (London: Hodder & Staughton, 1997); Neal Stephenson, *The Diamond Age* (New York: Bantam, 1995); Adrian Mathews, *Vienna Blood* (London: Jonathan Cape, 1999).

62. See Om Prakash Mathur, "Sustaining India's Megacities," in Toh Thian Ser, ed.,

Megacities, Labour, and Communications (Singapore: Institute for Southeast Asian Studies, 1998).

63. Michael Dutton, *Streetlife China* (Cambridge: Cambridge University Press, 1998), 10–11.

64. George Yudice, Jean Franco, and Juan Flores, introduction to *On Edge: The Crisis of Contemporary Latin American Culture* (Minneapolis: University of Minnesota Press, 1992), viii.

65. Benjamin Barber, "Jihad versus McWorld," *Atlantic Monthly*, March 1992, 53 (later expanded as *Jihad versus McWorld* [New York: Times Books, 1995]).

66. "Tunisia" (sponsored section), *International Herald Tribune*, November 7–8, 1998, 22.

67. See, e.g., George Ritzer, *The McDonaldization of Society* (Thousand Oaks, CA: Pine Forge Press, 1993), and *The McDonaldization Thesis* (London: Sage, 1998); James Watson, *Golden Arches East* (Stanford, CA: Stanford University Press, 1997). The last of these gives several examples of the impact of McDonald's on cultural practices, such as improved standards of hygiene.

68. Friedman, *The Lexus and the Olive Tree*, 235, 195–96.

69. Eric Reguly, "The Devouring of Corporate Canada," *Report on Business* (Toronto), September 4, 1999. At the time this article was published it seemed likely that the two major Canadian airlines would be merged and come under the control of a Canadian company with very close ties to United Airlines.

70. Gearoid Tuathail, Andrew Herod, and Susan Roberts, "Negotiating Unruly Problematics," in Herod, Tuathail, and Roberts, *An Unruly World?* (London: Routledge, 1998), 12.

71. Bales estimates that there are 27 million slaves in the world today, defining slavery as "the total control of one person by another for the purpose of economic exploitation" (Kevin Bales, *Disposable People: New Slavery in the Global Economy* [Berkeley: University of California Press, 1999], 6).

72. Anatol Lieven, "History Is Not Bunk," *Prospect*, October 1998.

73. Lester Thurow, *The Future of Capitalism* (New York: Morrow, 1996), 119.

74. Thus one "turbofolk" song in Serbia, strongly supportive of the Milosevic regime, invoked "Coca-Cola, Marlboro, Suzuki/Discotheques, guitars and bouzouki." Quoted in Laura Secor, review of Eric Gordy, *The Culture of Power in Serbia*, *Lingua Franca*, fall 1999, B27.

75. Harold Pinter, *"Party Time" and "The New World Order": Two Plays* (New York: Grove, 1993).

76. As do Jozsef Borocz and David Smith in their introduction to Smith and Borocz, eds., *A New World Order?* (Westport, CT: Greenwood, 1995), 2. Paul Ekins uses the term to discuss quite different approaches to those envisaged by Bush in his *A New World Order: Grassroots Movements for Global Change* (London: Routledge, 1992).

77. Neal Stephenson, *Snow Crash* (London: Bantam, 1992), 3.

78. Greider, *One World, Ready or Not*, esp. 192–93. Stephenson's preoccupation with Japan is echoed in William Gibson's *Idoru* (New York: Putnam, 1996).

79. Martin Walker, "The Clinton Doctrine," *New Yorker*, October 7, 1996, 6–8.

80. This is the argument of Alfredo Valladao, *The Twenty First Century Will Be American* (New York: Verso, 1996). Compare the various contributors to D. Slater and P. Taylor, eds., *The American Century* (Oxford: Blackwell, 1999).

81. For an argument about how CNN has helped globalize the fashion industry see Rebecca Mead, "Elsa's Reign," *New Yorker,* September 20, 1999, 76–83.

82. Mark Johnson, *Beauty and Power: Transgendering and Cultural Transformation in the Southern Philippines* (Oxford: Berg, 1997).

83. Deborah Amory, "*Mashoga, Mabasha,* and *Magai:* 'Homosexuality' on the East African Coast," in S. Murray and W. Roscoe, eds., *Boy-Wives and Female Husbands* (New York: St. Martin's, 1998), 85.

84. Salman Rushdie, *The Ground beneath Her Feet* (London: Jonathan Cape, 1999), 59.

85. Leo Ching, "Imaginings in the Empires of the Sun," in J. Treat, ed., *Contemporary Japan and Popular Culture* (Honolulu: University of Hawaii Press, 1997), 171.

86. Michael Keane, "Ethics and Pragmatism: China's Television Producers Confront the Cultural Market," *Media International Australia,* November 1998, esp. 77–78.

87. Sam Quinones, "Hooked on Telenovelas," *Hemispheres* (American Airlines), November 1997.

88. Wim Lunsing, "The 5th Asian Congress of Sexology, Seoul, November 1998," *Sexualities* 2:2 (1999): 383.

89. See James Larson and Heung-Soo Park, *Global Television and the Politics of the Seoul Olympics* (Boulder: Westview, 1993).

90. Beryl Langer, "Coca-Colonials Write Back," in K. Burridge, L. Foster, and G. Turcotte, eds., *Canada-Australia, 1895–1995: Towards a Second Century of Partnership* (Ottawa: Carleton University Press, 1997), 487. Compare John Street, "The Limits of Global Popular Culture," in A. Scott, ed., *The Limits of Globalization* (New York: Routledge, 1997), 75–89.

91. Edward Herman and Robert McChesney, *The Global Media* (London: Cassell, 1997), 19.

92. "Star Wars," *Economist,* March 22, 1997.

93. Thurow, *Future of Capitalism,* 133.

94. See Simon During, "Popular Culture on a Global Scale," *Critical Inquiry* 23 (summer 1997): 808–33.

95. For a discussion of the importance of "cultural multinational corporations," all of which are either American-owned or depend upon a sizeable American base, see Held et al., *Global Transformations,* 346–50.

96. "Survey: Technology and Entertainment," *Economist,* November 21, 1998, 12.

97. Wayne Ellwood, "Inside the Disney Dream Machine," *New Internationalist,* December 1998, 7. It is worth going back to Ariel Dorfman and Armand Mattelart, *How to Read Donald Duck* (New York: International General, 1975; originally published in 1971 in Chile), one of the first analyses of the impact of American comic-book culture on the south.

98. Kathi Maio, "Disney's Dolls," *New Internationalist,* December 1998, 12–14.

99. For a warning against too triumphalist a view of the growth of English see Joshua Fishman, "The New Linguistic Order," *Foreign Policy,* winter 1998–99, 26–40.

100. Compare the extraordinary reticence surrounding gay characters in shows like *Melrose Place* and *Will and Grace* with the gritty realism of *This Life* or *Queer as Folk*.

101. "Video Quotas," *Straights Times* (Singapore), February 5, 1999.

102. Lexington, "The Versace Controversy," *Economist,* July 19, 1997, 40.

103. Christopher Hitchens, *Blood, Class, and Nostalgia* (New York: Farrar, Straus, 1990), 30.

104. Robert Kaplan, *The Ends of the Earth* (New York: Random House, 1996), 279.

105. Arjun Appadurai, *Modernity at Large* (Minneapolis: University of Minnesota Press, 1996), 40.

106. Cynthia Enloe, *The Morning After: Sexual Politics at the End of the Cold War* (Berkeley: University of California Press, 1993), 72–75.

107. Kasian Tejapira, "The Postmodernization of Thainess," Proceedings of the Sixth International Conference on Thai Studies, Chiang Mai, October 14–17, 1996, 397.

THREE

1. Nancy Folbre, "The Improper Arts: Sex in Classical Political Economy," *Population and Development Review* 18:1 (1992), 105–21.

2. See, e.g., Rhonda Gottlieb, "The Political Economy of Sexuality," *Review of Radical Political Economics* 16:1 (1984): 143–65.

3. I am thinking here in particular of Marcuse's *Essay on Liberation* (Boston: Beacon, 1969).

4. Joel Kovel, *The Radical Spirit* (London: Free Association Books, 1988), 5. Thanks to Robert Reynolds for directing me to Kovel.

5. Michaela di Leonardo and Roger Lancaster, "Gender, Sexuality, Political Economy," *New Politics,* summer 1996 , 29–43.

6. Pettman, *Worlding Women.* (I am more inclined than Pettman to see gender as only one axis of inequality.)

7. As Aijaz Ahmad writes: "This reduction of Marxism to an element amongst other elements in the analytics of textual reading means—at the very least, and even where that hostility is less marked—that the problem of the determinate set of mediations which connect the cultural productions of a period with other kinds of productions and political processes, which is one of the central problems of Marxist cultural historiography, is rarely addressed with any degree of rigour in precisely those branches of literary theory where issues of colony and empire are most lengthily addressed" (*In Theory* [London: Verso, 1992], 5). Compare Nigel Thrift, "The Rise of Soft Capitalism," in Herod, Tuathail, and Roberts, *Unruly World,* esp. 26–28; Etienne Balibar, "Has 'the World' Changed?" in A. Callari, S. Cullenberg, and C. Biewener, eds., *Marxism in the Postmodern Age* (New York: Guilford, 1995), 405–14.

8. Diane Nelson, *A Finger in the Wound: Body Politics in Quincentennial Guatemala* (Berkeley: University of California Press, 1999), 351.

9. See Nancy Fraser, *Justice Interruptus,* and her "Heterosexism, Misrecognition, and

Capitalism: A Response to Judith Butler," *Social Text* 52–53 (fall/winter 1997): 279–89.

10. Fraser, *Justice Interruptus*, 15.

11. Teresa Ebert, *Ludic Feminism and After* (Ann Arbor: University of Michigan Press, 1995), 214.

12. Megan Vaughan, "Syphilis in Colonial East and Central Africa: The Social Construction of an Epidemic," in T. Ranger and P. Slack, eds., *Epidemics and Ideas* (Cambridge: Cambridge University Press, 1992), 269–302.

13. E.g., Biliana Vassileva and Milena Komarova, "Young People, Social Relationships, and Sexuality in Bulgaria," in J.-P. Moatti et al., *AIDS in Europe* (London: Routledge, 2000), 135–46.

14. "Auto-da-fe," in *Candide*, music by Leonard Bernstein, lyrics by Richard Wilbur (final revised version, 1989).

15. R. W. Connell, "Sexual Revolution," in L. Segal, ed., *New Sexual Agendas* (London: Macmillan, 1997), 60–76. Compare Edward Lautmann, John Gagnon, Robert Michael, and Stuart Michaels, *The Social Organization of Sexuality* (Chicago: University of Chicago Press, 1994).

16. See "The Condom Controversy," *Asiaweek*, January 19, 1994, 30–31.

17. Francis Fukuyama, "Why Japan Has Been Right to Wonder about the Pill," *International Herald Tribune*, June 10, 1999.

18. During the 1990s worldwide sales of condoms increased by 15% a year, according to a report by one company. See "Go Forth and Don't Multiply," *Economist*, June 19, 1999, 68. UNAIDS claims there has been considerable success in promoting condoms in a number of poor countries, including Thailand, Senegal, and Uganda.

19. Churnrutai Kanchanchitra, "Income Generation and Reduction of Women Entering Sex Work in Thailand," paper presented at Meeting on Effective Approaches for the Prevention of HIV/AIDS in Women, Geneva, February 1995.

20. See Ronald Ingelhart, *Modernization and Postmodernization* (Princeton: Princeton University Press, 1997), 276–80.

21. Anthony Giddens, "Dare to Care, Conserve, and Repair," *New Statesman and Society*, October 29, 1994, 18.

22. Don DeLillo, *Underworld* (London: Picador, 1998), 786.

23. Arthur Golden, *Memoirs of a Geisha* (London: Chatto & Windus, 1997), 153.

24. The word *sekuhara* has become widely used to mean sexual harassment in Japan. See Yoshio Sugimoto, *An Introduction to Japanese Society* (Cambridge: Cambridge University Press, 1997), 157.

25. Nicholas Bornoff, *Pink Samurai* (London: Grafton, 1991), 119–20.

26. Marta Savigliano, "Tango in Japan and the World Economy of Pleasure," in Tobin, *Re-Made in Japan*, 237.

27. Jose Quiroga, "Homosexualities in the Tropic of Revolution," in Balderston and Guy, *Sex and Sexuality in Latin America*, 134.

28. Marina Warner, *No Go the Bogeyman* (London: Chatto & Windus, 1998), 363.

29. For a discussion of how reggae has changed as Jamaica has been more effectively incorporated into the "global economy" see Andrew Ross, "Mr. Reggae DJ, Meet

the International Monetary Fund," in Ross, *Real Love* (London: Routledge, 1998), 35–70.

30. Neville Hoad, "Arrested Development or the Queerness of Savages," *postcolonial studies* 3: 2 (July 2000): 138.

31. Vance, *Pleasure and Danger.*

32. Jill Julius Matthews, "The 'Present Moment' in Sexual Politics," in R. W. Connell and G. W. Dowsett, eds., *Rethinking Sex* (Melbourne: Melbourne University Press, 1992), 126.

33. See Christopher Murray and Alan Lopez, *Health Dimensions of Sex and Reproduction* (Boston: Harvard School of Public Health, 1998).

34. Lenore Manderson and Margaret Jolly, introduction to *Sites of Desire,* 24.

35. Enloe, *Morning After,* 104.

36. R. W. Connell, "New Directions in Gender Theory, Masculinity Research, and Gender Politics," *Ethnos* 61:3–4 (1996): 175.

37. MacInnes, *End of Masculinity,* 1.

38. Barbara Ehrenreich, *The Hearts of Men: American Dreams and the Flight from Commitment* (New York: Doubleday, 1983).

39. Claire Miller, "Women Fight for a Nation Losing Its Hope," *Age* (Melbourne), December 12, 1998.

40. Seager, *State of Women in the World Atlas,* 20–21.

41. Agnes Runganaga and Peter Aggleton, "Migration, the Family, and the Transformation of a Sexual Culture," *Sexualities* 1:1 (1998): 73.

42. *The Wedding Banquet* (1993), directed by Ang Lee; *Happy Together* (1997), directed by Wong Kar-wai.

43. See Karen Kelsky, "Intimate Ideologies: Transnational Theory and Japan's 'Yellow Cabs,'" *Public Culture* 6 (1994): 465–78.

44. See Janet Hadley, *Abortion: Between Freedom and Necessity* (London: Vintage, 1996), 15–23, 135.

45. Wan Yan-hai, "Sexual Work and Its Public Policies in China," paper presented at International Conference on Prostitution, Van Nuys, CA, March 1997. For one overview of the Chinese situation see Borge Bakken, "Never for the First Time: 'Premature Love and Social Control in Today's China,'" *China Information* (Leiden) 7:3 (1992/93).

46. Compare current descriptions of sex in China—e.g., George Wehrfritz, "Unbuttoning a Nation," *Newsweek,* April 16, 1996—with Steven Mosher, *Broken Earth: The Rural Chinese* (New York: Free Press, 1986).

47. National AIDS Committee and UNAIDS, *Partnership in Action: HIV/AIDS in Vietnam* (Hanoi, 1998), 7.

48. Todd Crowell and Anne Naham, "A Communist Theme Park," *Asiaweek,* January 22, 1999, 34–37.

49. These figures were reported at an AIDS conference in 1999. See Daniel Kwan, "HIV Cases to Reach 1.2m. Next Year," *South China Morning Post,* February 1, 1999. For one vision of what this might mean see Stephenson, *Diamond Age.*

50. "STD Rise Highest in Decade," South China Morning Post Online, May 7, 1999 (www.scmp.com).

51. Francis Fukuyama, "Asian Values and the Asian Crisis," *Commentary,* February 1998, 27.

52. See Julia Suryakusuma, "The State and Sexuality in New Order Indonesia," in L. Sears, ed., *Fantasizing the Feminine in Indonesia* (Durham: Duke University Press, 1996), 92–119.

53. David Hill and Krishna Sen, "Rock'n'Roll Radicals," *Inside Indonesia,* October–December 1997, 27.

54. See Aihwa Ong, "State versus Islam: Malay Families, Women's Bodies, and the Body Politic in Malaysia," in Ong and Peletz, *Bewitching Women, Pious Men,* 159–94.

55. Anthony Pramualratana, "HIV/AIDS in Thailand," UNAIDS Position Paper, January 1998.

56. Michel Caraël, Anne Buvé, and Kofi Awusabo-Asare, "The Making of HIV Epidemics: What Are the Driving Forces?" *AIDS* 11, supp. B (1997): S27.

57. "The Price of Honor," *Time Magazine,* January 18, 1999.

58. Karen Thomas, "Women Fight Jordan's Licence to Kill," *Age* (Melbourne), September 8, 1999.

59. See, e.g., Marlise Simons, "Unmarried Mothers Outcasts in Morocco," *International Herald Tribune,* February 2, 1999, 2.

60. See, e.g., Sugimoto, *Introduction to Japanese Society,* 241; Prangtip Daorueng, "Sole Sisters," *Far Eastern Economic Review,* September 3, 1998, 36–37.

61. Ruth Adam, *A Woman's Place* (London: Chatto & Windus, 1975); Tuula Gordon, *Single Women* (London: Macmillan, 1994).

62. By the end of the century same-sex relationships enjoyed various forms of legal recognition in about a dozen European countries, mainly in northwest Europe but including the Czech Republic and Catalonia.

63. "Having It Both Ways, à la Francaise," *Economist,* September 26, 1998, 60.

64. Rex Wockner, "Canada Defines Marriage Heterosexually," International News, San Francisco, June 14, 1999.

65. See Jonathan Goldberg-Hiller, "The Status of Status: Domestic Partnership and the Politics of Same-Sex Marriage," *Studies in Law, Politics, and Society* 19 (1999): 3–38.

66. Sue Willmer, "Lesbians in Mexico," in R. Phillips, D. Watt, and D. Shuttleton, eds., *Decentering Sexualities* (London: Routledge, 2000): 177–8.

67. "Activists Battle to Preserve Constitutional Rights for Sexual Minorities," International Gay and Lesbian Human Rights Commission (San Francisco), *Action Alert* 7:1 (1999). In various ways sexual orientation has constitutional protection in Canada, South Africa, and Ecuador, in the last case having been introduced after local activists took the South African constitution as a model.

68. National Coalition for Gay and Lesbian Equality, "A Lesbian and Gay Guide to the 1999 Election" (Johannesburg, 1999).

69. Quoted in *8th May Newsletter* (London), May 1999.

70. Peter Drucker, "Introduction: Remapping Sexual Identities," in P. Drucker, ed., *Different Rainbows* (London: Gay Men's Press, 2000): 15.

FOUR

1. There is an interesting comment on the successes of at least part of the sexual liberationist agenda in Henning Bech, "After the Closet," *Sexualities* 2:3 (1999): 343–46.
2. See Margaret Keck and Kathryn Sikkink, *Activists beyond Borders* (Ithaca: Cornell University Press, 1998), chap. 2.
3. Kenneth Dutton, *The Perfectible Body* (New York: Continuum, 1995), 12.
4. See Bryan Turner, *The Body and Society*, 2nd edition (London: Sage, 1996), 172.
5. Dennis Wrong, "The Over-socialized Conception of Man in Modern Sociology," *American Sociological Review*, no. 26 (1961): 129.
6. Michel Foucault, "Nietzsche, Genealogy, History," quoted by Deborah Lupton, *The Imperative of Health* (London: Sage, 1995), 6. This is one of a plethora of books written in the 1990s which were strongly influenced by a Foucauldian reading of governmentality and the body.
7. A recent—and rather underrated—attempt to explore ways of linking a Marxist and a postmodern approach to the body is Donald Lowe, *The Body in Late-Capitalist USA* (Durham: Duke University Press, 1995).
8. Turner, *Body and Society*, 2.
9. Jean Starobinski, "A Short History of Body Consciousness," *Humanities in Review* (New York Institute for the Humanities) 1 (1982): 38.
10. Rosalyn Baxandall, "Marxism and Sexuality: The Body as Battleground," in Callari, Cullenberg, and Biewener, *Marxism in the Postmodern Age*, 244.
11. Emily Martin, "The End of the Body?" *American Ethnologist* 19:1 (1992): 121–22.
12. John D'Emilio, "Capitalism and Gay Identity," in A. Snitow, C. Stansell, and S. Thompson, eds., *Powers of Desire* (New York: Monthly Review Press, 1983); Dennis Altman, *The Homosexualization of America* (New York: St. Martin's, 1982), chap. 3. Much of the standard literature on the body ignores gay/lesbian writings. A typical example is Anthony Synnott, *The Body Social* (London: Routledge, 1993), which given its publication date is remarkably unaware of any of the relevant literature.
13. A good example of this is the stringent reading of Rubin in Nancy Hartsock, *The Feminist Standpoint Revisited and Other Essays* (Boulder: Westview, 1998), 192–204.
14. See David Halperin, *Saint Foucault* (New York: Oxford University Press, 1995), 31.
15. The literature here is immense. See, e.g., Jeffrey Escoffier, "From Community to University," in Escoffier, *American Homo* (Berkeley: University of California Press, 1998), 118–41; Steven Seidman, *Difference Troubles* (New York: Cambridge University Press, 1997); and such feminist postmodern theorists as Jane Flax, Joan Scott, and Judith Butler.
16. Shulamith Firestone, *The Dialectic of Sex* (New York: Morrow, 1970).
17. Agatha Christie, *At Bertram's Hotel* (London: Fontana, 1967), 97–98.
18. Thomas Disch claims the term "cyberpunk" was first used in 1982, by the Australian writer Damien Broderick, and quotes William Gibson's definition of "cyberspace" in his 1986 novel *Burning Chrome*: "Mankind's extended electric nervous system, rustling data and credit in the crowded matrix, monochrome nonspace where

the only stars are dense concentrations of information, and high above it all burn corporate galaxies and the cold spiral arms of military systems" (Thomas Disch, *The Dreams Our Stuff Is Made Of* [New York: Free Press, 1998], 216).

19. Donna Haraway, "A Manifesto for Cyborgs: Science, Technology, and Socialist Feminism in the 1980s," *Socialist Review*, no. 80 (1985): 65–66. Haraway had been writing about cyborgs for at least two years before this article was published.

20. Roland Tolentino, "Bodies, Letters, Catalogs: Filipinas in Transnational Space," *Social Text* 14:3 (fall 1996): 53.

21. John Nguyet Erni, "Queer Figurations in the Media: Critical Reflections on the Michael Jackson Sex Scandal," *Critical Studies in Mass Communication* 15:2 (1998): 162.

22. Advertisement for Robbie Davis-Floyd and Joseph Dumit, eds., *Cyborg Babies* (New York: Routledge, 1998), in *New York Review of Books*, September 24, 1998, 39.

23. Carole Parker, "Getting It on Line," *Australian Magazine*, May 30–31, 1998, 43.

24. Ziauddin Sardar, "alt.civilizations.faq: Cyberspace as the Darker Side of the West," in Z. Sardar and J. Ravetz, *Cyberfutures* (London: Pluto, 1996), 35.

25. See, e.g., Tad Williams, *Otherland* (New York: New American Library, 1996); Gibson, *Idoru*.

26. Dominic Eichler, exhibition catalogue essay, *Diagnostic Tools for the New Millennium*, Berlin, 1997, quoted by Josephine Starrs and Leon Cmielewski, *Embodying the Information Age* (Sydney: New Media Arts Fund and Audience Development and Advocacy Division, Australia Council, 1998), 4.

27. See, e.g., Frances Negron-Muntaner, "Jennifer's Butt," *Aztlan* 22:2 (1997): 181–94.

28. Michael Tan, "Walking the Tightrope: Sexual Risk and Male Sex Work in the Philippines," in P. Aggleton, ed., *Men Who Sell Sex* (London: UCL Press, 1998), 256.

29. Amelia Simpson, *Xuxa: The Mega-marketing of Gender, Race, and Modernity* (Philadelphia: Temple University Press, 1993), 39.

30. Perry Johansson, "White Skin, Large Breasts: Chinese Beauty Product Advertising as Cultural Discourse," *China Information* 12:2–3 (1998): 59–84.

31. John Thornhill, "Marx and Spenders," *Weekend Financial Times*, September 28, 1998, 8.

32. See Colleen Ballerino Cohen and Richard Wilk with Beverley Stoeltje, introduction to Cohen, Wilk, and Stoeltje, eds., *Beauty Queens on the Global Stage* (New York: Routledge, 1996), 5.

33. Seager, *State of Women in the World Atlas*, 50–51.

34. Penny van Esterik, "The Politics of Beauty in Thailand," in Cohen, Wilk, and Stoeltje, *Beauty Queens on the Global Stage*, esp. 206–11.

35. See Elizabeth Waters, "Soviet Beauty Contests," in Kon and Riordan, *Sex and Russian Society*. Compare Lena Moskalenko, "Beauty, Women, and Competition: 'Moscow Beauty 1989,'" in Cohen, Wilk, and Stoeltje, *Beauty Queens on the Global Stage*, 61–74.

36. Harry Knowles, "Beauty with a Conscience as Party Pressures Pageant," *South China Morning Post*, November 11, 1998.

37. Nicodemus Odhiambo, "Tanzania Lifts 'Bikini Ban,'" *Mail and Guardian* (Johannesburg), June 18–24, 1999, 16.

38. Vanessa Baird, "The World Made Flesh," *New Internationalist*, April 1998, 9.

39. Erica Goode, "Fijians Starving on TV-Rich Diet," *Age* (Melbourne), May 22, 1999.

40. Germaine Greer, *The Whole Woman* (London: Doubleday, 1999), 5.

41. On the obsession with thinness see Chilla Bulbeck, *Re-Orienting Western Feminism* (Cambridge: Cambridge University Press, 1998), 213.

42. Hamideh Sedghi, "Women, the State, and Development," in Turpin and Lorentzen, *Gendered New World Order*, 113–26.

43. Poroma Rebello, "Politics of Fashion in Dubai," *ISIM Newsletter* (International Institute for the Study of Islam in the Modern World, Leiden), October 1998, 18. For a sophisticated analysis of these issues see Arlene Elowe MacLeod, "Hegemonic Relations and Gender Resistance: The New Veiling as Accommodating Protest in Cairo," in B. Laslett, J. Brenner, and Y. Arat, eds., *Rethinking the Political* (Chicago: University of Chicago Press, 1995), 185–209.

44. Arzu Merali, "Ataturk's Children," *New Internationalist*, August 1999, 35. There is a sympathetic view of this argument in John Keane, *Civil Society: Old Images, New Visions* (Cambridge: Polity, 1998), 28.

45. See Sam Fussell, *Muscle* (New York: Poseidon, 1991); and the wonderful novel by Harry Crews, *Body* (New York: Simon & Schuster, 1990).

46. Ralph Austen, "The Moral Economy of Witchcraft," in J. Comaroff and J. Comaroff, eds., *Modernity and Its Malcontents* (Chicago: University of Chicago Press, 1993), 102.

47. Betsy Hartmann, *Reproductive Rights and Wrongs*, revised edition (Boston: South End Press, 1995), 50–51.

48. Gail Kligman, "Political Demography: The Banning of Abortion in Ceaucescu's Romania," in F. Ginsburg and R. Rapp, eds., *Conceiving the New World Order* (Berkeley: University of California Press, 1995), 234–55.

49. "Happy Family? Survey: The Nordic Countries," *Economist*, January 23, 1999, 4.

50. See Enloe, *Morning After*, 241–43.

51. "Stresses of Milosevic's Rule Blamed for a Decline in the Serbian Birth Rate," *New York Times*, July 5, 1999.

52. Marcus Warren, "Abortions Rise as Economy Falls in Russia," *Sunday Telegraph* (London), January 24, 1999.

53. World Health Organization, *Abortion: A Tabulation of Available Data on the Frequency and Mortality of Unsafe Abortion* (Geneva: World Health Organization, 1994).

54. Stephanie Boyd, "Secrets and Lies," *New Internationalist*, July 1998, 16. For a discussion of sterilization in a number of countries, including Brazil, Mexico, and the United States, see Petchesky and Judd, *Negotiating Reproductive Rights*.

55. Seager, *State of Women in the World Atlas*, 38–40.

56. "Abused Women Have Special Needs," *Network* (Family Health International), no. 18 (summer 1998): 4.

57. See Tola Olu Pearce, "Women's Reproductive Practices and Biomedicine: Cultural Conflicts and Transformations in Nigeria," in Ginsburg and Rapp, *Conceiving the New World Order*, 195–208.

58. Hadley, *Abortion*, 23–29; Ulla Kite, "Post-Unification: The Impact of Social Transformation on Women in Eastern Germany," *Contemporary Politics* 5:2 (1999): esp. 185–86.

59. See Susan Greenhaigh, "The Social Construction of Population Science: An Intellectual, Institutional, and Political History of Twentieth Century Demography," *Comparative Studies in Society and History* 38:1 (1996): 26–66.

60. For a sample see T. Disch, ed., *The Ruins of Earth* (London: Hutchinson, 1973); John Brunner, *Stand on Zanzibar* (New York: Random House, 1968).

61. E.g., P. D. James, *The Children of Men* (London: Faber, 1992); Liz Jensen, *Ark Baby* (London: Bloomsbury, 1998); Greg Bear, *Darwin's Radio* (New York: HarperCollins, 1998).

62. See Stanley Johnson, *World Population and the United Nations* (Cambridge: Cambridge University Press, 1987), chap. 5.

63. Betsy Hartmann, *Reproductive Rights and Wrongs*, revised edition (Boston: South End, 1995), 113–24.

64. On trials in Puerto Rico see Grant, *Sexing the Millennium*, chap. 3.

65. See "A History of Reproduction, Contraception, and Control," *New Internationalist*, July 1998, 26–27.

66. See Betsy Hartmann, *Reproductive Rights and Wrongs* (New York: Harper & Row, 1987), 179–82.

67. See C. Alison McIntosh and Jason Finkle, "The Cairo Conference on Population and Development: A New Paradigm?" *Population and Development Review* 21:2 (1995): 223–60.

68. Most reports list Argentina, Benin, Ecuador, Honduras, and Malta as the Vatican's strongest allies. The world's most populous Catholic and Islamic nations are conspicuously absent from this list.

69. Paul Lewis, "Conference Adopts Plan on Limiting Population," *New York Times*, July 3, 1999. For a discussion of some of the consequences of the Cairo conference see Sonia Correa and Gita Sen, "Cairo + 5: Moving Forward in the Eye of the Storm," paper written for DAWN, December 1998 (www.dawn.org.fj).

70. See, e.g., Hartmann, *Reproductive Rights and Wrongs*, revised edition, 159–70.

71. See Steven James, "Reconciling International Human Rights and Cultural Relativism: The Case of Female Circumcision," *Bioethics* 8:1 (1994): 1–26.

72. See Semra Asefa, "Female Genital Mutilation: Violence in the Name of Tradition, Religion, and Social Imperative," in S. G. French, W. Teays, and L. M. Purdy, eds., *Violence against Women: Philosophical Perspectives* (Ithaca: Cornell University Press, 1998), 94.

73. "Is It Crime or Culture?" *Economist*, February 13, 1999, 49.

74. Bronwyn Winter, "Women, the Law, and Cultural Relativism in France: The Case of Excision," in Laslett, Brenner, and Arat, *Rethinking the Political*, 315–50.

75. Zillah Eisenstein, *Global Obscenities: Patriarchy, Capitalism, and the Lure of Cyberfantasy* (New York: New York University Press, 1998), 136–37. See also Nikki Craske, "Remasculisation and the Neoliberal State in Latin America," in V. Randall and G. Waylen, eds., *Gender, Politics, and the State* (London: Routledge, 1998), 100–120.

FIVE

1. Laurence Altman, "AIDS Is on Course to Ravage Africa," *International Herald Tribune,* June 24, 1998.
2. On the epidemiology of HIV/AIDS see J. Mann and D. Tarantola, eds., *AIDS in the World II* (New York: Oxford University Press, 1996); and regular updates from UNAIDS.
3. Richard Parker, "Sexual Cultures, HIV Transmission, and AIDS Prevention," *AIDS* 8, supp. 1 (1994): S312.
4. Appadurai, *Modernity at Large,* 31.
5. "Three Kings," *Economist,* December 19, 1998, 89.
6. Ita Buttrose, *A Passionate Life* (Sydney: Viking, 1998), 166.
7. Mark Merlis, *Pyrrhus* (London: Fourth Estate, 1998), 232.
8. Anthony Smith, "AIDS Is . . . Reflections on the Australian Research Response to the HIV and AIDS Epidemics," *International Journal of Health Services* 28:4 (1998): 794.
9. Edward Hopper, *The River: A Journey Back to the Source of HIV and AIDS* (Boston: Little, Brown, 1999).
10. See Ted Conover, "Trucking through the AIDS Belt," *New Yorker,* August 16, 1993.
11. There has been some debate about the particular strains of HIV prevalent in Cambodia, and whether they indicate that the emphasis on the role of UN troops has been overemphasized. Nonetheless the general point about transmission through military involvement remains.
12. Richard Stern, "AIDS Taking Grim Toll in Poverty-Stricken Honduras," message from Triangulo Rosa, Costa Rica, July 27, 1998. Compare Stephanie Kane, "Prostitution and the Military: Planning AIDS Intervention in Belize," *Social Science and Medicine* 36:7 (1993): 965–79.
13. "A Global Disaster," *Economist,* January 2, 1999, 43.
14. For a detailed account of how these relationships are played out in the Haitian epidemic see Paul Farmer, *The Uses of Haiti* (Monroe, ME: Common Courage Press, 1994), esp. 321–44.
15. Doug Porter, "A Plague on the Borders," in Manderson and Jolly, *Sites of Desire,* 213–14.
16. See "The Hidden Epidemic," *Asian Harm Reduction Network Newsletter,* no. 10, January–February 1998.
17. "The Flourishing Business of Slavery," *Economist,* September 21, 1996, 49.
18. "AIDS: Economic Crisis May Intensify AIDS Risk," UNAIDS press release, Bangkok, April 2, 1999.
19. For a striking example of the trade in children see Gilberto Dimenstein, "Little Girls of the Night," *NACLA Report on the Americas,* May–June 1994.
20. E.g., Josef Decosas, "AIDS and Development: What Is the Link?" paper presented at International AIDS Conference, Vancouver, 1996 (available in Development Express, www.acdi-cida.gc/xpress/dex/dev9607.htm); Porter, "Plague on the Borders."
21. This is based on a report on ongoing research from the Asian Research Center for

Migration at Chulalongkorn University, Bangkok, reported in a posting to SEA-AIDS (sea-aids@bizet.inet.co.th), August 20, 1998.

22. Kelley Lee and Richard Dodgson, "Globalisation and Cholera: Implications for Global Governance," *Global Governance* 6:2 (2000): 216.

23. Gita Sen, "Globalization and Citizenship: Health and Reproductive Rights," paper presented at Globalization and Citizenship Conference, United Nations Research Institute for Social Development, Geneva, December 1996, 18–19.

24. See Peter Lurie, Percy Hintzen, and Robert Lowe, "Socioeconomic Obstacles to HIV Prevention and Treatment in Developing Countries," *AIDS* 9:6 (1995): 539–46. For a graphic account of the impact of structural adjustment on Mozambique—a country very vulnerable to HIV—see Mark Whitaker, "Means Streets," *New Internationalist,* January–February 1997, 19–20. For an overview of the impact on health see Gita Sen and Anita Gurumuthy, "The Impact of Globalisation on Women's Health," *Arrows for Change* (Kuala Lumpur), May 1998, 1–2.

25. See Daniel Whelan, "Gender and AIDS: Taking Stock of Research and Programmes," unpublished paper, UNAIDS, Geneva, 1999.

26. John Grobler, "Battle over Namibian Rape Bill," *Mail and Guardian,* June 11–17, 1999, 6.

27. Sheila Pelizzoni and John Casparis, "World Human Welfare," in T. Hopkins and I. Wallerstein, eds., *The Age of Transition* (London: Zed, 1996), 117–47.

28. On GPA see Jonathan Mann and Kathleen Kay, "Confronting the Pandemic: The WHO's GPA, 1986–1989," *AIDS* 5, supp. 2 (1991): S221–29; Daniel Tarantola, "Grande et petite histoire des programmes sida," *Journal du Sida,* June–July 1996, 109–16.

29. The original cosponsors of UNAIDS were the World Health Organization, the United Nations Development Programme, UNESCO, the United Nations Children's Fund, the United Nations Population Fund, and the World Bank. In 1999 they were joined by the United Nations Drug Control Program.

30. Carol Jenkins, "The Homosexual Context of Heterosexual Practice in Papua New Guinea," in P. Aggleton, ed., *Bisexualities and AIDS* (London: Taylor & Francis, 1996), 192.

31. Statement by Patrick Levy, Israel AIDS Task Force, to NGO Workshop on HIV/AIDS and Human Rights, Geneva, June 26, 1998.

32. Suzanne LeClerc-Madladla, "Enemy of the People," *New Internationalist,* June 1999, 35.

33. See, e.g., "Ashok to the System," interview with Ashok Row Kavi by William Hoffman, *Poz,* July 1998, 92–97.

34. Report from Support Proyecto Girasol, NGO Workshop on HIV/AIDS and Human Rights, Geneva, June 1998. Compare Timothy Wright and Richard Wright, "Bolivia: Developing a Gay Community," in D. West and R. Green, eds., *Sociolegal Control of Homosexuality* (New York: Plenum, 1997), 97–108.

35. D. Civic and D. Wilson, "Dry Sex in Zimbabwe and Implications for Condom Use," *Social Science and Medicine* 42:1 (1996): 91–98; L. Sandala et al., "'Dry Sex' and HIV Infection among Women Attending a Sexually Transmitted Diseases Clinic in Lusaka, Zambia," *AIDS* 9, supp. 1 (1995): S61–68.

36. Muosa Kalid Nsubuga et al., "The Dilemmas of Cultural Reform in the Era of HIV/AIDS: The Case of Polygamy in the Muslim Community in Uganda," paper presented at Twenty-second International Conference on HIV/AIDS, Geneva, July 1998.

37. See Chris Beyrer, *War in The Blood* (London: Zed, 1998), 32–34.

38. Dennis Altman, *AIDS in the Mind of America* (New York: Doubleday, 1986), 161–62; Edward King, *Safety in Numbers* (London: Cassell, 1993), 47–50; Simon Watney, "Safer Sex as Community Practice," in P. Aggleton, P. Davies, and G. Hart, eds., *AIDS: Individual, Cultural, and Policy Dimensions* (London: Falmer, 1990), 19–34; John-Manuel Andriote, *Victory Deferred* (Chicago: University of Chicago Press, 1999), chap. 4.

39. There are a number of examples of such prevention programs in A. Klusacek and K. Morrison, eds., *A Leap in the Dark: AIDS, Art, and Contemporary Cultures* (Montreal: Vehicule, 1992), and in Dennis Altman, *Power and Community: Organizational and Cultural Responses to AIDS* (London: Taylor & Francis, 1994), 44–47.

40. American coyness about condoms was noted by Mike Merson when he took up a position at Yale after heading the Global Program on AIDS ("Returning Home: Reflections on the USA's Response to the HIV/AIDS Epidemic," *Lancet,* June 15, 1996, 1673–76).

41. Eda Chavez, "When Women Say No," in Martin Foreman, *AIDS and Men* (London: Panos/Zed, 1999), 52.

42. Brendan Lemon, "Female Trouble," *Christopher Street*, no. 116 (1987): 48.

43. Linda Singer, "Bodies—Pleasures—Powers," *Differences*, no. 1 (1989): 47.

44. Frank Mort, *Cultures of Consumption* (London: Routledge, 1996), 79.

45. E.g., John Wagenhauser, "Safe Sex without Condoms," *Outlook* (San Francisco), no. 11 (1991): 65–70.

46. See A. M. Johnson, J. Wadsworth, K. Wellings, and J. Field, *Sexual Attitudes and Life-styles* (Oxford: Blackwell, 1994). For a detailed case study see Anthony Smith, Heidi Reichler, and Doreen Rosenthal, *An Analysis of Trends over Time in Social and Behavioral Factors Related to the Transmission of HIV among the General Community, Sex Workers, and Sex Travellers,* Evaluation of the National HIV/AIDS Strategy Technical Appendix 5 (Canberra: Commonwealth of Australia, 1996).

47. Molara Ogundipe-Leslie, "Nigeria: Not Spinning on the Axis of Maleness," in R. Morgan, ed., *Sisterhood Is Global* (New York: Anchor, 1984), 501.

48. In a recent research study 100% of the 759 participants reported that they had been abused by a sexual partner, while 77.5% had an STI. But whereas 90% of the women said they would inform their partner if they had an STI, only 19% believed their partners would inform them. These inequalities carry though into relative risks of HIV infection ("An Investigation into the Relationship between Domestic Violence and Women's Vulnerability to Sexually Transmitted Infections and HIV/AIDS" [Harare, Zimbabwe: Musasa Project, 1998]).

49. See Dennis Altman, "Globalization and the AIDS Industry," *Contemporary Politics*, September 1998, 233–46. Compare Paula Treichler, "AIDS, HIV, and the Cultural Construction of Reality," in G. Herdt and S. Lindenbaum, eds., *The Time of AIDS* (London: Sage, 1992), 65–98.

50. Norman Spinrad, *Journals of the Plague Years* (New York: Bantam, 1995), 141.

51. By 1990 John Brunner postulated a South Africa in which apartheid was kept viable through possession of a vaccine against AIDS. See his *Children of the Thunder* (London: Sphere, 1990).

52. Roger Lancaster, *Life Is Hard: Machismo, Danger, and the Intimacy of Power in Nicaragua* (Berkeley: University of California Press, 1992), 256.

53. On the commercialization of the ribbon see Simon Watney, "Signifying AIDS: 'Global AIDS,' Red Ribbons, and Other Controversies," in P. Buchler and N. Papastergiadis, eds., *Random Access* (London: Rivers Oram, 1995), 193–210.

54. For an overview see Gregory Woods, *A History of Gay Literature* (New Haven: Yale University Press, 1998), esp. chaps. 29 and 31.

55. Christopher Bram, *Gossip* (New York: Dutton, 1997), 52–53. There is illuminating discussion of the impact of AIDS in Douglas Crimp, "Mourning and Militancy," *October* 51 (winter 1989): 3–18; Simon Watney, "Representing AIDS," in T. Boffin and S. Gupta, eds., *Ecstatic Antibodies* (London: Rivers Oram, 1990), 165–90; Jeff Nunokawa, "'All the Sad Young Men': AIDS and the Work of Mourning," in D. Fuss, ed., *Inside/Out* (New York: Routledge, 1991), 311–23; and the special edition of *Ethnologie française*, "AIDS: Mourning, Memory, New Rituals," January–March 1998.

56. There has certainly been a significant literary response in French, Spanish, and, I suspect, Italian, German, and Portuguese (at least). For an overview of many of the themes in the French literary response see J.-P. Boule and M. Pratt, eds., "AIDS in France," *French Cultural Studies*, special issue, October 27, 1998.

57. Jewelle Gomez, "Silence Equals Forgetting," *Harvard Gay and Lesbian Review* 4:2 (1997): 25–27.

58. Robert Dessaix, *Night Letters* (Sydney: Macmillan, 1996).

59. Rushdie, *Ground beneath Her Feet*, 542.

60. DeLillo, *Underworld*, 243.

61. Suzanne Poirier, "Writing AIDS: Introduction," in S. Poirier and T. Murphy, eds., *Writing AIDS: Gay Literature, Language, and Analysis* (New York: Columbia University Press, 1993), 7.

62. Woods, *History of Gay Literature*, 418.

63. Richard Parker mentions several Brazilian works in his *Beneath the Equator*, 253 n. 7, and Alberto Sandoval discusses Puerto Rican works in "Staging AIDS: What's Latinos Got to Do with It?" in D. Taylor and J. Villegas, eds., *Negotiating Performance* (Durham: Duke University Press, 1994), 54–55.

64. Boris Davidovich, *Serbian Diaries;* Colm Toibin, *The Story of the Night* (London: Picador, 1996); E. Lynn Harris, *Just as I Am* (New York: Doubleday, 1994); Witi Ihimaera, *Nights in the Gardens of Spain* (Auckland: Secker & Warburg, 1995); Nigel Krauth, *JF Was Here* (Sydney: Allen & Unwin, 1990).

65. There is less being written, however, than one might expect. See Barbara Browning, "Babaluiaye: Searching for the Text of the Pandemic," in E. Nelson, ed., *AIDS: The Literary Response* (New York: Twayne, 1992); "The Emergence of AIDS Literature," in Mots Pluriels (www.arts.uwa.edu.au/AIDS/Guide/).

66. On the impact on identity of AIDS programs, see Dennis Altman, "Political Sexualities: Meanings and Identities in the Time of AIDS," in R. Parker and J. Gagnon, eds., *Conceiving Sexuality* (New York: Routledge, 1995), 97–106; Michael Bartos, "Community versus Population: The Case of Men Who Have Sex with Men," in P. Aggleton, P. Davies, and G. Hart, eds., *AIDS: Foundations for the Future* (London: Taylor & Francis, 1994); Eric Ratliff, "Women as 'Sex-Workers,' Men as 'Boyfriends': Shifting Identities in Philippine Go-Go Bars," *Anthropology and Medicine* 6:1 (1999): 79–101.

67. Judith Walkowitz, *Prostitution and Victorian Society* (New York: Cambridge University Press, 1980).

68. Susan Sontag, *AIDS and Its Metaphors* (New York: Penguin, 1990).

69. R. Myers, "Nothing Mega about It Except the Applause," *New York Times*, May 25, 1997.

70. See, e.g., Amy Spindler, "The Decade That Just Won't Go Away," *New York Times*, October 13, 1997. The sense of nostalgia for a pre-AIDS freedom runs through Stephen Barber, *Edmund White: The Burning World* (London: Picador, 1999).

71. For an extensive—but exclusively American—survey see David Roman, *Acts of Intervention* (Bloomington: Indiana University Press, 1998).

72. For examples of the artistic response see Ted Gott, ed., *Don't Leave Me This Way: Art in the Age of AIDS* (Canberra: Australian National Gallery, 1994); Frank Wagner, *Les Mondes du SIDA,* catalogue from exhibition held at Centre d'Art Contemporain, Geneva, June–October 1997.

73. Arlene Croce, "Discussing the Undiscussable," *New Yorker*, December 26, 1994, 54–60. See the comment by Adam Mars-Jones, "Survivor Art," in *Blind Bitter Happiness* (London: Chatto & Windus, 1997), 80–84.

74. Randy Shilts, *And the Band Played On: People, Politics, and the AIDS Epidemic* (New York: St. Martin's, 1987). *Zero Patience* is discussed in Paula Treichler, *How to Have Theory in an Epidemic* (Durham: Duke University Press, 1999), 312–14.

75. Collard's work has been praised effusively by the historian Theodore Zeldin (*An Intimate History of Humanity* [London: Sinclair-Stevenson, 1994], 126–28).

76. See discussion in Kenneth McKinnon, *The Politics of Popular Representation* (Madison, NJ: Fairleigh Dickinson University Press, 1992). The best novel that I have read in this genre which evokes AIDS is Elizabeth Hand, *Glimmering* (London: HarperCollins, 1997).

77. Mark Edmundson, *Nightmare on Main Street* (Cambridge: Harvard University Press, 1997), 28.

78. Originally published as *The Night Inside* (New York: Ballantine, 1993).

79. See, e.g., Claudia Springer, *Electronic Eros* (Austin: University of Texas Press, 1996).

80. Sarah Schulman, "Freedom Summer," *Ten Percent,* June 1994, 22.

81. E.g., Leavitt's stories "The Term Paper Artist" and "Saturn Street," in David Leavitt, *Arkansas* (New York: Houghton Mifflin, 1997).

82. There is a detailed discussion of the AIDS Memorial Quilt, though one which ignores its international dimension, in Marita Sturken, *Tangled Memories* (Berkeley: University of California Press, 1997), chap. 6.

83. On Mardi Gras see R. Wherrett, ed., *Mardi Gras! From Lock Up to Frock Up* (Melbourne: Penguin, 1999).

84. But see Stephanie Kane, *AIDS Alibis* (Philadelphia: Temple University Press, 1998), 77–80, for a description of rites in Belize.

85. Halperin, *Saint Foucault,* 15–16.

86. See Dennis Altman, "Globalization, Political Economy, and HIV/AIDS," *Theory and Society* 28 (1999): 559–84.

SIX

1. E.g., Frances Fox Piven, "Globalizing Capitalism and the Rise of Identity Politics," in L. Panitch, ed., *Socialist Register* (London: Merlin, 1995), 102–16; Leslie Sklair, "Social Movements and Global Capitalism," in F. Jameson and M. Miyoshi, eds., *The Cultures of Globalization* (Durham: Duke University Press, 1998), 291–311; Kaldor, *New and Old Wars,* 76–86.

2. For a clear exposition of this view of social constructionism see Jeffrey Weeks, *Sexuality and Its Discontents* (London: Routledge & Kegan Paul, 1985).

3. E.g., Beverley Hooper, "Chinese Youth: The Nineties Generation," *Current History* 90:557 (1991): 264–69.

4. See Sherrie Inness, ed., *Millennium Girls* (Lanham, MD: Rowman & Littlefield, 1999); Marion Leonard, "Paper Planes: Travelling the New Grrrl Geographies," in T. Skelton and G. Valentine, eds., *Cool Places: Geographies of Youth Cultures* (London: Routledge, 1998), 101–18.

5. Much of this section draws on work originally published in the mid-1990s. See especially Dennis Altman, "Rupture or Continuity? The Internationalization of Gay Identities," *Social Text* 14:3 (1996): 77–94; Altman, "On Global Queering," *Australian Humanities Review,* no. 2, July 1996 (electronic journal, www.lib.latrobe.edu.au); Altman, "Global Gaze/Global Gays," *GLQ* 3 (1997): 417–36.

6. See the bibliography in Balderston and Guy, *Sex and Sexuality in Latin America,* 259–77; the chapters on Brazil and Argentina in B. Adam, J. W. Duyvendak, and A. Krouwel, eds., *The Global Emergence of Gay and Lesbian Politics* (Philadelphia: Temple University Press, 1999); and the special issue of *Culture, Health, and Society* (1:3 [1999]) on "alternative sexualities and changing identities among Latin American men," edited by Richard Parker and Carlos Carceres.

7. For a discussion of the French position see David Caron, "Liberté, Egalité, Seropositivité: AIDS, the French Republic, and the Question of Community," in Boule and Pratt, "AIDS in France," 281–93. On the Netherlands see Judith Schuyf and Andre Krouwel, "The Dutch Lesbian and Gay Movement: The Politics of Accommodation," in Adam, Duyvendak, and Krouwel, *Global Emergence of Gay and Lesbian Politics,* 158–83. On Australia see Dennis Altman, "Multiculturalism and the Emergence of Lesbian/Gay Worlds," in R. Nile, ed., *Australian Civilisation* (Melbourne: Oxford University Press, 1994), 110–24.

8. I owe thanks to a long list of people who over the years have discussed these issues with me, including Ben Anderson, Eufracio Abaya, Hisham Hussein, Lawrence

Leong, Shivananda Khan, Peter Jackson, Julian Jayaseelan, Ted Nierras, Dede Oetomo, and Michael Tan.

9. Jim Marks, "The Personal Is Political: An Interview with Shaym Selvadurai," *Lambda Book Report* (Washington) 5:2 (1996): 7.

10. The original Indonesian term was *banci*. The term *waria* was coined in the late 1970s by combining the words for "woman" and "man." See Dede Oetomo, "Masculinity in Indonesia," in R. Parker, R. Barbosa, and P. Aggleton, eds., *Framing the Sexual Subject* (Berkeley: University of California Press, 2000), 58–59 n. 2.

11. See Peter Jackson, "Kathoey><Gay><Man: The Historical Emergence of Gay Male Identity in Thailand," in Manderson and Jolly, *Sites of Desire*, 166–90.

12. See Jeffrey Weeks, *Coming Out* (London: Quartet, 1977); John Lauritsen and David Thorstad, *The Early Homosexual Rights Movement* (New York: Times Change Press, 1974).

13. A. T. Fitzroy, *Despised and Rejected* (London: Gay Men's Press, 1988; originally published 1918), 223.

14. George Chauncey, *Gay New York* (New York: Basic Books, 1994), 65.

15. John Rechy, *City of Night* (New York: Grove, 1963).

16. E.g., Annick Prieur, *Mema's House, Mexico City* (Chicago: University of Chicago Press, 1998); Jacobo Schifter, *From Toads to Queens* (New York: Haworth, 1999); Peter Jackson and Gerard Sullivan, eds., *Lady Boys, Tom Boys, Rent Boys* (New York: Haworth, 1999); *Woubi Cheri*, (1998), directed by Philip Brooks and Laurent Bocahut.

17. Saskia Wieringa, "Desiring Bodies or Defiant Cultures: Butch-Femme Lesbians in Jakarta and Lima," in E. Blackwood and S. Wieringa, eds., *Female Desires: Same-Sex Relations and Transgender Practices across Cultures* (New York: Columbia University Press, 1999), 206–29.

18. Gloria Wekker, "What's Identity Got to Do with It? Rethinking Identity in Light of the Mati Work in Suriname," in Blackwood and Wieringa, *Female Desires*, 119–38. Compare the very complex typologies of "same-sex" groups in Murray and Roscoe, *Boy-Wives and Female Husbands*, 279–82, and the chapter by Rudolph Gaudio on "male lesbians and other queer notions in Hausa," 115–28.

19. Herdt, *Third Sex, Third Gender*, 47.

20. See Serena Nanda, "The Hijras of India: Cultural and Individual Dimensions of an Institutionalized Third Gender Role," in E. Blackwood, ed., *The Many Faces of Homosexuality* (New York: Harrington Park Press, 1986), 35–54. And read her comments in light of Shivananda Khan, "Under the Blanket: Bisexualities and AIDS in India," in Aggleton, *Bisexualities and AIDS*, 161–77.

21. See Niko Besnier, "Polynesian Gender Liminality through Time and Space," in Herdt, *Third Sex, Third Gender*, 285–328. Note that the subtitle of Herdt's book is "Beyond Sexual Dimorphism in Culture and History."

22. See Ramon Gutierrez, "Must We Deracinate Indians to Find Gay Roots?" *Outlook* (San Francisco), winter 1989, 61–67.

23. Besnier, "Polynesian Gender Liminality," 300.

24. See Lee Wallace, "*Fa'afafine: Queens of Samoa* and the Elision of Homosexuality," *GLQ* 5:1 (1999): 25–39.

25. Roger Lancaster, "'That We Should All Turn Queer?' Homosexual Stigma in the Making of Manhood and the Breaking of Revolution in Nicaragua," in Parker and Gagnon, *Conceiving Sexuality*, 150.

26. See Henning Bech, *When Men Meet: Homosexuality and Modernity* (Chicago: University of Chicago Press, 1997); Kenneth Plummer, *The Making of the Modern Homosexual* (London: Hutchinson, 1981); Seidman, *Difference Troubles*.

27. See Laurence Wai-teng Leong, "Singapore," in West and Green, *Sociolegal Control of Homosexuality*, 134; and the remarkable Singapore film *Bugis Street* (1995), directed by Yon Fan—remarkable for having been made at all.

28. E.g., Sandy Stone, "The Empire Strikes Back: A Posttranssexual Manifesto," in P. Treichler, L. Cartwright, and C. Penley, eds., *The Visible Woman* (New York: New York University Press, 1998), 285–309.

29. See Niko Besnier, "Sluts and Superwomen: The Politics of Gender Liminality in Urban Tonga," *Ethnos* 62:1–2 (1997): 5–31.

30. Thanks to Arthur Chen of the AIDS Prevention and Research Center, Taipei, for this information.

31. Jennifer Robertson, *Takarazuka: Sexual Politics and Popular Culture in Modern Japan* (Berkeley: University of California Press, 1998), 207.

32. For some of the complications in reading cinematic versions of cross-dressing see Marjorie Garber, *Vested Interests* (New York: Routledge, 1992).

33. See Leslie Feinberg, *Transgender Warriors* (Boston: Beacon, 1996); Kate Bornstein, *Gender Outlaw* (New York: Routledge, 1993).

34. Sereine Steakley, "Brazil Can Be Tough and Deadly for Gays," *Bay Windows* (Boston), June 16, 1994.

35. Jerry Z. Torres, "Coming Out," in N. Garcia and D. Remoto, eds., *Ladlad: An Anthology of Philippine Gay Writing* (Manila: Anvil, 1994), 128.

36. Chris Berry and Fran Martin, "Queer'n'Asian on the Net: Syncretic Sexualities in Taiwan and Korean Cyberspaces," *Inqueeries* (Melbourne), June 1998, 67–93.

37. Pheng Cheah, "Posit(ion)ing Human Rights in the Current Global Conjuncture," *Public Culture* 9 (1997): 261.

38. Pedro Bustos-Aguilar, "Mister Don't Touch the Banana," *Critique of Anthropology* 15:2 (1995): 149–70.

39. Kai Wright, "Industrializing Nations Confront Budding Movement," *Washington Blade*, October 23, 1998.

40. Pedro Albornoz, "Landlocked State," *Harvard Gay and Lesbian Review* 6:1 (1999): 17.

41. Ann Ferguson, "Is There a Lesbian Culture?" in J. Allen, ed., *Lesbian Philosophies and Cultures* (Albany: State University of New York Press, 1990), 63–88.

42. See, e.g., the interview by William Hoffman with Mumbai activist Ashok Row Kavi, *Poz*, July 1998, which proclaims him "the Larry Kramer of India."

43. Bing Yu, "Tide of Freedom," *Capital Gay* (Sydney), May 1, 1998.

44. In July 1999 the paper ManilaOUT listed over twenty gay, lesbian, and "gay and lesbian-friendly" organizations in Manila.

45. Naeko, "Lesbian = Woman," in B. Summerhawk et al., eds., *Queer Japan* (Norwich, VT: New Victoria Publishers, 1998), 184–87.

46. Malu Marin, "Going beyond the Personal," *Women in Action* (ISIS International Manila) 1 (1996): 58–62.

47. Manifesto of Chinese Tongzhi Conference, Hong Kong, December 1996. Thanks to Graham Smith for providing this source.

48. See Andrew Matzner, "Paradise Not," *Harvard Gay and Lesbian Review* 6:1 (winter 1999): 42–44.

49. Peter Jackson, "Beyond Bars and Boys: Life in Gay Bangkok," *Outrage* (Melbourne), July 1997, 61–63.

50. Statement from *Male* magazine, quoted in *Brother/Sister* (Melbourne), September 16, 1999, 51.

51. There is a similar argument in Barry Adam, Jan Willem Duyvendak, and Andre Krouwel, "Gay and Lesbian Movements beyond Borders?" in Adam, Duyvendak, and Krouwel, *Global Emergence of Gay and Lesbian Politics*, 344–71.

52. Mark Gevisser, "Gay Life in South Africa," in Drucker, *Different Rainbows:* 116.

53. Dean Murphy, "Zimbabwe's Gays Go 'Out' at Great Risk," *Los Angeles Times,* July 27, 1998.

54. For one view of the situation in Kenya see Wanjira Kiama, "Men Who Have Sex with Men in Kenya," in Foreman, *AIDS and Men,* 115–26.

55. Chris McGreal, "Gays Are Main Evil, Say African Leaders," *Guardian Weekly,* October 7–13, 1999, 4.

56. See Carl Stychin, *A Nation by Rights* (Philadelphia: Temple University Press, 1998), chap. 3.

57. *Times of India,* November 9, 1994, quoted by Sherry Joseph and Pawan Dhall, "No Silence Please, We're Indians!" in Drucker, *Different Rainbows:* 164.

58. Rodney Jones, "'Potato Seeking Rice': Language, Culture, and Identity in Gay Personal Ads in Hong Kong," *International Journal of the Sociology of Language* 143 (2000): 31–59.

59. James Farrar, "Disco 'Super-Culture': Consuming Foreign Sex in the Chinese Disco," *Sexualities* 2:2 (1999): 156.

60. John Clark, "The Global Lesbian and Gay Movement," in A. Hendriks, R. Tielman, and E. van der Veen, eds., *The Third Pink Book* (Buffalo: Prometheus Books, 1993), 54–61.

61. "The Asian Lesbian Network," *Breakout* (newsletter of Can't Live in the Closet, Manila) 4:3–4 (1998): 13.

62. On South Africa see Graeme Reid, "'Going Back to God, Just as We Are': Contesting Identities in the Hope and Unity Metropolitan Community Church," *Development Update* (Johannesburg) 2:2 (1998): 57–65. For a discussion of a gay church in Azcapotzalco, on the outskirts of Mexico City, see "Living la Vida Local," *Economist,* December 18, 1999, 85–87.

63. Coverage of the 1994 games in New York by the Brazilian press is discussed in Charles Klein, "'The Ghetto Is Over, Darling': Emerging Gay Communities and Gender and Sexual Politics in Contemporary Brazil," *Culture, Health, and Society* 1:3 (1999): 239–41.

64. This legislation, it might be argued, is another form of western discourse being

deployed to counter a largely western-generated phenomenon. See Eliza Noh, "'Amazing Grace, Come Sit on My Face,' or Christian Ecumenical Representations of the Asian Sex Tour Industry," *Positions* 5:2 (1997): 439–65.

65. Kathleen Barry, *Female Sexual Slavery* (New York: New York University Press, 1984). This should be read alongside the very different views of G. Phetersen, ed., *A Vindication of the Rights of Whores* (Seattle: Seal Press, 1989). A more contemporary statement drawing on Barry's work is Sheila Jeffreys, *The Idea of Prostitution* (Melbourne: Spinifex, 1997). For an overview of some of the relevant literature see Lynn Sharon Chancer, "Prostitution, Feminist Theory, and Ambivalence," *Social Text*, no. 37 (1993): 143–71; Wendy Chapkis, *Live Sex Acts* (London: Cassell, 1997).

66. Jo Bindman with Jo Doezema, *Redefining Prostitution as Sex Work on the International Agenda* (London: Anti-Slavery International, 1997), 1. See also Cheryl Overs and Paulo Longo, *Making Sex Work Safe* (London: Network of Sex Work Projects, 1997).

67. *Sex Workers' Manifesto*, theme paper of the First National Conference of Sex Workers organized by Durbar Mahila Samanwaya Committee, Calcutta, November 14–16, 1997. Compare Wendy Chapkis's statement that "[t]here is no such thing as The Prostitute; there are only competing versions of prostitution" (*Live Sex Acts*, 211).

68. See Valerie Jenness, *Making It Work: The Prostitutes' Rights Movement in Perspective* (New York: Aldine de Gruyter, 1993).

69. Cecilie Hoigard and Liv Finstad, *Backstreets: Prostitution, Money, and Love*, translated by K. Hanson, N. Sipe, and B. Wilson (Cambridge: Polity, 1992), 181.

70. See Kemala Kempadoo, "Introduction: Globalizing Sex Workers' Rights," and Angelita Abad et al., "The Association of Autonomous Women Workers, Ecuador," in K. Kempadoo and J. Doezema, eds., *Global Sex Workers* (New York: Routledge, 1998), 1–28, 172–77.

71. "The 'Fallen' Learn to Rise," and "Sex Worker's Co-operative," publications of Durbar Mahila Samanwaya Committee, Calcutta, 1998–99.

72. "Prostitutes Seek Workmen Status," *Statesman Weekly*, November 22, 1997.

73. There is an interview with the central figure in the development of NSWP, Cheryl Overs, in Kempadoo and Doezema, *Global Sex Workers*, 204–9. Overs here pays tribute both to her "mates in the global village" and to her Australian background.

74. Guenter Frankenberg, "Germany: The Uneasy Triumph of Pragmatism," in D. Kirp and R. Bayer, eds., *AIDS in the Industrialized Democracies* (New Brunswick: Rutgers University Press, 1992), 121.

75. "Sex Appeal," *Far Eastern Economic Review*, February 4, 1999, 29–31.

76. This sort of "transactional sex" is discussed in Lori Heise and Chris Elias, "Transforming AIDS Prevention to Meet Women's Needs," *Social Science and Medicine* 40 (1995): 931–43.

77. Chris Jones, "Making a Users Voice," paper presented at the Fifth International Conference on Drug-Related Harm, Toronto, March 1994, 7.

78. See Alfred Neequaye, "Prostitution in Accra," in M. Plant, ed., *AIDS, Drugs, and Prostitution* (London: Routledge, 1993), 178–79.

79. Matt Forney, "Voice of the People," *Far Eastern Economic Review*, May 7, 1998, 10.

80. Heather Montgomery, "Children, Prostitution, and Identity," in Kempadoo and Doezema, *Global Sex Workers*, 147.

81. Lenore Manderson, "Public Sex Performances in Patpong and Explorations of the Edges of Imagination," *Journal of Sex Research* 29:4 (1992): 473. See also Barbara Zalduondo, "Prostitution Viewed Cross-Culturally: Toward Recontextualizing Sex Work in AIDS Intervention Research," *Journal of Sex Research* 28:2 (1991): 232–48.

82. On the sexual radicals see Paul Robinson, *The Freudian Left* (New York: Harper & Row, 1969).

83. See Frantz Fanon, *Black Skin, White Masks* (London: Pluto, 1986), and the introduction to that volume by Homi Bhabha, vii–xxvi.

SEVEN

1. It is often claimed that tourism is the world's largest employer. By 1995 international tourist numbers had reached half a billion people, with annual expenditures of over $380 billion. See Held et al., *Global Transformations*, 361.

2. Jakob Arjouni, *One Man, One Murder* (Harpenden, England: No Exit Press, 1997; originally published in German in 1991).

3. Jeremy Seabrook, *Travels in the Skin Trade* (London: Pluto, 1996), 169–70. Compare Truong, *Sex, Money, and Morality.*

4. Caulfield, "Birth of Mangue," 100 n. 33.

5. Christopher Cox, "The Body Snatchers," *Boston Herald*, August 3, 1999.

6. Chris Ryan, *Recreational Tourism* (New York: Routledge, 1991), 163.

7. On the links between neoliberalism, tourism, and prostitution see the statement by one of the Philippines' major umbrella women's organizations, GABRIELA: "Fleshing Out the Flesh Trade," in *Human Rights Defender* (Sydney: University of NSW, 1998).

8. Don Greenlees, "New Life for Oldest Profession," *Weekend Australian*, May 30–31, 1998. On the history of "official prostitution complexes" see Terence Hull, Endang Sulistyaningsih, and Gavin Jones, *Prostitution in Indonesia* (Jakarta: Pustaka Sinar Harapan, 1998), 25–32.

9. Mick Blowfield, "Working the Graveyard Shift," *WorldAIDS* (Panos), May 1994, 2.

10. "Health: Sexually Transmitted Disease Sweeps the Former Soviet Union," IPS wire, May 26, 1998.

11. "Plenty of Muck, Not Much Money," *Economist*, May 8, 1999, 58.

12. Lynne Attwood, "Sex and the Cinema," in I. Kon and J. Riordan, eds., *Sex and Russian Society* (Bloomington: Indiana University Press, 1993), 72. Zillah Eisenstein discusses the impact of the end of Communism on sexuality in *Hatreds: Racialized and Sexualized Conflicts in the 21st Century* (New York: Routledge, 1996), 155–60.

13. Alma Guillermoprieto, "Love and Misery in Cuba," *New York Review of Books*, June 11, 1998, 10–14.

14. Shu-mei Shih, "Gender and a New Geopolitics of Desire: The Seduction of Mainland Women in Taiwan and Hong Kong Media," *Signs* 23:2 (1998): 297.

15. Anita Pleumarom, "'Make Love Not War' in New Social Order," *Nation* (Bangkok), November 3, 1997.

16. Enloe, *Morning After*, 145.

17. Keith Richburg, "New AIDS Victims," *International Herald Tribune*, August 14, 1998.

Compare Chris Beyrer, "Burma and Cambodia: Human Rights, Social Disruption, and the Spread of HIV/AIDS," *Health and Human Rights* 2:4 (1998): 85–96.

18. Stephen Grey, "War on Women," *Australian Magazine,* June 27–28, 1998, 17; Rabih Alameddine, *Koolaids* (New York: Picador, 1998), 156.

19. Patrick Larvie, "Natural Born Targets: Male Hustlers and AIDS Prevention in Urban Brazil," in Aggleton, *Men Who Sell Sex*, 159–77. Compare the description of sex work in Santo Domingo by E. Antonio de Moya and Rafael Garcia in the same volume, 127–40.

20. See John Rechy, *Numbers* (New York: Grove, 1967), esp. chap. 2.

21. For an interesting example of this see Matti Bunzl, "The Prague Experience: Gay Male Sex Tourism and the Neo-colonial Invention of an Embodied Border," in M. Bunzl, D. Berdahl, and M. Lampland, eds., *Altering States: Ethnographies of Transition in Eastern Europe and the Former Soviet Union* (Ann Arbor: University of Michigan Press, 1998), 70–95.

22. See J. Mann, D. Tarantola, and T. Netter, eds., *AIDS in the World* (Cambridge: Harvard University Press, 1992), 376.

23. David Elias, "A Growing Interest in Women, Sex, and Money," *Age* (Melbourne), November 19, 1998.

24. Peter Kellner, "We Are Richer Than You Think," *New Statesman*, February 19, 1999.

25. The brothel apparently became part of a local power struggle in mid-1999, in the course of which at least one worker was murdered (message posted by Asia Pacific Network of Sex Work Projects, July 30, 1999).

26. "Sex Industry Assuming Massive Proportions in Southeast Asia," ILO press release, August 19, 1998, Geneva and Manila. The study is Lin Lean Lim, *The Sex Sector: The Economic and Social Bases of Prostitution in Southeast Asia* (Geneva: International Labour Organisation, 1998). Compare Shyamala Nagaraj and Sit Rohani Yahya, *The Sex Sector: An Unenumerated Economy* (Kuala Lumpur: Penerbit Universiti Pertanian Malaysia, 1997).

27. "Rampant Prostitution the Darker Side of Growing Tourism in Nepal," *Asian Age*, November 11, 1997, republished in *Ki Pukaar* (London), April 1998, 10.

28. Alan Morris, *Bleakness and Light: Inner-City Transition in Hillbrow, Johannesburg* (Johannesburg: Witwatersrand University Press, 1999), 258–63.

29. M. Fisher, "Cunanan Fit the Pattern of 'Preppy Gigolo,'" *International Herald Tribune,* July 26, 1997.

30. Edmund White, *The Farewell Symphony* (London: Chatto & Windus, 1997), 245.

31. Francois Vauglin, "La prostitution: HIV comme parcours exploratoire," *Ex Aequo* (Paris), February 1998, 8 (my translation).

32. Shivananda Khan, "Through a Window Darkly: Men Who Sell Sex to Men in India and Bangladesh," in Aggleton, *Men Who Sell Sex*, 196.

33. See Francine Pickup, "Deconstructing Trafficking in Women: The Example of Russia," *Millennium* 27:4 (1998): 995–1021; and Jo Doezema, "Loose Women or Lost Women?" paper presented at International Sociological Association Conven-

tion, Washington, DC, February 1999 (www.walnet.org/csis/papers/doezema-loose.html).

34. Prostitution was banned under the authoritarian government of Marshal Sarit Thanarat in 1960. It remains outlawed under the provisions of the Prevention and Suppression of Prostitution Act (1996), which, despite being widely disregarded, continues to stigmatize and marginalize sex workers. See Sukanya Hantrakul, "Legalise Prostitution to Save Victims," *Nation* (Bangkok), March 26, 1999.

35. This information comes from a 1996 study in Bindman and Doezema, *Redefining Prostitution as Sex Work,* 25–27.

36. Hoigard and Finstad, *Backstreets,* 182.

37. Bishop and Robinson, *Night Market,* chap. 8.

38. "Improving the Lives of Tribal Sex Workers," International Family Health (London) Annual Report, 1998, 12.

39. Pek Siok Lian, *Mail Order Brides,* Drama Centre, Singapore, 1998. See Venny Villapando, "The Business of Selling Mail-Order Brides," in Asian Women of California, ed., *Making Waves: An Anthology of Writings by and about Asian Women* (Boston: Beacon, 1989); Ara Wilson, "American Catalogues for Asian Brides," in J. Cole, ed., *Anthropology for the Nineties* (New York: Free Press, 1988), 114–25.

40. Cecille Sese, "The Dark Side Down Under," *Observer* (University of the Philippines), June–July 1998, 16.

41. Julie Lewis, "The American Dream Heads to Russia for Love," *Weekend Australian,* November 7–8, 1998.

42. Dennis Altman, *Defying Gravity* (Sydney: Allen & Unwin, 1997), 75.

43. The literature on the "porn debate" is enormous. For various feminist views see Andrea Dworkin, *Pornography: Men Possessing Women* (New York: Perigee, 1979); Linda Williams, *Hard Core: Power, Pleasure, and the "Frenzy of the Visible"* (Berkeley: University of California Press, 1989); Lynne Segal and Mary McIntosh, *Sex Exposed: Sexuality and the Pornography Debate* (London: Virago, 1992). For an overview of debates on pornography see Alan Soble, *Pornography: Marxism, Feminism, and the Future of Sexuality* (New Haven: Yale University Press, 1986); for a specific defense of homosexual porn see Stan Persky, *Autobiography of a Tattoo* (Vancouver: New Star, 1997).

44. "Erotica or Smut?" *Economist,* February 13, 1999, 61.

45. Laurence O'Toole, *Pornocopia* (London: Serpent's Tail, 1998), 128.

46. Andrew Masterson, "Sex Circus: Sensuality Slides as Sales Soar," *Sunday Age,* November 22, 1998.

47. Frank Rich, "What's the Point of This Story? Sex! So Quit the Pontificating," *International Herald Tribune,* February 5, 1998. A story the following year upped the value of the industry to $4.5 billion. See Christopher Reed, "Porn-Again Hollywood," *Bulletin* (Sydney), March 16, 1999.

48. "Vivid Imagination: Technology and Entertainment Survey," *Economist,* November 21, 1998, 15.

49. Karl Taro Greenfeld, *Speed Tribes* (New York: Harper, 1994), 88–89.

50. Ian Buruma, *Behind the Mask* (New York: Meridian, 1984), 55–63.

51. "The Darker Side of Cuteness," *Economist*, May 8, 1999, 28. Compare Tim Larimer, "Japan's Shame," *Time Magazine*, April 19, 1999.
52. "The Sex Industry," *Economist*, February 14, 1998, 23.
53. "X-Rated Russian Channel Hooks Bangla," *Asian Age*, August 12, 1999, reprinted in *Pukaar* (London), no. 27 (1999): 9.
54. Dick Hebditch and Nick Anning, *Porn Gold* (London: Faber & Faber, 1988), 2.
55. Ibid., 35.
56. See Ehrenreich, *Hearts of Men*, chap. 3.
57. Bernard Arcand, *The Jaguar and the Anteater*, translated by Wayne Grady (Toronto: McClelland & Stewart, 1993), 168.
58. Ray Eccleston, "The Respectable Pornographer," *Weekend Australian*, Review section, March 13–14, 1999, 6–8.
59. Nina Munk, "Wall Street Follies," *New Yorker*, July 12, 1999, 25–26.
60. Dorelies Kraakman, "Pornography in Western European Culture," in F. Eder, L. Hall, and G. Hekma, eds., *Sexual Cultures in Europe* (Manchester: Manchester University Press, 1999), 117 n. 2.
61. See Bruce Handy, "Ye Olde Smut Shoppe," *Time Magazine*, February 23, 1998.
62. Hebditch and Anning, *Porn Gold*, 193.
63. Barbara Creed, "The Public Erotic and the Culture of Display," *Australian Book Review*, November 1998, 28.
64. Bill Thompson, *Soft Core* (London: Cassell, 1994), 248–50.
65. See "Porn Goes Mainstream," *Time Magazine*, October 5, 1998.
66. By the end of 1999 one reporter claimed there were a million "sex sites" on the World Wide Web, with 10,000 being added every week (Garry Barker, "Boom in Sex Sites on Internet," *Age* (Melbourne), November 6, 1999.
67. "Inside the Dark Web," and "Behind IT," *Weekend Australian*, December 5–6, 1998, 12.
68. James Willwerth and Mark Thompson, "Cooling Off Hotseattle," *Time Magazine*, October 4, 1999.
69. Advertisement, *Sunday Times* (Singapore), January 31, 1999.
70. In 1997 almost 2,500 women were registered as "exotic dancers" in Toronto. See E. Maticka-Tyndale et al., "Social and Cultural Vulnerability to Sexually Transmitted Diseases: The Work of Exotic Dancers," *Canadian Journal of Public Health* 90:1 (1999): 19–22.
71. "Small but Perfectly Formed," *Economist*, January 3, 1998, 65.
72. Thomas Boggs, *Tokyo Vanilla* (London: Gay Men's Press, 1998), 50.

EIGHT

1. Crucial writings about gender and human rights in the 1990s include Charlotte Bunch, "Women's Rights as Human Rights: Towards a Re-vision of Human Rights," *Human Rights Quarterly* 12 (1990): 486–98; Katerina Tomasevski, *Women and Human Rights* (London: Zed, 1993); R. Cook, ed., *Human Rights of Women: National and International Perspectives* (Philadelphia: University of Pennsylvania Press, 1994); Maila Stivens, "Theoretical Perspectives on Human Rights and Gender Politics

in the Asia Pacific," in Hilsdon et al., *Human Rights and Gender Politics: Asia-Pacific Perspectives,* 1–36.

2. Macintyre, "Melanesian Women and Human Rights": 147.

3. See Keck and Sikkink, *Activists beyond Borders,* chap. 5.

4. George Hicks, *The Comfort Women: Japan's Brutal Regime of Enforced Prostitution in the Second World War* (New York: Norton, 1994).

5. Enloe, *Morning After,* 244. This point is developed by Rosalind Petchesky, "Sexual Rights," in Parker, Barbosa, and Aggleton, *Framing the Sexual Subject,* 81–103.

6. Boutros Boutros-Ghali, "Democracy, Development, and Human Rights for All," *International Herald Tribune,* June 10, 1993.

7. See Alice Miller, Ann Janette Rosga, and Meg Satterthwaite, "Health, Human Rights, and Lesbian Existence," *Health and Human Rights* 1:4 (1995): 433.

8. The 1995 UNICEF *State of the World's Children* reported that violence against women is the most common crime in the world. See Pettman, *Worlding Women,* 187.

9. Stuart Whitmore and Suvendrini Kakuchi, "Silent Screams," *Asiaweek,* April 9, 1999, 50.

10. See Clive Archer, *International Organizations,* 2nd edition (London: Routledge, 1992), chap. 1.

11. See A. M. Clark, E. Friedman, and K. Hochstetler, "The Sovereign Limits of Global Civil Society," *World Politics,* October 1998, 1–35. (They claim a far higher figure, but this seems doubtful. Peter Waterman suggests an attendance of 20–30,000 (*Globalisation, Social Movements, and the New Internationalism* [London: Cassell, 1998], 157).

12. The growth in nongovernmental activity around human rights is discussed in Jackie Smith and Ron Pagnucco, "Globalizing Human Rights: The Work of Transnational Human Rights NGOs," *Human Rights Quarterly* 20:2 (1998): 379–412. See, too, Manisha Desai, "From Vienna to Beijing," in Peter van Ness, *Debating Human Rights* (London: Rutgers, 1999), 184–96.

13. DAWN began in 1984 and has since been an active participant in most of the large UN conferences of the past decade, as well as publishing important material about globalization and sexual and reproductive rights.

14. For examples see Sasha Roseneil, "The Global Common," in Scott, *Limits of Globalization,* 55–71; Ellen Dorsey, "The Global Women's Movement: Articulating a New Vision of Global Governance," in P. Diehl, ed., *The Politics of Global Governance* (Boulder: Lynne Rienner, 1997), 335–59.

15. R. Grosfoguel, F. Negron-Muntaner, and C. Geroas, "Beyond Nationalist and Colonialist Discourses," in Negron-Muntaner and Grosfoguel, *Puerto Rican Jam: Rethinking Colonialism and Nationalism* (Minneapolis: University of Minnesota Press, 1997), 35 n. 53.

16. See Miranda Morris, *The Pink Triangle: Struggle for Gay Law Reform in Tasmania* (Sydney: University of New South Wales Press, 1995); Tim Tenbensel, "International Human Rights Conventions and Australian Political Debates," *Australian Journal of Political Science* 31:1 (March 1996): 7–23; Stychin, *Nation by Rights,* 164–84.

17. Reported in *Hankyurae* (newspaper), November 27, 1997 (information from International Gay and Lesbian Human Rights Commission).

18. Nancy Scheper-Hughes, "AIDS and the Social Body," *Social Science and Medicine* 39:7 (1994): 996–97.

19. See, e.g., Maxine Ankrah, "AIDS and the Social Side of Health," *Social Science and Medicine* 32:9 (1991): 972.

20. With a South African colleague I have tried to deal with some of these dilemmas in relation to HIV/AIDS. See Mark Heywood and Dennis Altman, "Confronting Aids: Human Rights, Law, and Social Transformation," *Health and Human Rights* 5:1 (2000, forthcoming).

21. Derek Davies, former editor of the *Far Eastern Economic Review,* believes the appeal to Confucianism as a current political ploy was devised as a strategy by Lee Kuan Yew and Dr. Mahathir as recently as 1987. See his "Neo-Confucianism Ploys Just a Cynical Abuse of Power," *Weekend Australian,* December 31, 1994, 16. And compare Ben Anderson, *The Spectre of Comparisons* (London: Verso, 1998), 17 n. 35.

22. Kyi Kyi Hla in *Myanmar Perspectives* (Rangoon) 5:12 (1996): 53–54 (a publication handed to visitors to Burma).

23. Tu Wei-ming, *Ways, Learning, and Politics* (Singapore: IEAPE, 1989). There is a useful discussion in Ruth Macklin, *Against Relativism: Cultural Diversity and the Search for Ethical Universals in Medicine* (New York: Oxford University Press, 1999), 228–33.

24. Anwar Ibrahim, *The Asian Renaissance* (Singapore: Times Books, 1996), 28.

25. Fauzi Abdullah et al., "Human Rights," in A. Milner and M. Quilty, eds., *Comparing Cultures* (Melbourne: Oxford University Press, 1997), 48.

26. Ken Booth, "Human Wrongs and International Relations," *International Affairs* 71:1 (1995): 115.

27. Saskia Sassen, "Towards a Feminist Analytics of the Global Economy," *Indiana Journal of Global Studies* 4:1 (1996): 8.

28. For an overview see Fred Halliday, "Gender and IR: Progress, Backlash, and Prospect," *Millennium* 27:4 (1998): 833–46.

29. See D. Kulick and M. Wilson, eds., *Taboo: Sex, Identity, and Erotic Subjectivity in Anthropological Fieldwork* (London: Routledge, 1995).

30. See Cynthia Enloe, *Bananas, Beaches, and Bases* (Berkeley: University of California Press, 1990). See also Katherine Moon, *Sex among Allies: Military Prostitution in U.S.–Korea Relations* (New York: Columbia University Press, 1997); Saundra Sturdevant and Brenda Stolzfus, *Let the Good Times Roll* (New York: New Press, 1992); Richard Setlowe, *The Sexual Occupation of Japan* (New York: HarperCollins, 1999).

31. Enloe, *Morning After,* 253.

32. Sara Ruddick, "Pacifying the Forces: Drafting Women in the Interests of Peace," *Signs* 8:3 (1983): 477.

33. Eisenstein, *Global Obscenities,* 17.

34. J. K. Gibson-Graham, "Queer(y)ing Globalization," in H. Nast and S. Pile, eds., *Places through the Body* (London: Routledge, 1998), 23–41.

35. See Lionel Tiger, *Men in Groups* (New York: Random House, 1969).

36. Nancy Hartsock, *Money, Sex, and Power* (New York: Longman, 1983), 186. Thomas Dunn, one of the few political scientists to develop this theme, discusses male bonding, sex, and power in his *united states* (Ithaca: Cornell University Press, 1994), 49–55.

37. Adam Farrar, "War: Machining Male Desire," in Paul Patton and Ross Poole, *War/Masculinity* (Sydney: Intervention Publications, 1985), 68.

38. See Pettman, *Worlding Women,* 92–95.

39. There is the beginning of such an analysis in Neil Garcia, "Knowledge, Sexuality, and the Nation State," *Buddhi* (Ateneo de Manila University) 3:1 (1999): 107–17.

40. Kaldor, *New and Old Wars.*

41. Barbara Ehrenreich, *Blood Rites: Origins and History of the Passions of War* (New York: Henry Holt, 1997), 129.

42. Connell, *Masculinities,* 10.

43. For a sophisticated Foucauldian critique see Ann Stoler, "Educating Desire in Colonial Southeast Asia: Foucault, Freud, and Imperial Sexualities," in Manderson and Jolly, *Sites of Desire,* 27–47.

44. bell hooks, *Yearnings* (Boston: South End Press, 1990), 227.

45. Sigmund Freud, "Psycho-analytic Notes on an Autobiographical Account of a Case of Paranoia," *Complete Works,* translated by James Strachey (London: Hogarth, 1958), 12:61.

46. Varda Burstyn, *The Rites of Men* (Toronto: University of Toronto Press, 1999), 178.

47. See Hal Cohen, "A Secret History of the Sexual Revolution: The Repression of Wilhelm Reich," *Lingua Franca,* March 1999, 24–33.

48. E.g., Guy Hocquenghem, *The Problem Is Not So Much Homosexual Desire as the Fear of Homosexuality* (London: Allison & Busby, 1978); Mario Mieli, *Homosexuality and Liberation* (London: Gay Men's Press, 1980); Dennis Altman, *Homosexual: Oppression and Liberation* (New York: New York University Press, 1994; originally published 1971); David Fernbach, *The Spiral Path* (Boston: Alyson, 1981).

49. Cynthia Weber, "Something's Missing: Male Hysteria and the U.S. Invasion of Panama," in Zalewski and Parpart, *"Man" Question in International Relations,* 160.

50. Organized religion is a factor in hate crimes in many parts of the world. For examples see R. Kelly and J. Maghan, eds., *Hate Crime: The Global Politics of Polarization* (Carbondale: Southern Illinois University Press, 1998), although the editors fail to fully synthesize the evidence of their contributors on the importance of religious hatreds.

51. Joel Kovel, "The Crisis of Materialism," in Kovel, *Radical Spirit,* 320.

52. Tony Kushner, *Angels in America,* part 1 (New York: Theater Communications Group, 1993), 46.

53. One of the most interesting explorations of the connection between sexuality and the Cambridge spies is found in John Banville, *The Untouchable* (London: Picador, 1997).

54. This relationship is explored, albeit in a rather confused way, in Klaus Theweleit, *Male Bodies: Psychoanalyzing the White Terror,* translated by Erica Carter and Chris Turner (Minneapolis: University of Minnesota Press, 1989; originally published 1978).

55. Quoted in Robert Dreyfuss, "The Holy War on Gays," *Rolling Stone,* March 18, 1999.

56. George Orwell, *1984* (Harmondsworth: Penguin, 1954), 109. It is interesting that

Robin Morgan uses this same quotation in her introduction to *Sisterhood Is Global*, 14.

57. Keumsoon Lee, "Gender and Security," paper presented at Asia-Pacific Roundtable, Kuala Lumpur, June 1996, 8.

58. Ricardo Llamas and Fefa Vila, "Passion for Life: A History of the Lesbian and Gay Movement in Spain," in Adam, Duyvendak, and Krouwel, *Global Emergence of Gay and Lesbian Politics*, 216.

59. See Scott Long, *Public Scandals: Sexual Orientation and Criminal Law in Romania* (New York: Human Rights Watch and International Gay and Lesbian Human Rights Commission, 1998).

NINE

1. S. M. Lee, "Am I a Fuddy-Duddy?" *New Paper* (Singapore), February 1, 1999.

2. See Nancy Hatch Dupree, "Afghan Women under the Taliban," in W. Maley, ed., *Fundamentalism Reborn?* (London: Hurst, 1999), 145–66.

3. Psychiatrist Yuri Shevchenko, quoted in "Russians Protest Sex Education," *Toronto Star*, November 22, 1997, quoted in *Naz*, April 1998.

4. On "masculine fundamentalism" see R. W. Connell, "Masculinities and Globalization," *Men and Masculinities* 1:1 (July 1998): 17.

5. Karen McCarthy Brown, "Fundamentalism and the Control of Women," in J. S. Hawley, ed., *Fundamentalism and Gender* (New York: Oxford University Press, 1994), 190.

6. "A Fight for the Faithful," *Economist*, May 8, 1999, 48.

7. V. S. Naipaul, *Beyond Belief: Islamic Excursions amongst the Converted Peoples* (New York: Random House, 1998), 361–408.

8. Thomas Friedman, "Time to Draft Fundamentalists into the New Israeli Century," *International Herald Tribune*, June 23, 1999.

9. Jenkins, " Homosexual Context of Heterosexual Practice," 193.

10. Lynn Freedman, "The Challenge of Fundamentalisms," *Reproductive Health Matters*, no. 8 (1996): 57.

11. See McIntosh and Finkle, "Cairo Conference," 242–49.

12. See Jane Mansbridge, *Why We Lost the ERA* (Chicago: University of Chicago Press, 1986).

13. Frank Gibney, "The Kids Got in the Way," *Time Magazine*, August 23, 1999. According to this story the Phineas Priesthood is a group of individuals who earn membership through killing or maiming Jews, homosexuals, or anyone who is not "white."

14. "Free at Last," *Economist*, June 13, 1998, 72.

15. Stanley Cohen, *Folk Devils and Moral Panics* (London: MacGibbon & Kee, 1972), 24. The term seems to have been coined by Cohen's colleague Jock Young. See Erich Goode and Nachman Ben-yehuda, *Moral Panics* (Oxford: Blackwell, 1994), 12.

16. Kenneth Thompson, *Moral Panics* (London: Routledge, 1998), 140–42.

17. Igor Kon, "Sexuality and Culture," in Kon and Riordan, *Sex and Russian Society*, 35–44.

18. Doezema, "Loose Women or Lost Women?" 24.

19. See Kenneth Plummer, "The Lesbian and Gay Movement in Britain," in Adam, Duyvendak, and Krouwel, *Global Emergence of Gay and Lesbian Politics,* 143; David Evans, *Sexual Citizenship* (London: Routledge, 1993), chap. 5.

20. See Joel Krieger, *Reagan, Thatcher, and the Politics of Decline* (Cambridge: Polity, 1986); Thomas Ferguson and Joel Rogers, *Right Turn: The Decline of the Democrats and the Future of American Politics* (New York: Hill & Wang, 1986).

21. George Gilder, *Wealth and Poverty* (New York: Basic Books, 1981); Charles Murray, *Losing Ground* (New York: Basic Books, 1984).

22. Charles Murray, "The Coming White Underclass," *Wall Street Journal,* October 29, 1993, quoted in Brendon O'Connor, "American Liberalism, Conservatism, and the Attack on Welfare," unpublished Ph.D. thesis, La Trobe University, 1999.

23. Ian Buruma, "Sex and Democracy in Taiwan," *New York Review of Books,* February 4, 1999, 15.

24. Already in 1990 John O'Neill had identified AIDS as a "potential globalizing panic" ("AIDS as a Globalizing Panic," *Theory, Culture, and Society* 7 [1990]: 334).

25. On Japanese views of HIV/AIDS see Sandra Buckley, "The Foreign Devil Returns," in Manderson and Jolly, *Sites of Desire,* 262–91.

26. John Treat, *Great Mirrors Shattered* (Oxford: Oxford University Press, 1999).

27. Kane, *AIDS Alibis,* 170.

28. "800 Suffering from AIDS in Pakistan," Internet version of *The Dawn,* August 20, 1998 (www.dawn.com).

29. Examples can be found in a number of countries, and have been analyzed for particular cases in Canada and New Zealand. See, e.g., Ron Patterson, "'Softly, Softly': New Zealand Law Responds to AIDS," in P. Davis, ed., *Intimate Details and Vital Statistics: AIDS, Sexuality, and the Social Order in New Zealand* (Auckland: Auckland University Press, 1996), 31–47.

30. "When Fear and Fury Took Over," *Hindu,* May 11, 1998 (www.webpage.com/hindu/daily).

31. David Lamb, "Catholic Church Frowns on Anti-AIDS Ads in Philippines," Los Angeles Times Online, February 1, 1999 (www.latimes.com).

32. A posting to the SEA-AIDS network identified the source as an *Indian Youth and Family Planning Programme Council Newsletter,* May 1998 (see www.owner-sea-aids @biznet.inet.co.th, June 23, 1998). I have read similarly unsupported claims that "snuff movies are common in Europe."

33. Supawadee Susanpoolthong, "Key Hurdle for Tough Bill on Child Prostitution," *Bangkok Post,* March 28, 1996.

34. "For Lust or Money," *Far Eastern Economic Review,* December 14, 1995, 23.

35. John Zubrzycki, "Clarke: A Sex Odyssey," *Weekend Australian,* February 7–8, 1998.

36. Richel Langit, "Pedophiles in RP Are Mostly Pinoys—Unicef," *Manila Times,* August 12, 1998. Compare Maggie Black, "Home Truths," *New Internationalist,* February 1994, 11–13.

37. Paul Daley, "Women's Sex Abuse of Boys Stirs Outcry," *Age* (Melbourne), August 6, 1999.

38. See Weeks, *Sexuality and Its Discontents,* 224.

39. J. R. Wood, *Report of the Royal Commission into the New South Wales Police Service* (Sydney, 1997).

40. There is a large literature on Jackson, but little of it refers to media coverage outside the United States. See, e.g., Stephen Hinerman, "(Don't) Leave Me Alone: Tabloid Narrative and the Michael Jackson Child-Abuse Scandal," in J. Lull and S. Hinerman, eds., *Media Scandals* (New York: Columbia University Press, 1997), 143–63.

41. Scott Heim, *Mysterious Skin* (New York: Harper, 1996); Neal Drinnan, *Glove Puppet* (Melbourne: Penguin, 1998); Matthew Stadler, *Allan Stein* (New York: Grove, 1999).

42. Andrew Vachss, *Batman: The Ultimate Evil* (New York: Warner, 1995).

43. Chris Gelken, "Row over Call to Boycott 'Paedophile' Playground," Pangaea, February 28, 1997 (www.panagaea.org/street_children/asia/asiasex2.htm).

44. A. M. Homes, *The End of Alice* (New York: Simon & Schuster, 1996).

45. Steven Seidman, *Embattled Eros* (New York: Routledge, 1992), 212.

46. Richard Hofstadter, *The Paranoid Style in American Politics* (New York: Vintage, 1967), 34.

47. Compare Daniel Bell, *The Cultural Contradictions of Capitalism* (New York: Basic Books, 1976).

48. Newt Gingrich, *To Renew America* (New York: HarperCollins, 1995), 78. (This of course is the book for which Gingrich received a huge advance from a Murdoch-owned company, leading to allegations of conflict of interest.) Thanks to Brendon O'Connor for this reference.

49. See the interview with Gilbert Herdt in Joseph Geraci, *Dares to Speak* (London: Gay Men's Press, 1997).

50. Sylvia Walby makes this point in comparing Britain and the United States in her "'Backlash' in Historical Context," in M. Kennedy, C. Lubeslska, and V. Walsh, eds., *Making Connections* (London: Taylor & Francis, 1993), 86–87.

51. Barry Gilheany, "The State and the Discursive Construction of Abortion," in Randall and Waylen, *Gender, Politics, and the State*, 58–79; Lisa Smith, "Abortion and Family Values: The X Case, Sexuality, and 'Irishness,'" in D. Epstein and J. Sears, eds., *A Dangerous Knowing* (London: Cassell, 1999), 195–209.

52. Writing in the 1820s Alexis de Tocqueville already pointed to the importance of religion in American political culture. For a discussion of the historic roots of American religiosity see Jon Butler, *Awash in a Sea of Faith* (Cambridge: Harvard University Press, 1990). For a comparison with other rich societies see Steve Bruce, *Conservative Protestant Politics* (New York: Oxford University Press, 1998).

53. Susan Faludi, *Backlash* (New York: Vintage, 1991), 14.

54. See Didi Herman, *The Antigay Agenda* (Chicago: University of Chicago Press, 1997), 194–200.

55. See John D'Emilio and Estelle Freedman, *Intimate Matters: A History of Sexuality in America* (New York: Harper & Row, 1988), chap. 15; Rosalind Petchesky, *Abortion and Woman's Choice* (Boston: Northeastern University Press, 1985); Barbara Ehrenreich, Elizabeth Hess, and Gloria Jacobs, *Re-making Love* (New York: Doubleday, 1986), chap. 5.

56. For an overview see Sara Diamond, *Roads to Dominion* (New York: Guilford, 1995); Geoffrey Hodgson, *The World Turned Right Side Up* (New York: Houghton Mifflin, 1996).

57. In a 1989 ruling on a Missouri law the Court upheld banning the use of state moneys for "encouraging or counselling" women to have abortions and forbidding state employees or hospitals from taking part in an abortion not necessary to save a woman's life (*Webster versus Reproductive Health Services*, 1989).

58. In fact discharges from the military for homosexual behavior have increased under Clinton. See Tim Weiner, "Military Discharges of Homosexuals Soar," *New York Times*, April 7, 1998.

59. There is now a large literature on contemporary debates within the gay/lesbian movement. See, e.g., Urvashi Vaid, *Virtual Equality* (New York: Anchor, 1995); Daniel Harris, *The Rise and Fall of Gay Culture* (New York: Hyperion, 1997); Jeffrey Escoffier, *American Homo* (Berkeley: University of California Press, 1998).

60. See "Mad about the Boy," *Time Magazine*, February 16, 1998.

61. Roger Angell, "Lo Love, High Romance," *New Yorker*, August 25, 1997, 156–59.

62. There is a review of some of the issues involved in Amitai Etzioni, *The Limits of Privacy* (New York: Basic Books, 1999), chap. 2.

63. See Douglas Sanders, "Getting Lesbian and Gay Issues on the International Human Rights Agenda," *Human Rights Quarterly* 18 (1996): 98–103.

64. "The Christian Voter's Guide to the '99 Elections" provided justification for its free market position by reference to Proverbs 10:2–4, Matthew 25:14–27, and Thessalonians 3:10 (*Today: The Magazine for Christian Living*, May 1999).

65. See Johnson, *World Population and the United Nations*, 254–57.

66. For the debate over "sex panic" see the various feature articles in the *Harvard Gay and Lesbian Review* 5:2 (spring 1998); Caleb Crain, "Pleasure Principles," *Lingua Franca*, October 1997, 26–37.

67. See Ken Silverstein, "Still in Control," *Mother Jones*, September–October 1999, 55.

68. Paul Freston, "Brother Voted for Brother: The New Politics of Protestantism in Brazil," in V. Garrard-Burnett and D. Stoll, eds., *Rethinking Protestantism in Latin America* (Philadelphia: Temple University Press, 1993), esp. 87–92.

69. Martin's is a complex and persuasive argument. See David Martin, *Tongues of Fire* (Cambridge: Blackwell, 1990), esp. 278–84. For a statement of the indigenous development of Protestantism in Latin America see Jeff Haynes, *Religion in Global Politics* (New York: Addison Wesley Longman, 1998), 51–61.

TEN

.1. Manuel Castells, *The Power of Identity* (Oxford: Blackwell, 1997), 268.

2. Connell, *Masculinities*, 243.

3. This is not true, of course, of everything claiming to be "queer." See, e.g., some of the leads in G. Ingram, A. M. Bouthilette, and Y. Retter, *Queers in Space* (Seattle: Bay Press, 1997), and some of the tentative steps toward a "homo-economics" in M. Duberman, ed., *A Queer World* (New York: New York University Press, 1996).

4. R. W. Connell, "Democracies of Pleasure: Thoughts on the Goals of Radical Sexual Politics," in Linda Nicholson and Steven Seidman, *Social Postmodernism* (Cambridge: Cambridge University Press, 1995), 385.

5. Lisa Duggan, "Making It Perfectly Queer," *Socialist Review* 22:1 (1992): 26. Compare Tim Edwards, "Queer Fears: Against the Cultural Turn," *Sexualities* 4:1 (1998): 471–84.

6. Gilbert Herdt, *Guardians of the Flutes* (New York: McGraw-Hill, 1981); Herdt, *The Sambia: Ritual and Gender in New Guinea* (New York: Holt, Rinehart & Winston, 1987).

7. A film about the arrival of disco in Singapore in the 1970s, first released under the name *Forever Fever* (1998), directed by Glen Goei.

8. Stadler, *Allan Stein*, 153.

9. Altman, *Homosexual: Oppression and Liberation*, 86.

10. Jeffrey Weeks, "The Rise and Fall of Permissiveness," *Spectator* (London), March 17, 1979, 17.

11. Julie Burchill, "Pleasure Principle," *Age* (Melbourne), June 6, 1998.

12. Rita Mae Brown, "Queen for a Day: A Stranger in Paradise," in K. Jay and A. Young, eds., *Lavender Culture* (New York: Jove, 1979), 69–76.

13. Annie Sprinkle, "Post Porn Modernist Manifesto," quoted in Grant, *Sexing the Millennium*, 244.

14. J. C. Ballard, *Cocaine Nights* (London: Flamingo, 1997), 232.

15. Lance Morrow, "The Madness of Crowds," *Time Magazine*, August 9, 1999, 64.

16. Elizabeth Jelin, "Engendering Human Rights," in E. Dore, ed., *Gender Politics in Latin America* (New York: Monthly Review Press, 1997), 76.

17. Dowsett and Aggleton, "Young People and Risk-Taking in Sexual Relations," 37–38.

18. See Jeffrey Weeks, *Invented Moralities: Sexual Values in an Age of Uncertainty* (Cambridge: Polity, 1995), and works by R. W. Connell and Nancy Fraser already cited.

19. Robin Morgan, introduction to *Sisterhood Is Global*, 34.

20. Andrews, "Violence against Women in South Africa," 436.

Index

abortion, 39, 45, 63, 64, 65, 141, 149, 150–2
ACT UP, 126
Adorno, Thomas, 134
advertising, 58, 76, 142
Afghanistan, 109, 123, 132, 138
African National Congress, 98, 160
"Africanness," 98, 128, 163
Aggleton, Peter, 5, 44
Agnew, Spiro, 150
AIDS. *See* HIV/AIDS
AIDS Conferences, International, 78, 84, 126
AIDS-Hilfen, 102
AIDS literature, 79–80, 186n.56
AIDS Memorial Quilt, 79, 83
AIDS panics, 144–5
Alameddine, Rabih, 109, 148
Albania, 136
Albright, Madeleine, 135
Algeria, 139
All National Women's Conference (India), 102
Almodovar, Pedro, 34
Altman, Dennis, 54
Ambon, 133
"Americanization," 26–7, 28–32, 58, 79, 126, 155–6
Amnesty International, 123, 127
Amory, Deborah, 29
Amsterdam, 10
And the Band Played On, 81
Andrews, Penny, 163
androgyny, 91

Angels in America, 79, 81, 135
Anglicans. *See* Church of England
Angola, 70
Anjaree, 96–7
Annan, Kofi, 68
anorexia, 59
anthropology, 60, 130
Anwar, Ibrahim, ix, 94, 129
Appadurai, Arjun, 19, 32–3, 69
Araki, Gregg, 81
Argentina, 18, 39, 49, 96
Asian Lesbian Network, 99
"Asian values," 43, 128–9
Asimov, Isaac, 25
Attwood, Lynne, 108
Atwood, Margaret, 62
Austen, Ralph, 61
Australia, 18, 20, 62, 67, 69, 87, 102, 111, 115, 127, 153
Austria-Hungary, 12–3

"backlash," 150
Baird, Vanessa, 59
Baker, Josephine, 41
Baker, Russell, ix
bakkla, 88
Bales, Kevin, 27
Bali, 44, 110
Ballard, J. C., 162
Banana, President (Zimbabwe), ix–x, 43
Bangkok, 10–14, 41, 97, 107, 109, 147
Bangladesh, 18, 23, 111, 118
bantut, 29
Barbados, 44